360/ND

The Soundless Sahara

BOOKS BY R. V. C. BODLEY

Biography

ADMIRAL TOGO

GERTRUDE BELL

THE MESSENGER

INDISCRETIONS OF A YOUNG MAN

THE WARRIOR SAINT

Fiction

YASMINA

OPAL FIRE

LILAC TROLL

THE GAY DESERTERS

Travel

ALGERIA FROM WITHIN

THE QUEST

A JAPANESE OMELETTE

FLIGHT INTO PORTUGAL

INDISCREET TRAVELS EAST

THE DRAMA OF THE PACIFIC

WIND IN THE SAHARA

and

IN SEARCH OF SERENITY

R. V. C. BODLEY

The Soundless Sahara

*Illustrated
and with maps*

ROBERT HALE LIMITED
LONDON

© *R. V. C. Bodley* 1968
First published in Great Britain 1968

SBN 7091 0066 3

Robert Hale Limited
63 Old Brompton Road
London S.W.7

PRINTED IN GREAT BRITAIN
BY EBENEZER BAYLIS AND SON LIMITED
THE TRINITY PRESS, WORCESTER, AND LONDON

Contents

		page
	Prologue	11
1	Mysteries of the Sahara	17
2	René Caillé	26
3	Aurélie Picard	47
4	The Twareg	73
5	The Flatters Disaster	85
6	Cardinal Lavigerie and the White Fathers	99
7	Viscount Charles de Foucauld	120
8	General Laperrine	129
9	Isabelle Eberhardt	141
10	The Murder of the Marquis de Mores	167
11	The Finding of Petroleum in the Sahara	189
	Epilogue	201
	Appendix I: The Islamic Faith	207
	II: Glossary	213
	Bibliography	217
	Index	219

Illustrations

~~~~~~

facing page

The author in his ceremonial Arab dress outside the Caid Isa's house in the oasis of Laghouat   48

Caid Isa in the first car to come to the Sahara shows it off to the author   49

Caid Isa ben Abdallah using another form of transport   49

The corsair palace in Algiers which belonged to the author's grandfather   64

Before the toothache-curing episode: patient and dentist to the right of the tent and Caid Isa inside   64

Laghouat, where Aurélie Picard had her "town" residence and where the author lived for many years   65

Si Ahmed Tidjani *(Photo: Librairie baconnier)*   65

Aurélie Picard *(Photo: Librairie baconnier)*   65

The Hoggar country in the region of Tamanrasset *(Photo: Esso)*   112

A Twareg tribesman *(Photo: Documentation Française)*   112

Top: Father Richard *(left)* Father Pouplard *(right)*
Bottom: Father Paulnier *(left)* Father Bouchard *(right)*
Centre: Cardinal Lavigerie *(Photo: Documentation Française)*   128

René Caillé *(Photo: Documentation Française)*   128

Colonel Flatters *(Photo: Documentation Française)*   128

Charles de Foucauld *(Photo: French Embassy Press and Information Division)*   128

General Laperrine *(Cahiers Charles de Foucauld)*   128

One of Laperrine's Meharist scouts *(Photo: Cmidom)*   129

The café in Bone where Isabelle Eberhardt first began to
drink absinthe and smoke *kief*   176

The flooded desert where Isabelle Eberhardt was drowned   176

Isabelle Eberhardt when a young girl   177

Sliman, Isabelle Eberhardt's husband   177

Ben Messis, the friend of the Marquis de Mores who
fruitlessly warned him of the ambush   192

The square in Kebili from which de Mores set out on the
journey to his death   192

One of the many oil fields that have broken the silence of
the Sahara *(Photo: Documentation Française)*   193

MAPS

I Caillé's exploration   29

II Explorers of the Central Sahara   49

Sayings of two women who loved the Desert as I did

For one is only free when one is alone
Isabelle Eberhardt
speaking of the Sahara

The great charm of life comes, perhaps, from the certainty of death
Isabelle Eberhardt
speaking of her rather disastrous life in the Sahara

To wake up on a fine morning in the desert is like waking up in an opal——I think that the old saying—"See Naples and die"—should be changed to—"See the desert on a Spring morning and die if you can"——

There is no name for it. The Arabs do not speak of the desert or wilderness as we do. Why should they? To them it is neither desert nor wilderness, but a land which they know every feature, a mother country whose smallest product has a sufficient use for their needs. They know it, or at least they knew it in the days when their thoughts shaped themselves in deathless verse, how to rejoice in the great spaces and how to honour the rush of the storm——They had watched, as they crossed the barren water courses, the laggard wonders of the night, when the stars seemed chained to the sky as though the dawn would never come.

From a letter from Gertrude Bell to her father Sir Hugh Bell.

I dedicate this book to
OSYTH LEESTON
without whose help and encouragement
it could never have been written
R.V.C.B.

Prologue

~~~~~~

I HAVE often been asked to explain what made me go and live with the Bedouin of the Sahara and remain there for over seven years with no status higher than that of a nomad shepherd. How was it that with my Eton and regular army background, the son of a distinguished historian and blessed with all the advantages which the world can offer, I could resign myself to living in a nomad's tent, no more than a shelter against the midday sun. How could I sleep on a carpet, sharing my shepherd's meagre fare, wearing the same sort of clothing as these desert wanderers, practising the Moslem faith, cut off from educated and thinking human beings and with no books to read and no newspapers, so that I had no idea of world events during those peaceful years in the Sahara.

The immediate cause of my going to live in the desert was T. E. Lawrence, Lawrence of Arabia. He never knew the Bedouins as intimately as I did, because underneath his Kufaya and his Abba there was always the uniform and the authority of a British officer and although he consorted with the shepherd nomads it was always in the capacity of an honorary Arab chief.

Under my bournous there was nothing but an unknown Roumi;[1] Lawrence knew less about Arabia and its people than did my cousin, Gertrude Bell, who explored the whole of the Arabian desert, and very much less than Richard Burton or St. John Philby or Charles Doughty who had lived with and studied the desert people during a great part of their lives.

At the end of the Paris Peace Conference of 1919, during which we had worked together trying to deal fairly with those who had

[1] The North African's name for any Occidental dating from the days when the only foreigners in N.W. Africa were Roman.

11

helped us defeat the Turks in the Middle East, Lawrence suggested that I should go and live in the desert. I was suffering from exhaustion after nearly five years in the trenches of the Western Front as well as from nervous tension engendered by the Peace Conference.

"But how?" I questioned, rather taken aback by what sounded like an order.

"Just go to the desert and say that you like the way of living of the Bedouins and want to join them. Buy some sheep, become a nomad shepherd. If these people see that you are sincere, they will accept you and in a year's time all your cares will be gone and you will have peace of mind as well as good health."

Lawrence paused and added peremptorily, "Go and live in the desert with Arabs. . . ."

There was another incentive for my seemingly strange behaviour.

My grandfather, John Bell, the uncle of Gertrude, was the head of one of the biggest steel concerns in the North Riding of Yorkshire, where his father had discovered iron ore. My grandfather suffered from poor health and could not stand the Yorkshire winters. So he would set sail on his all-weather yacht every year after the autumn equinox and make for the Mediterranean.

One year he landed in Algiers which had lately been taken over from the Turkish Corsairs by the French. There were few Europeans outside the soldiers in the neighbourhood and the Mustapha Hill dominating Algiers was dotted with moorish palaces which the Turks had built with slave labour. My grandfather decided to buy one of these, but no one knew what price to ask as the French had never imagined that anyone would want to acquire what were in reality miniature palaces. Finally it was agreed that the price should be between three and four thousand francs, about £150 at that time. After the Second World War my aunt sold the property for £200,000.

John Bell spent his winters at Mustapha Rais—the house was named after the old pirate who had built it—with his wife and three daughters, one of whom became my mother. She met my father at the Governor's ball at the Summer Palace. He had lately resigned as private secretary to Sir Charles Dilke and was gathering material for his history of modern France, which included the French colonies. They were married very soon afterwards in

Algiers and, although I was born in France, my mother who loved Algeria and its people kept me interested in all that went on there.

I had continued to visit my grandfather's home as a boy, and as I grew up, I made trips to the Sahara and became acquainted with the Berber chiefs. It was, therefore, natural for me to return to the Sahara when Lawrence suggested this as the perfect catalyst—the way to peace and tranquillity.

I soon found out that it was not as easy to become a Bedouin of the Sahara as Lawrence had suggested. I had made my way to the oasis of Laghouat, which lies on the northern borders of the Sahara and some three hundred miles from Algiers. This was the place I had visited as a boy and where I had made the acquaintance of various Bedouin chiefs. At first these sedentary oasis people as well as desert nomads suspected that I had been sent as a spy by the French government. When it became known that the French themselves believed that I was on some nefarious spying British-subsidized project to report on the Sahara this was thought by the nomads harmless enough. Nevertheless, they found it difficult to understand why an occidental should wish to live this wandering existence, but they welcomed me as a guest. My status was changed by the Caid Isa ben Addallah, an old friend of my mother's, who agreed to buy sheep for me and to let me share his life as a Bedouin, though such a thing had never been done before. I accordingly dressed as a Bedouin and lived in a tent which was no more than a black blanket made of camel's and goat's hair spread over three posts.

I was assigned to a tribe, the El Soffrane, one of the tribal groups making up the Federation of Larba nomads. My immediate chief was the Caid Isa, but he himself was under a Bash Agha called Jelloul Ben Yahia, head of the whole Larba Federation. This group had its allotted pasturing area, yet with no visible boundary marks and we never trespassed on the pastures of the other three neighbouring federation of tribes; the Ouled Nails to the north, the Zibans to the east and the Shamba to the south.

After I had learnt the tribal customs of my companions, a good deal of the Sahara Arabic dialect and enough about my sheep, I became curious about the Sahara itself and the lives of the men and women who had opened up the Sahara to occidental penetration. I could find out little of their history from the nomads, but I learnt a great deal from Casimir Champollion the *medecin major*

of the oasis of Laghouat, who was also a descendant of the famous
Jean Champollion who had deciphered the Rosetta Stone in
Egypt at the end of the eighteenth century. He had lived and
worked in the Sahara for some fifty years and was an acknow-
ledged authority on the strange history of the desert, its peoples
and the explorers who had lived and died there. I met survivors of
expeditions, descendants of some of those men and women,
talked to them and heard details of the tragic stories which are
not generally known. But to Casimir Champollion himself, his
wisdom and knowledge and his ability to assess the value of what
these courageous pioneers set out to do and the odds they encountered I owe an immeasurable debt. It is he who helped me to
gain some understanding of that strange force that draws men to
the Sahara, to define my own reasons for living as a Bedouin
shepherd and to draw on this experience in writing of these
explorers and inhabitants of the desert.

In addition to all I heard about the Sahara from Casimir
Champollion I later read every book I could on the subject. I also
obtained information from these survivors or descendants of those
men and women who had lost their lives in their attempts to
make this great desert known to future generations. I did not
attempt to go back to Anselm Salguier, the fifteenth-century
traveller who crossed the desert from north to south and from
south to north and lived to tell the tale. Nor did I investigate
Commander Clapperton, R.N. and Doctor Oudeney who both
lost their lives in the Sahara about 1818. So much has been
written on Mungo Park, who discovered the Niger at the end of
the eighteenth century, that I omitted him too. I began with more
contemporary pioneers, Major Gordon Laing and René Caillé,
travellers during the first half of the nineteenth century, who do
not seem to have left any descendants. I found it hard to obtain
first-hand information. Laing had been strangled by Moslem
fanatics north of Timbuktu. He had written some letters to his
fiancée, the daughter of the British consul in Tripoli, but they
give nothing of much interest to geographers. All his notes on the
journey from the Mediterranean to Timbuktu had been scattered
about the desert at the time of his death. I had to rely on reports
from E. W. Bovill and other writers who had taken the trouble
to write up what this gallant young officer had achieved.

René Caillé had died forgotten and in poverty in his native

France. He had left the notes of his incredible journey on foot from Senegal to Marseilles via Timbuktu and Morocco. These notes had been written on odd sheets of wrapping paper or anything he could get hold of and had been put together by the secretary of France's Geographical Society and published as a book in 1830. I managed to obtain a copy of this volume from the Bibliothèque Nationale.

I was fortunate in obtaining first-hand information on the Flatters disaster, for while living near the oasis of Laghouat, I met Aurélie Picard. She had been married to the Marabout of the Tidjani holy fraternity which had its headquarters at Ain Mahdi. She told me her own fantastic story and a great deal about the Flatters expedition. She had encouraged Colonel Flatters to lead his men into the Twareg country and after the massacre she had made contact with the survivors through her Tidjani connections.

My information about Cardinal Lavigerie and the White Fathers came from various sources, including the special study made by my father for his book on the church in France. Father David, who was the Superior of the White Fathers in Laghouat while I lived in the Sahara, gave me a great deal of data on the saintly martyrs who died futilely for a hopeless cause in the desert. Father Fournier, the Superior of the White Fathers in Washington, came to see me when he heard that I was writing the life of Father de Foucauld for the centenary of his birth in 1958. To celebrate this occasion an exhibition of Foucauld's relics was held in the crypt of the Basilique of the Sacré Cœur in Paris. The exhibition was in the charge of a number of White Fathers who had known de Foucauld and who were able to tell me about him and their colleagues who had died in the desert.

The research on Father de Foucauld brought me into contact with his friend General Laperrine and further details of his life and death came from Marshal Lyautey. I had met Marshal Lyautey through a friend of mine who was one of his A.D.C.s. He also gave me unpublished information about Isabelle Eberhardt. This information was supplemented by the Comtesse de Brazza, the widow of the Belgian explorer Savorgnan de Brazza who had opened up the Congo to occidentals. Madame de Brazza had been a friend and admirer of Isabelle Eberhardt's in spite of Isabelle's unorthodox way of life.

The Marquis de Mores' tragedy and the ugly political story

behind this came to me from Monsieur Steeg, the Governor-General of Algeria, who allowed me to have access to the files of the Mores murder. I also learned a great deal from the Marquis' grandson, I believe the Duc de Vallombrosa.

My own experience of living as a Bedouin in the desert has helped me to appreciate in some small measure what these pioneers endured in their search for knowledge of the Sahara.

I must take this opportunity to thank Monsieur Jules Massenet, a great nephew of the composer, and French Consul General in Boston, Massachusetts for setting me on the track of government officials in France able to supply me with maps and photographs to illustrate this book as well as to help me with my research work.

Also Father Coudray, Superior of the Order of the White Fathers in Paris, who generously helped me with photographs and material regarding the White Fathers who died martyrs of the Sahara.

And to Harriet who read and corrected my first set of proofs.

Finally to Valerie Green who gave me invaluable help with the final editing of this book which I could have never undertaken alone.

1

MYSTERIES OF THE SAHARA

~~~~~~

THE Sahara has a personal and mysterious charm which no one can explain. It is an enigma which no man so far has been able to solve. I once read in a French geographic magazine: "There is much we *think* we know but more that we do *not* know about the great Sahara Desert." And there was also the statement of General Laperrine, who had lived most of his life in this wilderness of stones and sand, made just before his death in this parched country which he so loved: "Neither I nor anyone else knows the Sahara."

During the first few years that I lived in this part of the world, I had rather taken the Sahara for granted. It was another remarkable phenomenon of nature like the Gobi Desert which I had once glimpsed with Roy Chapman Andrews, or the Mojave Desert or the desolate Nefuhd, into which I had once peered with T. E. Lawrence. But after a while, I began to think differently.

I remembered how Herodotus and Strabo and Pliny and other writers of ancient times had tried to describe the Sahara and interpret it, and had failed. I thought of men like Fromentin and Maupassant speaking of the Sahara as if they knew it intimately, merely because they had travelled on horseback a few hundred miles inland from Algiers to the fringe of the desert.

Until this day of pondering, I *had been* a Fromentin or a Maupassant. I *had talked* familiarly about these desolate plains, where I had made my home—without any qualification to do so! Because the country charmed me. I also knew of Frenchmen who

at the termination of their civilian or military services in the
Sahara could have retired to end their days in some fertile
province of France. Yet, after a few months away from this
glittering cruel desert, they had returned to die of their infatuation
for this waterless wilderness. Suddenly, I was a little afraid. I did
not understand. It was all too big, too bright. The perpetual lack
of sound, this absence of rock giving echoes, and the rare thunder
storms were not normal. Why was there rarely any noise as in
other countries, or as there is at sea? Who were these Shamba
and M'zabites and Twareg and other strange races, who lived
here by preference?

It was all now so confusing. It was the same with the nomads
of the federation of tribes to which I belonged. I was happy with
them. I was well. I had peace of mind. There were moments, too,
when I really felt that I belonged to this Bedouin way of living.
I could see before me a broad, sunlit path leading onward to
happiness. I almost felt that the contentment which every man
seeks was within my grasp. And then, down came a mist, blotting
out everything. I no longer had any notion of where I was;
whither I was going. The Bedouins became shadowy; their
minds became as impenetrable as the fog. I had no idea what they
thought of me, or if they thought at all. There was something
either in the country or in the people, or both, which eluded
me.

Added to this baffling sensation, there was the strange, natural
phenomena of the Sahara itself. There was that burning wind,
called in this part of the desert, the sirocco. The Bedouins who
live in the Sahara do not even try to understand the desert; they
accept strange phenomena as part of their lives just as they accept
the sirocco.

As darkness suddenly blacks out the glittering plains of the
desert one hears weird mutterings, mingled with the whispering
of the wind. In the middle of the night, ghostly grindings and
shattering cracks, like the firing of a rifle, waken one with a start.
One listens tensely for the sound of an approaching enemy and
sure enough, one can hear the rolling of a thousand drums as if
announcing an army which never gets any nearer.

Men of science, who have explanations for everything, including religious beliefs, say that the sudden drop of temperature
after sunset, which often causes a broiling day to be followed by a

frosty night, causes the rocks to be rent apart. The mutterings and the drummings are caused by the ever-blowing Sahara wind, charged with sand, hissing through the scrub. This is as it may be; but the nomad Bedouins who know nothing about refrigeration and erosion, attribute the uncanny sounds to djinns. I prefer to hold this belief too.

The mirages in the southern Sahara are, likewise, something which do not belong to an everyday, occidental world. My Bedouins were used to them and took little notice when the desert started its picture-making. But I was fascinated!

What we most often saw were expanses of water appearing about a mile away from us, but when I galloped hopefully towards the shimmering lake, it retreated or changed places. Sometimes I would find myself on an island with sparkling water in all directions. At other times, I would catch the sight of strange animals with long, stilt-like legs, which became distorted as I watched. Again I would ride towards them, and they would fly into the air like prehistoric monsters. Occasionally an oasis or a town would come into being, usually beside water. I would draw my friend the Caid Isa's attention to the domes and minarets and palms, but before he could comment, they had gone or changed into something else.

No one could tell me what caused these mirages, but this I learned: with the exception of the water illusions, which are reflections of the sky, no mirage can appear if there is nothing to reflect. If a town or trees or animals are seen in mirage form, somewhere, not far away there *is* a town, or trees, or animals. This is so true that nomads travelling over unfamiliar territory check their bearings by a mirage which, on clear mornings, often appears soon after dawn. According to them, it gives a picture of the country beyond the horizon.

The mirage is one of the strangest things in this strange land of purring winds, and shattering rocks, and no one tells the same tale about it. The *Encyclopædia Britannica* gives the explanation that it is the reflection caused by light rays undergoing refraction, but this does not get one much farther.

When the weather in the southern pastures began to warm up, we turned north again; that is, the flocks turned north. A nomad has really nothing to do with his wandering. He could just as well live in one place as in another. It is the flocks which wander in search of pasture, and the nomads follow the flocks. And it is not the sheep, either, who decide where to roam—it is the goats. The sheep are the stupidest animals in existence. If left to themselves, they would eat the pastures immediately before them, and then die of starvation. It would not occur to them that there might be food a little further on. If a mountain lion attacked them, they would unprotestingly submit to being killed and eaten.

The goats, on the other hand, are as alert as the sheep are lethargic. So little exaggerated is this, that my nomads always kept a dozen goats in every flock of two hundred and fifty sheep. The goats were forever looking for pastures and will skip off if danger is about. When the shepherds slept, they always had a goat at the end of a string attached to their wrists. In this way, they knew when something was amiss and could get up and fire a shot into the air which would frighten away marauders, human or animal. It also alerted the other shepherds.

Nevertheless, after hearing the cracking rocks and watching the ever-changing mirages, I knew little more about the Sahara than I did before I had begun to wonder about the desert phenomena.

The fact of the matter was that none of these people, were they Bedouin shepherds or oasis shopmen, cared what the Sahara might be. I really believe that the majority of my companions thought that the whole of the world was something like the Sahara for, as one of my men said to me one evening: "But if you have no Sahara in your country, where can you walk alone in peace?"

These desert men called this desolate land "The Garden of Allah", declaring that God had created it so that there would be one sure place on earth where he could walk unmolested by tiresome mortals. For this reason, they reverenced it as holy territory and generally walked on it on bare feet. That was about all the information which I could obtain from my Bedouin friends as answers to my reiterated questions.

The desert was there, always had been there and would probably continue to be there until the end of time. In any case, it was not their business, and certainly not mine, to query its origins.

My ethnic, geographic and historic knowledge of the Sahara really came to me by way of a toothache.

I had already been leading a nomad shepherd's life on the desert for over two years when I suddenly developed a terrible tooth-ache in one of my back molars. The pain was so great that I could not sleep, I could not even stay still in one place.

I confided my troubles to my friend and chief, Isa ben Abdallah. The Caid sympathized but said that I could not find a European doctor or dentist until our campers reached Laghouat, an oasis on the northern limits of this part of the desert. This palm-shaded city was used by my tribesmen as a kind of headquarters where they sold their sheep, their wool and replenished their groceries and other stores before setting out on another long sojourn in the desert.

He said that we were at present one hundred miles away from Laghouat, but on account of my obvious pain, he would order forced marches so as to reach the hospital as quickly as possible. In the meanwhile, he added that one of his own shepherds was suffering from the same complaint as I and at sundown that evening one of the *toubibs* (wise man or doctor) who travelled with the tribe was going to cure the aching tooth by using Bedouin methods. "If," he continued, "you would like to attend the operation, and see how it is done, you might like to confide your toothache to the *toubib*." The Caid assured me that whatever preliminary pain the operation caused, he himself would guarantee that my toothache would be instantly stopped.

I accordingly followed my shepherds to a place near the camp fire where the said *toubib* was making ready to perform his primitive dentistry.

Quite a few shepherds were assembled when the "dentist", an oldish man dressed in spotless white, appeared. Having summoned the patient, he looked into his mouth, located the decayed tooth, nodded knowingly, and ordered the shepherd to lie on the ground. He then called two stalwart Bedouins and told them to sit on the patient's chest. From the folds of his *gandourah*, the *toubib* then produced a lump of suet with which he covered the decayed tooth inside and out. Having done this to his satisfaction he produced what looked like a large ordinary nail and walking over to the camp fire dropped it into the glowing embers. In a few minutes he produced a pair of pincers with which he took the nail out of the fire. Satisfied that it was red hot, he carried it to the patient who lay on the ground. The "dentist" spoke a few words which led the man to open his mouth wide. Then, without a word of warning, the *toubib* took the red-hot nail and plunged it deep into the suet and then deeper into the decayed tooth.

As the suet sizzled and smoked, the man on the ground let out fearsome cries and struggled to get up. This was a futile gesture as the shepherds on his chest were hefty chaps who could not be moved. The *toubib* stepped back, made a few gestures with his right hand. The struggles and bellows of the patient diminished and stopped.

The *toubib* made a sign to the shepherds to get off the patient's chest. He immediately got up himself, spat out the nail, rubbed his cheek once or twice with his hand. His face melted into a broad grin which was followed by a laugh, after which he walked over to the *toubib* and kissed his forehead and walked away quite cured.

"You see," commented the Caid Isa, "desert dentistry may be primitive and painful, but it cures the toothache and will cost the sick one but one ewe. Perhaps you would like the *toubib* to deal with your tooth tomorrow at sundown."

However, although I was suffering great pain, what I had just seen had rather shaken me. So I replied: "No, thank you very much. I think that I would rather see the French doctor at Laghouat as soon as we get there."

"He is very skilful," commented Isa, "and he can answer all your questions about the Sahara which you seem so eager to learn about. His name is Colonel Casimir Champollion and he knows more about the Sahara than any other living man, Occidental or Berber. He has lived in this part of the world for over fifty years and has performed some life-saving cures. If you change your mind, let me know. Good night."

With that, I retired to my tent to pass a sleepless night in agonizing pain, wondering whether I had been unwise to refuse the services of the *toubib* and his red-hot nail.

However, two days later we reached the neighbourhood of Laghouat and mounting my horse I galloped as fast as I could to the hospital which Isa had pointed out to me on a rocky ridge in the middle of the oasis. When I reached the hospital I tethered my animal to a post in the courtyard.

There was no one who could tell me the whereabouts of the doctor's office. So, hearing a sound on the first floor, I climbed the stone staircase. Then, guided by voices, I entered what might have been termed a very large doctor's waiting-room. There, for the first time, I beheld Colonel Casimir Champollion. He was a heavily-built, red-faced man wearing the uniform of a Colonel of the French Army Medical Corps and was talking to a Bedouin who, I gathered, was a patient. After a few minutes' wait, the doctor went into what must have been a surgery and came out with a bottle of green liquid which he gave to his patient. The Bedouin thanked the doctor and went on his way.

The doctor then turned to me questioningly. "I presume, *mon Colonel*," I began "that you are the *medecin major*, Colonel Casimir Champollion?"

The Colonel formally bowed and replied, "I am, and I presume from your appearance and your European accent that you are the lunatic Englishman who, for reasons unexplained, has taken up residence in a nomad's tent and lives the life of a Bedouin shepherd?" He paused and went on at once. "But that is of no importance and none of my business. In what way can I help you?"

I explained my predicament and added: "Having seen dentistry as practised in the desert, I felt it safer to place myself in your care. The Caid Isa ben Abdallah told me that you had performed miracle cures among these desert people."

The doctor smiled. "I am afraid the Caid exaggerates. I am just a country doctor and no dentist, although I can probably extract your tooth without having recourse to red-hot nails. Show me the tooth which gives you pain."

I opened my mouth and indicated the source of my anguish.

"Ah, yes," said the doctor, "a deep cavity in a very decayed tooth. To relieve you, it must come out immediately. Kindly sit in that armchair," he added, pointing to an ordinary upholstered drawing-room chair, as he continued with a laugh. "We do not run to dentist chairs in Laghouat, and I'm afraid I have no cocaine to rub on your gum which might ease the pain and, of course, no laughing gas. But we'll do our best not to hurt you too much; I will have one of my orderlies hold you while I pull. If you'll wait a minute, I'll bring the forceps."

The Colonel went back into the surgery and on the way said a few words in Arabic to an orderly who stood by the door. The orderly nodded and led me back to the armchair in which I sat with the man standing by.

In a very few minutes the doctor returned, carrying a pair of bright steel forceps. The orderly simultaneously placed his strong hands on my shoulders, while the doctor inserted the forceps into my mouth. He then, after the manner of dentists, began pushing the tooth down into the gum and trying to turn it to right and to left. The tooth was, however, stubborn, and would not be moved. The doctor made clicking sounds with his tongue and muttered:

"I'm afraid I shall have to pull the tooth out by brute force."

With that, he leaned back and began tugging and tugging while the orderly prevented my following the doctor's tugs by holding me firmly in the chair. The pain in my jaw was great but less great, I felt, than the red-hot nails.

Finally, having taken hold of the forceps with both hands and putting all his weight into the pulling, the tooth suddenly gave and sent the doctor flying across the room still holding the forceps which imprisoned the tooth until he hit the far wall of the waiting-room.

With the agony through which I had gone during the previous three days, I felt so relieved that I burst out laughing.

The doctor laughed too. "That tooth seems to have been part of your jaw. I hope I didn't hurt you too much." He looked at the tooth in the forceps and added: "No wonder you had pain, you had a big abscess hanging on to the roots of your tooth. Look!"

So saying, he got up from the floor and showed me the white sack of the abscess clinging to the bottom of the tooth. "Thank you, *mon Colonel*," I said. "The pain was short and sharp and much less, I am sure, than that red-hot nail business."

The doctor nodded. "These nomads seem to be able to withstand unbelievable pain with no after effects."

"But how does the red-hot nail effect this sudden cure?" I asked.

"Quite simple," replied the doctor. "If one can destroy the source of pain, the pain goes. The red-hot nail destroys not only the tooth but also the nerve and, at the same time, cauterizes the wound. *Voila!* Incidentally, come into surgery and I will give you some disinfectant to clean your mouth."

I did as I was bid and, feeling very much better, I said: "I am most grateful for what you have done for me, although, as a matter of fact, I was intending to pay you a courtesy call anyway on the advice of the Caid Isa, who suggested that you would satisfy my insatiable curiosity over matters Saharan. As you know, the native inhabitants take the desert as a matter of course. They have always known it and things which seem strange to me do not seem worth explaining. I've been leading a nomad's life with the Federation of the Larba tribes, and I know no more about the history or origins of the Sahara than I did when I first came here two years ago. I have no idea what these people think of me or if they think anything. They seem to be very stupid, ignorant people. This Caid Isa told me that you had lived in the Sahara for nearly fifty years and knew more about this part of the world near Bamakao in 1806.

"Yes," interrupted Casimir, "these nomads are very stupid if you gauge intelligence by education. They have none to speak of, outside learning the Koran by heart, which entails the reading of Arabic. They are nevertheless very astute men and very courageous, as well as being staunch friends. As to my knowledge of the Sahara, I have lived in this desert so long with really not very much to do, that I set myself the task of learning all I could about this part of the world and its inhabitants. If you are really interested, I will pass on to you all that I know."

This is how, in a few days, I learned the history of the Sahara and of the courageous explorers who opened up the desert to Europeans.

2

RENÉ CAILLÉ

~~~~~~

RENÉ CAILLÉ, the most valiant and the greatest of French explorers, was the son of poor French peasants who lived in the Poitou near La Rochelle. He was an undersized youth who had become an orphan when quite young and placed under the guardianship of his uncle. However, in spite of his lack of money and his puny body, he was obsessed with the ambition to travel and explore unknown countries.

He had heard of the disastrous exploit of Major Gordon Laing and he made up his mind to complete what the British officer had failed to accomplish and find out whether the tales of Timbuktu, as a fabled city like Baghdad in the days of Haroun al Raschid, were true or false. These tales were told by the Andalusian Berber, Hassan ibn Muhammed, better known as Leo Africanus, in his *History and Description of Africa*, published during the sixteenth century.

Major Laing of the Yorkshire Light Infantry made his way from Tripoli to Timbuktu along a trail unknown even to the native inhabitants themselves. He wore his British uniform jauntily and told all who questioned him that he was an English officer as well as a staunch Christian. He did this in a country where Occidentals were detested, worthy only of beheading, while death and torture were all that a Christian could expect among fanatic Moslems. Needless to say, he succumbed to the inevitable fate of such brave men since he would not renounce his race or religion.

After passing through Timbuktu, at that time under the rule of
26

King Osman, a Moslem Sudanese, Caillé travelled on to the Mediterranean and eventually reached France where he could tell his story of an unprecedented journey from Senegal and across the Sahara accompanied by unbelievable hardships.

In order to achieve this seemingly impossible task for an almost uneducated child of peasants, Caillé scraped up enough money to buy a pair of new shoes and a presentable suit of clothes. He then walked to La Rochelle, where he found a job as a servant to a French naval officer called Deberré, who was about to sail for West Africa. The reason for the departure of this one and two other warships was to take possession again of Senegal, which the British were returning to France after the fall of Napoleon.

After a month's sea journey, during which time more than half the crew had died of scurvy, the ship reached St. Louis at the mouth of the Senegal river. However, the British governor had received no orders about handing over Senegal to the French. The ship, therefore, sailed on to Cape Verde where there was a French garrison. Here most of the survivors of the sea journey died of yellow fever. Those who were alive, including René Caillé, were then allowed to return to St. Louis.

Here he just missed the British expedition which was going to search for Mungo Park, the explorer who had set out to discover the source of the Niger and was found to have died somewhere near Bamakao in 1806.

Many writers suggest that Caillé now made his way directly to Timbuktu. This is a probably laudable desire to save space. However, the fact remains that before Caillé set out on his final expedition, which was to earn him France's Geographical Society's medal, he made three false starts under the worst possible conditions.

He first tried to join the Gray expedition in Gambia but a walk of nearly three hundred miles across desert country so exhausted him that he had to lie up and rest. When recovered, he joined a caravan led by a Monsieur Partarrieu, which was carrying a replenishment of stores for Major Gray. However, when he did reach the Gray expedition at Boulibany, he found that the paramount chief of the district had forbidden any further advance.

As it was impossible for a caravan of foreigners to move without native protection, Gray decided to retreat and, taking to boats on the Senegal, eventually reached St. Louis. Caillé had no money left so he took a job as cook at the local dockyard.

For a while after these setbacks Caillé enjoyed a short period of good fortune. He managed to join a caravan of Mandingos moving into the interior towards the Niger. However, finding that his companions were too exacting in the matter of gifts, which he could not afford to buy, he once more had to leave this caravan and return to the coast.

Here he met a Monsieur Castagnel who was so impressed by his audacity and determination to reach Timbuktu that he gave the weary little Frenchman some money.

When Caillé arrived in West Africa, he knew little Arabic and even less about Islam but he frequented the local market-place where he was quick to learn the local dialect and secretly read the Koran until he knew enough about the Moslem Faith to cook up the following story. He said that he had been captured when a small boy by Bonaparte's troops as they conquered Egypt. He had been to France where the French made him abandon his religion and forget the customs of his people. Owing to his diligent work and honesty, he had been released soon after the fall of the Empire. He had then learnt that his parents had died, and that he was a penniless orphan, but his one idea was to return to Egypt and pick up the threads of his old life and, above all, re-establish himself as a conscientious member of his old faith. He added to this pathetic tale, which he punctuated with sobs, that his name was Abdallahi, the servant of God.

The whole story went down well with the Moslem merchants and he was eventually able to find another caravan of Mandingo traders who were moving into the interior from Kaikondy[1] on the River Nunez in Gambia and were willing to take him as a servant and man of all work with them.

After suffering unbelievable hardships, including scurvy and lacerated feet, he reached a village called Kouroussa which lay on the banks of the Niger. This marked one of Caillé's most important discoveries as it filled in the space left blank on the maps between the mountains of Sierra Leone and the desert. However, the scurvy had by now taken such a hold on Caillé that his palate seemed to be rotting while his teeth were falling out and the ribs and other bones of his emaciated body strained against his skin

[1] Kaikondy has today been identified as Boké.

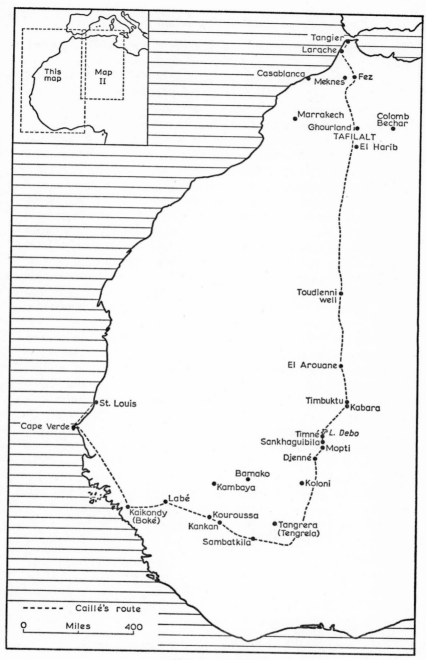

Caillé's exploration

and turned him into a veritable skeleton. In fact so ill did he feel
that he prayed God to take his life and put him out of his misery.

Nevertheless, he pushed on, his face covered with running
suppurating sores, until he reached Djenné, known as the Pearl of
the Niger. Here he placed himself courageously under the
protection of the local Moslem chief, who was of Arab extraction,
telling the story of his degrading life as a slave of the French and
begging the men who formed the staff of the chief to help him to
return to his kin and his religious duties, which the Christians had
forced him to neglect.

His story was accepted with compassion and understanding, so
that according to the custom of Arab hospitality and protection
of a guest, Caillé found himself treated like a normal human being
for the first time since he left Kaikondy. Now, he cared only about
reaching the fabled city of Timbuktu. Once there, he would be
in a position to try and fulfil the conditions laid down by the
Geographical Society to earn the Gold Medal. How this was
accomplished is the first personally recorded and authentic tale
of the crossing of the Great Sahara Desert by an Occidental.

While Timbuktu's existence had been known for a long time,
it was still regarded at the beginning of the nineteenth century as
a mysterious and magnificent city as well as the central market
of Morocco and Algiers, trafficking chiefly in gold and slaves.
Caillé, therefore, was the first to publish any accurate description
of this Sudanese Moslem town near the Niger. Thus, from the
time of his return to Europe, Timbuktu ceased to be a legendary
name on a map. This is how Caillé wrote about his first view of
Timbuktu:

> At length, we arrived safely at Timbuktu, just as the sun was
> reaching the horizon. I now saw this capital of the Sudan, to reach
> which had so long been the goal of my wishes. On entering the
> mysterious city which is an object of curiosity and research to the
> civilized nations of Europe, I experienced an indescribable satisfac-
> tion. I never before felt a similar emotion and my excitement was
> extreme. I was obliged, however, to restrain my feelings, and to
> God alone did I confide my joy. With what gratitude did I return
> thanks to Heaven for the happy result which attended my enter-
> prize! This duty being ended, I looked around and found that the
> sight before me did not answer my expectations. I had formed a
> totally different idea of the grandeur and wealth of Timbuktu.

At first view, the city presented nothing but a mass of ill-looking houses, built of earth. Nothing could be seen in all directions but immense plains of quicksand of yellowish ochre colour. The sky was pale red as far as the horizon: all nature wore a dreary aspect, and the most profound silence prevailed; not even the warbling of a bird was heard. Still, though I cannot account for the impression, there was something imposing in the aspect of a great mud city, raised in the midst of sands, and the difficulties surmounted by its founders cannot fail to excite the admiration. I am inclined to think that formerly the river flowed close to Timbuktu, though at present it is eight miles to the south of the city.

Caillé's problems of investigation as well as of his personal safety were facilitated by having this introduction from Djenné, to a merchant called Sidi-Abdallahi Chebir, who received him hospitably, lodged him and clothed him during his stay in Timbuktu. The introduction included the Egyptian orphan boy story and evidently led Sidi-Abdallahi to believe the alleged circumstances which had brought this strange Moslem, who did not look like an Egyptian, across West Africa. He seems to have liked Caillé, too, and was most helpful in arranging the continuation of his journey over the Sahara.

Owing to the rough treatment and the illnesses which Caillé had suffered during the trek from West Africa, he stayed on at Timbuktu for a few weeks to recuperate, at the same time making notes of all he saw. Most of this was done from memory in the privacy of a room which had been allotted to him by his host. He also made sketches which were sufficiently well drawn, and to such an accurate scale as to be reproduced by engravers in London and Paris. The way Caillé achieved these sketches which, apart from the dangerous conditions of their execution, show much artistic talent, is best described by himself:

Conceiving that the description alone would not convey an adequate idea of the construction of the mosque, I ventured to make a sketch of it, as well of the town. To make this sketch I squatted in the street in front of it and, covering myself in my large wrapper, which I folded over my knees, I held in my hand a sheet of white paper close to a leaf of the Koran. When I perceived anyone approaching, I hid my drawing and looking at the leaf of the Koran, I appeared to be absorbed in devotion. The passers-by, far from suspecting me, regarded me as one of the elect and applauded my zeal.

Yet had that white sheet slipped on to the ground Monsieur Caillé's life would have been brought to an abrupt end. But he never seems to have appreciated these dangers, or had any apprehensions about getting home. René Caillé belongs to the ranks of those heroes of exploration whose achievements were taken for granted and then forgotten.

Suddenly feeling that too much familiarity with his host might betray his true identity, Caillé decided to join a caravan which was leaving for Tafilalet on the southern borders of Morocco. Sidi-Abdallahi seemed to be genuinely sorry to see his guest go and went as far as to offer to lend him money so that he could set himself up in business in Timbuktu. However, Caillé begged to be allowed to go on his way as his reason for this journey had been originally undertaken so that he would eventually reach his home.

This was, in fact, true, although not in the sense in which his host interpreted it—he still believed the "Egyptian orphan" story—Caillé did have an urge to see his family and old friends in France. But above all, he wanted to win the Geographical Society's prize. His journey into the interior of West Africa from Sierra Leone was known only by the few in whom he had confided, and if he did not appear again, he would be written off as one of the many who had died on similar adventures. He must, therefore, reach Paris at all costs and present his case to the Geographical Society. In making this decision he was taking his life in his own hands and embarking on a journey even more trying and terrifying than that through the Sudanese tropical forests.

Sidi-Abdallahi Chebir, seeing that Caillé was determined to leave, did everything possible to help him. He hired a well-conditioned camel for him as well as a guide called Ali, and gave him provisions for the journey. It was the last generous gesture which Caillé was to receive for a long time.

On the morning of 24th May, 1828, the caravan, consisting of six hundred camels bearing merchandise and a great number of black slaves to be sold in Morocco, set off to cross one of the most arid sections of the Sahara, and probably the most waterless desert in the world. The weather was suffocatingly hot, but to begin with a fair ration of water was given to each person and moving was carried out in the early morning until the temperature became too high for anything but huddling in the shade of primitive tents.

While Caillé had a compass which showed him that the general course set was north, the leaders of that procession had nothing like it. By day they took their bearings from the sun, and by night by the pole star. However, more than anything else, they remembered the route by familiar landmarks. A dune, a rock, a difference of colour in the sand, a few tufts of herbage, were infallible indications that the right route was being followed. The eldest caravan conductor led the way and these men had such an instinct for observing the most minute things that they never went astray, although there was not a vestige of a road, and the ever-blowing wind covered tracks with sand which had been made but a half hour before. The average pace of the caravan was two miles per hour, yet it was very rare to arrive at the few desert wells later than anticipated by the leaders. The camels too, when a start was made, instinctively turned their heads towards the north.

Thus Caillé's caravan, crossing this interminable waste of sand and stone and shale and rock, never deviated from its course, and arrived at El Arouane, near where Major Laing had been murdered, some two hundred miles north of Timbuktu, for which it had been heading, and at almost the precise hour predicted. Up to that time, El Arouane had been marked on Sahara maps as a group of wells. Caillé showed it to be a comparatively important desert town where caravans travelling north or south, east or west, halted to replenish their supply of water or dates. It was also the last form of sedentary civilization which he would experience for a long time. From now on, these Sahara wells, some of which might be choked with sand, would be the only source of liquid until Morocco was reached.

Eight hundred more camels with a corresponding number of slaves and Bedouin had joined the original party. Gold, ostrich feathers, gum, ivory and cloth had been added to the merchandise. Caillé described the scene in his book published in 1830 as follows:

> One one side were camels laden with ivory, gum and bales of goods of all sorts; on the other, camels carrying on their backs negroes, men and children, who were on their way to be sold at the Morocco market, and further, men prostrate on the ground invoking the prophet.

This spectacle touched and excited my feelings, and in imitation of devout Moslems, I fell on my knees but it was to pray to the God of the Christians: with my eyes turned to the north to my country, my relations and friends, I besought the Almighty to remove from my path the obstacles which had stopped so many other travellers; in the ardour of my wishes, I imagined that my prayer was granted, and that I should be the first European who had set out from west Africa to cross this ocean of sand and succeed in the undertaking. The thought electrified me; and while gloom hung on all other faces, mine was radiant with hope and joy. Full of these sentiments, I hastened to mount my camel, and to penetrate fearlessly into the deserts which separate the fertile Sudan from the regions of northern Africa. I felt as if I was mounting the breach of an impregnable fort, and divesting myself of every kind of fear and braving this new peril.

A boundless horizon was already expanding before us, and we could distinguish nothing but an immense plain of shining sand, and over it a burning sky. At this sight the camels uttered long moans, the slaves became sullen and silent, and, with their eyes turned towards heaven, they appeared to be tortured with regret for the loss of their country and the recollection of the verdant plains from which avarice and cruelty had snatched them.

Poor Monsieur Caillé, he was on the eve of enduring as much as these wretched slaves. More so, perhaps, as these "almost savages" had none of the nervous or physical reactions of this sensitive man. He began to suffer from thirst, as not only was all drinking rationed, but the rich maize cooked in rancid butter and served to everyone at the end of the march parched his throat. Furthermore, his guide, Ali, who had been paid by Sidi-Abdallahi to look after his guest, was using his charge's water for himself and thus reducing what was due to him. This, too, was only the beginning of the rascally behaviour towards the man he had been hired to take care of.

Soon the camels, too, began to suffer from lack of pasture. They lay exhausted with their heads between their forelegs waiting for the caravan to start and bring them a little nearer to a well. Before the signal was given, Ali brought the rations for the group which had accompanied Caillé from Timbuktu. This consisted of a few handfuls of maize which he threw into a calabash and then poured water on it, mixing the stuff with his hands and thrusting in his arms up to the elbow. He had, of course, not been able to wash at all for days, so that the beverage was not only lukewarm but very dirty. However, under the circumstances everyone, including Caillé, swallowed the nauseating mess eagerly.

There were times, too, when Ali would make his "cuisine" after attending to the saddle sores from which some of the camels were suffering. When one of the animals became too exhausted or ill to continue the trek, it was killed. The stagnant water in its stomach reservoir was drunk and the flesh distributed to the cameleers and slaves nearby.

Added to the hardships of these scanty solid and liquid rations, there were occasional sandstorms which caused the caravan to halt and lie on the ground while the hot wind lashed the men and the animals with burning grit. Much of the water at the wells was sandy and brackish. For this precious liquid, men and beasts fought until their thirsts had been quenched. Even Caillé had to thrust his head among the animals to drink with them.

Ali was behaving with even greater insolence to his charge than at the start of the journey when the caravan might have retraced its steps to Timbuktu and his conduct been reported to Abdallahi. Other cameleers, and soon the slaves, noticing what was going on, also began to torment Caillé. Sometimes they would strike him with camelthorn branches; at other times they would threaten to drive little pieces of stick through his nose as if he were a camel. Caillé, however, never lost his head and behaved in such a humble manner that soon some of the more important members of the caravan took pity on him and gave him their protection. Nevertheless, he knew that he was suspected of being an infidel and if this were confirmed he could only look forward to the same fate as his hero Major Laing.

By 29th May life began to be a little less torturing. The caravan had reached an area where there were wells of some kind at the end of each march. There was also a little scrub pasture for the camels. By then, many of the animals were so dehydrated and underfed that it was too late for their recovery and they had to be killed and then eaten. It seemed also that Caillé, for the first time since he had left Sierra Leone, was showing signs of discouragement. On June 11th, he recorded among his geographical notes:

> I was so tired that it was with much difficulty that I could keep my seat upon my camel. I frequently called to mind that the only chance of surviving the journey lay in hastening the march; this

idea supported my courage and restored my exhausted strength: I confess, nevertheless, that I envied the fate of those who can purchase fame at a cheaper rate than by such painful trials and continually recurring dangers.

Fortunately for him the courageous Frenchman did not anticipate what was still in store for him before he saw France again. In spite of now having enough to drink and sometimes sufficient water with which to wash his hands and face, Ali and his colleagues would not give him his full ration of food. In fact, if it had not been for these other travellers who felt compassion for this supposedly friendless orphan, Caillé might have died of starvation in the midst of comparative plenty. On 20th June he was almost killed when his camel fell while trying to negotiate a steep and rocky path through a defile in the hilly country which leads towards the Atlas foothills. He was badly bruised and also sustained a slight concussion of the brain. For two days following this accident he was in terrible pain and might have been left by the roadside to die had not the same kind-hearted companions again defended him against his guide, who coveted his camel and his few belongings.

Finally on 30th June the caravan reached an encampment near El Harib in the midst of sagebrush pastureland below the Atlas. Here Ali's family were encamped and Caillé was received with curiosity mingled with suspicion by these shepherds. The women were especially interested in the story of the kidnapped boy trying to make his way back to his native land. But while suitably fed, he was by no means treated as an honoured guest.

The caravan remained in this place for nearly two weeks. The reason for the delay was that the next stage of the journey over the Tafilalt regions passed through the territory of the Atlas Berbers, who were, and still are, warlike people who could not resist the sight of a rich caravan which required little effort to capture. An escort supplied by the Berber chief of the district was, therefore, a necessity. The escort cost a high price, but it was much less expensive than having the whole caravan looted and many of its members killed.

Caillé was content to rest and edit his notes on the journey. This ability of his to write was noticed by the women, who made up their minds that here was a man of learning who could prepare charms to enable their daughters to find suitable husbands. In return for these magic services Caillé would be properly fed for the remainder of the time he was at El Harib. He was only too pleased to oblige on such terms and wrote charms which he ordered to be hung around the necks of the girls. He also inscribed mysterious words on pieces of wood and ordered that the ink be washed off and the water used for the purpose be drunk by the husband-seekers. This was at one time a common Moslem fallacy, since the people of Islam connected any kind of writing with the Koran, so that a man who could write must have some kind of God-sent gift which would produce magical results. Caillé took the precaution to emphasize that the charm would not begin to work for one lunar month, knowing that by that time he would be on his way to Morocco.

Everyone was delighted and Caillé soon found himself being overfed with greasy food which he could not digest. But he could now move freely about the camp and the neighbouring country. He was, nevertheless, relieved to learn that the necessary escort for the trek north had been hired in plenty of time before the efficacy of his charms could be put to the test.

On 12th July the caravan set out once more at 5 a.m. in a north-westerly direction. It was a rough country composed of great sand dunes covered with sparse vegetation and intersected with deep ravines. Soon, they came into a district which was actually being cultivated with primitive ploughs. There were also date palms and sufficient water to irrigate vegetable gardens.

Ten days later, on 23rd July, the caravan reached Ghourland in the really fertile region of Tafilalt, where palms grew by the thousands. It was here that the merchandise brought from Timbuktu found its market. Caillé, through the recommendations of his host in Timbuktu, found himself invited to breakfast in the house of the local Caid. He was not allowed to spend the night there owing to the strictness with which the women were kept from the view of strangers. He had to lodge at the mosque in the edifice set aside for the reception of travellers.

While there Caillé talked to an educated Moor, called Sidi-Baubacar, who had lived in Mogador where he had met Christians. He had also been to Tripoli. He then confessed that he had learned arithmetic from the Christians and to prove it, did some quite complicated calculations. He also showed Caillé a watch and added that, while he despised Christians, he considered their intelligence infinitely superior to that of the Berber Moslems. He went on to discuss Bonaparte's campaigns in Egypt. Caillé was completely dumbfounded to find someone who could talk like an educated Occidental. Nevertheless, he did not dare to represent himself as anyone other than what he was supposed to be. This required a great deal of self-restraint, especially when in Sidi-Baubacar's house he was shown the prismatic compass which had belonged to Major Laing. He did not even dare to ask how it had come into his possession.

Sidi-Baubacar was helpful to Caillé during his stay in Ghourland and took him into several houses where he was able to make notes on the customs of the inhabitants. Then on 29th August, the man to whom he had originally been recommended warned Caillé that the next caravan going to Fez would leave shortly.

This put him in a quandary. His fall from the camel had left him rather lame and he could not consider taking this two hundred mile trek across mountains on foot. Nor could he break the laws of Moslem etiquette by asking Sidi-Baubacar for money with which to hire a mule or a donkey. Finally, he was able to sell his tired camel and some fairly new clothing which had been given to him in Timbuktu by his host and hired an ass with the money. On 2nd August he joined the caravan to make the journey to Fez.

Although the sojourn at Ghourland sounds comparatively tame after the ordeal of the desert, it held dangers of another nature. During the caravanning period everyone was too preoccupied by the trials of the route to worry much about Caillé, except by insulting him. But, among the sedentary population in a town where gossip was one of the chief occupations, he was in constant danger of doing something which would show him to be an infidel. The very fact that he could write might have led to the searching of his baggage, when any of the educated Moors would have discovered that the notes had nothing to do with Holy Writ.

It would have been clear from these that he was an Occidental seeking information about this Moslem world closed to all Christians. Even when Charles de Foucauld penetrated into Morocco seventy years after Caillé's visit, he had to do so in disguise and in daily danger of having his identity revealed, which would have meant death.

The journey towards Fez was through a lush land where the

gardens of the villages were full of dates and vegetables, figs, melons and grapes. For Caillé there was little of this refreshing food. In fact, most of the time there was little food at all. Whereas in the desert feeding was more or less of a community problem, here meals had to be paid for and Caillé had no money, having sold all of his possessions to hire the donkey.

He was dependent on Moslem charity which, according to Koranic law, is one of the obligations of the faith. In other words, he had to go begging for enough to keep him alive. Sometimes he received no more than a handful of dates or a bowl of couscous. Occasionally he met generous men who took him to their houses and entertained him, providing a satisfying meal and showing him their gardens where he was gorged with fruit. He was never sure when he woke each morning whether or not he would eat that day.

This lack of nourishment was all the more trying as the caravan was now in the Atlas Mountains and the country was too steep for the animals to carry heavy loads. Caillé was, thus, forced often to walk when in a weak and emaciated condition. Yet all the while, he continued to observe and note a country which no European had ever seen. On 12th August he reached Fez.

The beauty of this ancient city with its splendid mosques and beautiful palaces was a joyous surprise to Caillé, who for nearly three months had seen nothing but native villages and encampments and primitive towns consisting of mud houses. However, he realized the dangers of being detected were daily becoming greater.

There was a majority of educated Moors in Fez who had travelled and could quickly detect any European peculiarities in Caillé's behaviour or way of speaking Arabic. So on 14th August he set out alone for Rabat, where he hoped to find a French consul.

Reaching Rabat on 19th August Caillé had himself directed to the French consulate by saying that he had some money which he wanted to change into Moorish currency. He was dismayed to find that there was only a consular agent there who was a Jew of French nationality.

Caillé decided not to take the risk of disclosing his identity, but while the agent accepted his story, he made it clear that, although he did not believe it, he would not betray his compatriot. On the other hand, he also declared that he could do nothing to protect a Christian in this, the fanatical capital of Morocco. The nearest French consul was in Tangier and to him Caillé must go if he wished to escape to France.

Caillé, having now no money, tried to get in touch with his sovereign's representatives in Tangier, but finding that either the consular agent was doing nothing about it or else that the letters were not getting through, set out on foot on September 2nd to cover the one hundred and fifty miles which separated Rabat from Tangier. He was in the last stages of mental and physical exhaustion and was suffering from bouts of fever. Nevertheless, he made this trip in five days and on the most meagre of rations, reaching Tangier on the night of 7th September.

Here Caillé discovered that the French consul had died the previous week. There was a vice-consul, Monsieur Delaporte who, after first closing the door of his house in the face of what seemed to be the dirtiest Arab beggar he had ever seen, recognized in Caillé's French an accent which did not even slightly resemble that of France's "colons" in Algeria, and therefore re-opened the door and let the little man in. He then listened with amazement to the fantastic story which this scrofulous, verminous creature began to tell him.

Nevertheless, Delaporte believed all that he was told and warned Caillé that he was not even safe in the consulate. The unfortunate man was forced to return to the local fondouk until the consul had made arrangements to repatriate him. This led to many awkward questions from some of the Moors who had seen Caillé emerge from the Frenchman's house.

After the necessary arrangements to repatriate Caillé were made the consul sent one of his Jewish employees to fetch him and, after letting him in through a side door of his house, set about trying to cure the ravages caused to his body and stomach by the ordeals which he had undergone. His first action was to lead Caillé to the bathroom where, for the first time since leaving Sierra Leone seventeen months before, he was able to wash from head to foot and then sleep in a bed. The next day his ragged and verminous clothing was burned and the consul dressed him in the clothes of a French sailor. On 28th September he was smuggled aboard a French sloop and a week later he landed at Toulon.

The immediate reaction in France to Caillé's story was

incredulity. It seemed impossible that any human being could have survived such a journey. In fact, some people were sure that the whole story had been invented. Caillé did not protest but merely handed his notes and maps to Monsieur Jommard, the Vice-President of France's Geographical Society.

Monsieur Jommard had read a good deal about African travel and had in his possession fairly accurate maps of the area where Caillé said he had been, and was soon convinced that what Caillé had reported tallied with his own data on the subject. Furthermore, no impostor could have understated an adventure as had this rather retiring little Frenchman. This is what Monsieur Jommard wrote to his colleagues:

On the first arrival of the letters which I received from M. Delaporte, I entertained some doubts of the authenticity of his narrative, and I immediately arranged some questions by way of trial on the language spoken in Timbuktu, the customs of the country, its natural products, etc. For this purpose, I also requested the traveller to see me in Paris. The very day of his arrival, he submitted to my inspection a journal of his travels, modestly observing: "I do not know if I can answer all your questions, but here are my notes."

After reading these and asking a few questions, I could entertain no further doubts as to the authenticity of M. Caillé's exploits. It remains for members of the Geographical Society to share my convictions.

On 5th December, 1828, René Caillé was received officially on the premises of the Geographical Society by the illustrious naturalist George Cuvier and the committee of the Society. Everyone of importance in Paris was in the hall to listen to Cuvier's eulogious report on what Caillé had achieved. He was followed on to the platform by Monsieur Jommard, who emphasized that Monsieur Caillé's success was the more worthy of interest and praise for having been accomplished on his own very limited resources and without either participation or assistance from anyone else.

In fact, he had sacrificed everything he possessed to supply the requirements for this journey of exploration. The Geographical Society had, therefore, decided to award him ten thousand francs bonus in addition to the original sum proposed, as well as the Gold Medal of the Society.

The two speeches were acclaimed with thunderous applause from all those present, much to the embarrassment of René Caillé, who was already feeling ill at ease in his suit with the frilled shirt and high collar. A little later on Charles X, who had just launched his first military expedition against the Turks in northwest Africa, decorated Caillé with the Legion of Honour.

The only people who seemed quite indifferent to what this gallant man had done were the cabinet ministers of the French government, who took little notice of the Geographic Society's pleas for some official monetary recognition for the Frenchman whose name had become famous all through Europe. The various ministers passed on these requests to their colleagues in some other ministry—the Secretary of State of the Interior saying that this was a matter depending on the Secretary of State for War who, in turn, declared that it depended on the Ministry of the Navy, to which was attached the newly formed Ministry, for the still non-existent colonies. With this particular ministry, Caillé's cause was aided by Baron Roger, who, having been governor of France's West African provinces, was well aware of the riches of Senegal and pointed out that, without Caillé's reports, any exploitation of the country in France's interests would have been impossible.

The Secretary of State for the Navy, harassed on all sides by angry criticisms for his behaviour towards this heroic man, awarded him a further sum of three thousand francs, while this new Ministry of the Colonies in April 1829 appointed him French Resident at Bamako, which lies above the rapids which separate the Upper Niger from the Middle Niger, at a salary which was to be six thousand francs a year. Bamako was, incidentally, the place where Caillé had passed as a penniless Egyptian orphan two years before. It was soon to become the capital of French Sudan.

This position was never to be realized, in spite of Caillé's humbly going back to school to learn subjects neglected in his childhood which were necessary for the representative of France in this, then remote, jungle town of tropical Africa. At the same time and with the help of Monsieur Jommard, he put together his diary and notes, scribbled almost illegibly on the backs of pages of the Koran, and sometimes on wrapping paper in which rations had been packed for that terrifying journey from Sierra Leone.

He carried out this work chiefly to refute insinuations from certain sections of the press that he had never really reached Timbuktu, while a religious magazine severely criticized Caillé for having practised the Moslem faith during his heroic journey, declaring that, "even for the sake of security, a Christian has no right to abjure his own religion". The British, too, who were smarting over the failure of Major Laing to reach Timbuktu and return in safety, took the side of the French critics in suggesting that René Caillé was an impostor.

However, in 1830, the notes and diaries were all classified and were published by the Royal Press in three volumes at the expense of the government. They were entitled as follows: *Journal of a journey to Timbuktu and to Jenné in Central Africa with Observations made among the Moors of Braknas, the Nalous and other peoples during the years 1825, 1826, 1827 and 1828.*

Included in these volumes was a map showing the route followed by René Caillé with Franco-Mandigo and Franco-Kissour vocabularies. This book was an instantaneous success and by the details which it gave of places and peoples, distances and geographical aspects of the countries covered, closed the mouths of all Caillé's critics.

The satisfaction of feeling himself exonerated was short-lived. Caillé's health had been ruined by his illnesses in tropical Africa and the ordeals of the Sahara trek began to take their toll. In fact so ill did he become that he was sent to a sanitorium where he met another invalid, Caroline Tétu, with whom he fell in love. She was already married to an adventurer who turned out to be a bigamist. Caroline was thus able to get rid of her husband and was married to Caillé by a Justice of the Peace.

Caillé was now supremely happy, yet he still had hallucinations and suffered from those hardships with which he had had to cope. Neither he nor his bride had any reliable source of income but they were in love and settled down contentedly in Caillé's rooms in Paris. Moreover, this happy life with someone to care for him seemed to be improving his health so that it looked as if he might be able to throw off those weakening, insidious fevers of Central Africa.

He had not been quite forgotten. One day the new king of France, Louis Philippe, summoned him and his wife to the Tuilleries, where he was received in the friendliest of fashion by the royal family. However, in spite of the evident admiration which the king showed for Caillé, the Resident's position at Bamako was showing no signs of materializing. The fact of the matter was that with the abdication of Charles X and the replacement of the House of Bourbon with that of the Orleans Dynasty, a new set of statesman had taken the place of those who, under the previous reign, had voted those small emoluments for the great explorer. These new men, too, were bent on setting off the new reign on a sound economic basis.

Thus in the month of November 1830 René Caillé received a cold and impersonal letter from the Ministry of the Navy informing him that owing to reductions in the budget, no money could be voted for an official trading post at Bamako. Furthermore, wrote the official, the pension of three thousand francs a year which had been allotted to Caillé until such time as he took up his post at Bamako would cease on 1st January, 1831.

When Monsieur Jommard heard of this decision he went to the king, who ordered that Caillé should always receive his pension and that it should be increased to four thousand francs a year, which then amounted to one hundred and sixty pounds or eight hundred dollars. This was not much for a man who had paved the way for France's occupation of Central Africa and the southern Sahara with all their riches, to say nothing of losing his health in so doing, but it kept him out of real want.

Caillé took this destruction of his dreams of living again in Africa, which he still loved very much, to heart, and decided to return to his native village, Mauze. His reception was regal and boisterous, but Caillé was a shy and retiring man and his old friends mistook this for pride or disdain for the poverty of the men and women who had once been his equals. The reception was a fiasco owing to his inability to talk about himself and this made his friends treat him with a deference which he disliked.

Furthermore, he had no family ties left in Mauze. His grandmother was dead as was his guardian and uncle, Barthelemy Lepine. His sister had left the neighbourhood to marry a well-to-do mason. In fact, Caillé was so completely disillusioned by the return to his home town, which he had so often visualized in the steaming jungles of Senegal and on the waterless waste of the Sahara, that he returned to Paris.

Paris with its fogs which irritated his heavy cough and gave him constant colds further undermined his physical resistance. Soon his bronchial troubles were diagnosed as tuberculosis. Consequently, on hearing that a small property in a village which was not far from Mauze called Beurlay was for sale, he bought this land and settled down to be a farmer. There were vines to cultivate and wheat to grow.

Caillé and his new wife moved into their home during the autumn of 1832. In May 1833 his wife bore him a daughter and in the same month of 1835, a son, which compensated a great deal for the disappointments of the past two years. He even had the joy of finding his sister again, who lived nearby.

The citizens of Beurlay knew all about Caillé's heroic exploits in Africa and did their best to make him feel important. He even wrote letters to various ministries explaining wisely and accurately why Bamako should be made an official French trading centre. But by this time the government bureaucrats had forgotten who René Caillé was. They were far too occupied with the campaign in North Africa to even consider matters to do with Senegal, and so did not even reply to his letters. The only encouragement Caillé received came from Monsieur Jommard, who still hoped to rouse someone's interest in this distinguished explorer.

In the meantime Caillé had the honour bestowed on him of being elected mayor of his village. This did not involve much work and allowed him a position which made him feel that he had not been entirely abandoned. His health was failing rapidly and on 15th May 1838 the tired little man who had seen death come so close from scurvy and thirst in the swamps of Senegal and on the stony wastes of the Sahara, where he could never be certain that he would be alive before the next day dawned, slipped his "mortal coil" while lying between the clean white sheets of his own bed in the presence of his wife and four children.

The oak coffin in which lay the hero of the Niger and Timbuktu was carried to the cemetery in a bullock cart followed by village dignitaries as well as representatives of the Navy from La Rochelle and from the Prefecture of the Charente. No official representative of the French government seems to have attended this humble funeral.

However, in 1886, the Marquis de Chasseloup Laubat, who was then Minister of the Navy under Napoleon III, had a commemorative monument erected at Kaikondy, whence Caillé had set out so courageously into the interior of unknown Senegal. Mauze also erected a bust to its distinguished citizen and there is now a memorial plaque on the wall of what remains of the house where René Caillé was born.

This is a sad and rather unrewarding story. Nevertheless, Caillé must be counted as one of the greatest contributors to the opening of Northwest Africa and the consequent discovery of its underground riches which are causing such a stir in the commercial world of today. In fact, it is possible to say that, without any heroics, the story of René Caillé is the greatest and noblest to come out of the Sahara.

3

AURÉLIE PICARD

CAILLÉ'S exploits, although unrewarded were to set in motion a number of expeditions with the object of crossing the Sahara from north to south. Most of these expeditions ended in disaster. The first and most famous was that of Colonel Flatters which was inadvertently encouraged by a French woman called Aurélie Picard.

Aurélie Picard, who was to die a Maraboute of the Tidjani Fraternity, one of the largest Moslem organizations of the world, was born in June of 1849, at Montigny le Roy in the department of the Haute Marne. Her father was a French gendarme in the employ of the new French government, which had lately dethroned their king, Louis Phillippe. The head of this government was Prince Louis Napoleon, later to be the emperor Napoleon III, the son of Napoleon I's brother Jerome. The gendarme had carried out his military service in Algeria with the army of General de Bourmont and then with Marechal Bugeaud's, had been several times wounded, and had retired with the Legion of Honour on his chest, to become a village gendarme.

He had married a local girl of no particular education and Aurélie was their first-born when the couple were already middle-aged. There were four more children, so that to make ends meet Aurélie had to leave school early, which disappointed her as she was avid to learn. However, she was a dutiful daughter and obedient to her parents, and they found her a place in the local milliner's and dressmaker's shop.

Aurélie led a humdrum existence, running errands, heating the pressing irons, which gave her no opportunity to use her natural intelligence. She had no friends of her own age, because her colleagues were all dull country bumpkins with few ambitions and no horizons beyond the village cemetery. On Sundays she went to Mass early and for the rest of the day when she was not in the shop, she helped her mother with her housekeeping.

When she was just eighteen, the wife of the deputy of the Haute Marne, a Madame Steinakers, came into the dressmaker's shop to buy some hats. Aurélie was told to serve the deputy's wife, who took an immediate liking to the girl, appreciating her quick mind and the way she kept to herself, which was quite unlike the other gossiping, chattering, dowdy shopgirls of the firm.

When the hats were finished Madame Steinakers asked that Aurélie Picard deliver them herself to the château. Here Aurélie was much impressed by the lovely gardens and the interior of the house into which she was ushered and requested to wait until Madame Steinakers could see her.

When Madame Steinakers appeared she asked Aurélie if she would like to come and live in the château as her companion. She would receive higher wages than at the dressmaker's and would also lead a life of less drudgery. Aurélie was so taken aback by this offer that she did not know what to reply, and Madame Steinakers, believing that this modest girl wanted to think things over, told her that she need not decide for a few days. Aurélie immediately declared that her silence had not meant any hesitation and that she would be delighted and honoured to accept the generous offer.

The next day Aurélie started work in an atmosphere of luxury and refinement for which she had so often longed. This ideal existence came to an abrupt end in 1870 with the outbreak of the Franco-Prussian War. Monsieur Steinakers, who was Postmaster-General, had to follow the French government which had fled before the rapid Prussian advance after the Battle of Sedan to Bordeaux, where the Cabinet had set up its temporary headquarters. With the two Steinakers went Aurélie Picard.

Arriving in Bordeaux, Aurélie found herself quartered in a local hotel. She had never left her native village before and this large provincial town on the Gironde was, to her, something unbelievable. What was even more unbelievable was to find in the

The author in his ceremonial Arab dress outside the Caid Isa's house
in the oasis of Laghouat

Caid Isa in the first car to come to the Sahara shows it off to the author

Caid Isa ben Abdallah using another form of transport

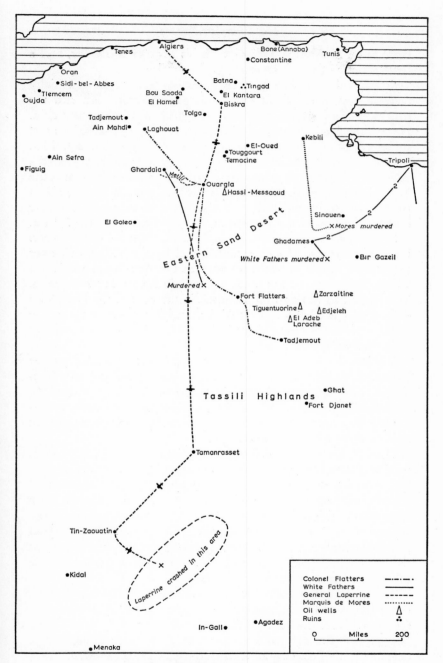

Explorers of the Central Sahara

Tenes
Algiers
Bone (Annaba)
Tunis
Oran
• Constantine
Sidi-bel-Abbes
Batna•
..•Tingad
Tlemcem
Bou Saada•
•El Kantara
Oujda
El Hamel
Biskra
Tadjemout •
Tolga•
Ain Mahdi•
•Laghouat
•El-Oued
Kebili
•Ain Sefra
•Touggourt
•Temacine
•Figuig
Ghardaia•
Melili
Ouargla
△Hassi-Messaoud
El Golea•
Sinauen•
X Mores murdered
Eastern Sand Desert
Ghadames•
2
White Fathers murdered X
•Bir Gazeil
Tripoli
Murdered X
•Fort Flatters
△Zarzaitine
Tiguentuorine△
△Edjeleh
△El Adeb
Larache
•Tadjemout

Tassili   Highlands
•Ghat
•Fort Djanet

•Tamanrasset

Tin-Zaouatin
Laperrine crashed in this area
•Kidal

In-Gall•
•Agadez
Menaka•

Colonel Flatters   —·—·—·
White Fathers   ————
General Laperrine   ————
Marquis de Mores   ··········
Oil wells   △
Ruins   ∴

0   Miles   200

Explorers of the Central Sahara

4

same hotel Si Ahmed Tidjani with his brother Si Bachir, and a large retinue of negro servants, probably slaves.

Si Ahmed was then twenty years old and of an essentially negroid type with a flat nose, a large sensual mouth and the suspicion of a growing beard fringing his flabby cheeks and chin. He was the head of the Tidjani fraternity, a political-religious sect suspected by the French government of subversive activities. The headquarters of this sect were at Ain Mahdi and consisted of a *zaouia*, seminary, and an ancient mosque where the holy men of the Tidjani were buried. Ain Mahdi itself was a small village, about twenty or thirty miles from Laghouat, and to a casual visitor looked like one of the poorest mud-walled towns of the Sahara.

In spite of his poor exterior, Si Ahmed, the head of the order, received a fabulous fortune contributed by the Tidjanis all over the world, rather in the same way as the Aga Khan receives a tribute from members of the Ismaili sect in Africa, India or Persia. Si Ahmed had distinguished himself in the eyes of the French by defending Ain Mahdi against Abd el Kader, the last of the native chiefs to defy the French invasion of North Africa, who had laid siege to it in 1836 for eight months.

Si Ahmed was only fifteen when he was confirmed as head of the order, thereby automatically becoming a marabout to whom Tidjani delegates from Arabia, Egypt, Tunisia, Morocco and the Sudan paid homage. This adulation, together with his now un-limited income, made him feel all-powerful, and he began to act as if he were a reigning sovereign.

One of his first megalomaniac actions was to intervene as mediator between the French and some tribes of the Sahara who had staged a small rebellion, and dictate the peace terms. The French, nervous of their hold over the native inhabitants, took exception to this behaviour, to Si Ahmed setting himself up as the arbitrator in Franco-Berber disputes. Consequently Si Ahmed and Si Bachir were deported to Algiers and housed in a village on the coast where they were held, more or less as hostages, in case of any further trouble in the Sahara.

The marabout, who had been brought up in the broad expanses of the desert and was accustomed to being treated like a monarch, resented this confinement, as did his brother. In 1870, however, an opportunity for comparative freedom came with France's first defeats by the Prussians at Wissenbourg and Reichshoffen.

Fighting in the ranks of the French army were Algerian Tirailleurs and a number of Saharan chiefs. Si Ahmed and Si Bachir offered to go to the "front" and encourage these Moslems, many of whom belonged to the Tidjani sect. The French, appreciating that this could raise the morale of the Moslem troops defending France in this disastrous war, arranged for the departure of the holy men and had them received in Paris with all the ceremony due to their rank and position.

However, there was no longer any "front" since the complete defeat of Napoleon III at Sedan, and what little was left of the French army was streaming towards the Loire where it was hoped that the next stand could be made. The two holy men were, therefore, moved as fast as possible to Bordeaux, and to the hotel where Aurélie Picard was living.

Aurélie was fascinated by these dark-skinned creatures in their snow-white robes, who never moved without an escort of slaves wearing scarlet jackets and carrying curved scimitars. Since the time when her father had told her stories about his campaigns against the Berbers during the days of the French conquest, she had been enthralled by the Sahara. There was no opportunity for a girl in her position to meet a man like Si Ahmed. Nevertheless, the threads of her destiny were still being unwound faster than she imagined. One evening, the Paris Opera Company which had moved with the government to Bordeaux gave a gala performance in the magnificent Louis XVI period theatre which is still used in Bordeaux. Madame Steinakers asked Aurélie if she would like to sit with her in a box. Aurélie demurred. She had never been inside a theatre and had no proper clothes for such an occasion as this gala performance. Madame Steinakers quickly settled that problem by calling in a seamstress and had one of her own gowns altered so that it would fit her shy companion.

Aurélie could hardly eat her dinner, so excited was she about going to the opera, and when she entered the box and saw the red velvet seats and the huge chandeliers and all the golden furnishings of the auditorium she felt as if she had stepped into fairyland. Then, as she looked at everything with astonishment and delight, an orchestra in the pit struck up a martial air.

The Prefect of the Gironde, followed by the commanding general of the district with his staff, all in full dress uniform, entered the official double box in the centre of the box circle, facing the stage. With this group came Si Ahmed Tidjani in his snow-white robes and turban. As he appeared the audience spontaneously sprang to its feet and applauded and cheered the marabout and his brother, who both returned this acclamation by waving their hands.

Aurélie, who had never had the opportunity to look at Si Ahmed for more than a second as she passed him in the corridor or on the staircase of the hotel, could now do so. For some reason which she could not explain to herself, she was strangely attracted by this negroid face, looking out of the frame of white linen. It may have been the setting with all those men sparkling with decorations in the red plush box which gave her this sensation, but she felt herself captivated by this negro holy man who, she had learned, owed his dark skin to his mother, a Sudanese concubine of his father.

But that did not matter. Si Ahmed Tidjani, one of the wealthiest marabouts in the world, had done something to Aurélie which she knew she could not get over.

The next day, however, the fairy tale was ended and Aurélie was back again attending to her duties as a lady's companion, to which had been added the tending of the carrier pigeons which brought news every day—bad news generally—of what was going on at the new battle front.

She saw no more of Si Ahmed than before as she passed him when he left or entered his apartments. One evening, as the marabout was leaving the hotel with his slaves, he met Aurélie face to face. She was carrying five white pigeons in her arms. Si Ahmed stopped to enjoy the picture, which reminded him of his own country where these birds were regarded by the Arabs as messengers from God and venerated accordingly. He stared at the pretty, slim girl with the masses of naturally wavy, black hair.

Aurélie noticed, too, that he had kindly eyes which suggested sensitiveness and goodness. It was a look which she could not forget when she found herself back in her rooms in a state of emotion which she had never experienced before.

Shortly after this meeting the news of the complete defeat of the last of the French armies followed by the destruction of the Tuilleries by the communards reached Bordeaux. Si Ahmed immediately asked permission to return to Ain Mahdi where his financial affairs were in a bad state owing to the dishonesty of a

Caid appointed by the French to administer the marabout's estates during his semi-exile. It was expedient that he should go back immediately, as he had been receiving no income for some months and living on borrowed money from his *zaouia*.

He had fallen completely under the charm of the gendarme's daughter, and he knew that he must have her for himself. In his own country all that he would have to do under similar circumstances would be to give the word and the girl would be handed over to him without question, while the family thanked God for being found worthy of such an honour. But here in France his position was entirely different. The bride-to-be would have to give her consent.

Every day Si Ahmed loitered about the hotel hoping to catch a glimpse of his beloved and smiling whenever he saw her. However, Aurélie, who returned the marabout's passion but had been strictly brought up, passed him without even a glance in his direction. The marabout in despair asked the advice of one of the French officers of his suite and at his suggestion requested an interview with Madame Steinakers. She told her companion of this call and asked her to be present.

Aurélie herself could not imagine why the marabout was taking this step and remained shyly in the background when the call was made. After a few banalities Si Ahmed went straight to the point, explaining that since encountering the girl with the pigeons he had been unable to think of anyone else and would pay any price to have her with him always. Madame Steinakers, taken aback by the whole proposal, assured the marabout that, while Aurélie was available for marriage, she was not for sale.

Si Ahmed had not intended to commit himself to the extent of marrying Aurélie, appreciating all the complications which such a union with a Christian would cause among the devout and rather fanatic Tidjanis. He realized, too, that he had made an error in etiquette by offering money. Accordingly, he began to apologize and to explain that he was not accustomed to European ways.

Madame Steinakers explained that Aurélie Picard was not her daughter and that if he wanted to pursue the matter he must go to Monsieur Picard, who exercised the profession of gendarme in the Haute Marne. With this, she indicated that the interview was over and Si Ahmed left. Madame Steinakers then called Aurélie, who had kept herself concealed at the far end of the drawing-room, and asked her what she felt about this proposal. To her surprise, Aurélie did not scoff at the idea, but said that she was much honoured that so great a man should want her.

"Do you realize that his sparkling white teeth are false?" questioned Madame Steinakers.

Aurélie blushed and said that she did not mind what his teeth were made of. Madame Steinakers, realizing to her surprise that these emotions were not one-sided, wrote to Gendarme Picard to hasten to Bordeaux.

In the meantime Si Ahmed, who was no fool, had two worrying problems on his mind—the first, the chaotic financial situation at Ain Mahdi; the second, that by offering to buy Aurélie he might have ruined his chances of getting her.

On the other hand the very fact of the grand master of the order of the Tidjanis marrying an infidel might cause misunderstandings with the holy men who governed his *zaouia*. At the same time the sacrifice he was making, since it concerned his faith, might convince the French that he was loyal to their flag. In any case he felt so deeply in love with Aurélie that he did not mind very much what happened, provided she would be his.

While these thoughts were disturbing the marabout Monsieur Picard arrived in Bordeaux in not too good a mood. He had served as a soldier in North Africa and on the borders of the Sahara, and he knew a good deal about Moslems and their ways, and of the unfairness and one-sidedness of the Koranic law as it concerned women. Nor could he imagine his beloved daughter living with a negro Moslem in a small oasis where there was not a white man within thirty miles and no women, except the White Sisters and a few officers' wives at Laghouat.

His first condition, therefore, for giving his consent to this marriage was as Si Ahmed had anticipated—that it should be solemnized according to French law. With that condition agreed to, he went to find out what Aurélie felt about the whole thing.

Aurélie had never had the opportunity to attach herself to a beau, but, being a normal young girl, she had had other dreams of a lover than one who was extremely ugly as well as black and, as she had now learned, with a complete set of false teeth.

If she remained in France the future was not bright for Aurélie. The war was over and times were hard, so that it seemed unlikely that Madame Steinakers would be able to keep her in her employ. What then? The local dressmaker's shop and helping her mother at home seemed the only future left for her, as no man would be interested in the daughter of a gendarme without the hope of even a small dowry. She could not let this chance slip by. She would not go back to drudgery in a village of the Haute Marne. When father and daughter were talking matters over with Si Ahmed, and the gendarme was being difficult, the marabout exclaimed rather petulantly: "You don't want your daughter to be one of the richest women in the world?" Aurélie intervened, telling her father that she would marry the Lord of the Tidjanis or no one.

There followed an official meeting in the drawing-room of Madame Steinakers' house. The Postmaster General's wife presided from a large armchair with the gendarme beside her. Aurélie and Si Ahmed sat opposite. The gendarme spoke first: "My daughter, have you completely made up your mind?"

Aurélie hesitated and looked at the splendid diamond ring which Si Ahmed had given her, but she did not reply.

"Mademoiselle," the marabout said in French, "I love you; all that I possess is yours. Will you be my wife? I swear to you that I will make you happy."

The gendarme then proclaimed that in addition to the marriage, according to the laws of France, he asked that he be permitted to accompany his daughter as far as her new home. Si Ahmed agreed and added that he would, furthermore, pay all expenses. He also informed his bride-to-be that while he already had two legitimate wives at Ain Mahdi, he had every intention of repudiating them both.

As soon as the authority of Marshal MacMahon, now President of France's Third Republic, had been granted to the brothers Tidjani to return to Ain Mahdi, preparations for departure for Algiers where the wedding was to be celebrated were accelerated. Before embarking at Marseilles Aurélie made a flying visit to her village and proudly told her friends and colleagues in the dressmaker's shop of the "Arabian Night" fiancé she was to wed, dazzling them at the same time with her regal jewels. She also convinced her mother of the wisdom of her decision, and made her promise to visit her in the Sahara soon.

The wedding was to take place at the Tidjani residence in

Algiers which was rather of the same structure as my grand-father's house, Mustapha Rais, and had undoubtedly belonged to another Barbary corsair. Aurélie was delighted by the marble hall with its fountain splashing in the centre, its wonderfully sculptured cedarwood doors and its bright tiles looted by the corsairs from Dutch merchantmen.

But her delight was soon spoiled. What Si Ahmed did not know, or if he did, had not told Aurélie, was that at this period of the conquest of Algeria, marriage between a French citizen and a Moslem was illegal and the most that the mayor of the local municipal council could do was to give Si Ahmed an authorization for a Moslem and a Frenchwoman to live together, but without any mention of marriage.

Si Ahmed immediately wrote a personal letter to the Governor-General asking for an exception to be made in his case. The answer was a curt refusal. The reasons the Governor gave were the French authorities' fear for the safety of a Frenchwoman transported into the still little-known Sahara, where she would be out of touch with French people and might disappear without a trace.

The second reason was the outbreak of a fanatical religious war, proclaimed by some marabouts of Kabylie who paid tribute to the Tidjanis, whose followers had actually been able to defeat a French punitive column and might at any time attack Algiers.

Si Ahmed was persistent as well as in love, and he took his case to his own people—to the Cadi, who combines the duties of lawyer and judge in all matters where Koranic law is involved. The Cadi, however, said that anything he did in favour of Si Ahmed would not be recognized by the French government. Si Ahmed therefore went to the French Court of Appeals in Algiers which also threw out his plea.

The gendarme began to be restless, but when he suggested to his daughter that it might be a good idea to forget about the whole project and return to France, she flatly refused. She could not bear the prospect of telling her friends in the village about the end of her Arabian Nights' dream and this Oriental life with all its luxuries and beauty appealed to her. She now wanted to be the wife of Si Ahmed more than anything else in the world.

The problem was eventually solved by Aurélie's father meeting Cardinal Lavigerie, whose affection for the Berberized Arabs was well known. The gendarme told the cardinal of the quandary in which he found himself and the cardinal listened with interest. The next day Lavigerie sent for Aurélie and Si Ahmed, and, after cross-examining them both and seeing that the marriage project was no whim, said that he was ready to perform the ceremony on condition that Si Ahmed swore to get rid of the two wives who waited the return of the marabout in the Sahara. This Si Ahmed did with his hand on the Koran. Cardinal Lavigerie then blessed the union of Si Ahmed with Aurélie Picard in the vestry of Nôtre Dame d'Afrique.

This was followed by the Moslem ceremony, presided over by the Grand Mufti of Algiers. An Arab feast concluded these ceremonies at the Tidjani house with musicians and Ouled Nail dancing suggestively, accompanied by an endless series of Arab dishes.

Virginal and religiously brought up, Aurélie seems to have accepted this most unchristian celebration, as well as the marriage bed which she now had to occupy with her black Moslem marabout, as a matter of course. Nor did she ever regret the step which she had taken or, in any way betray the kindness and affection of this man, whose instincts were in no way European and belonged to the Moslem world of Haroun el Raschid and Scheherazade.

Aurélie never "went native", or even wore native dress. She always remained a Frenchwoman who, in spite of her humble origins, had the dignity befitting the wife of the head of this all-powerful and wealthy order of the Tidjanis.

What has never been recorded, however, were the reactions of the Governor-General of Algeria and the Court of Appeal when they found out that the laws of France had been broken. Nor did Aurélie or the gendarme care—in their Catholic minds the marriage was much more secure than any performed by the Mayor of Algiers. Cardinal Lavigerie had a position in North Africa which put him above criticism or censure. Moreover, this marriage did a great deal to facilitate France's occupation of Algeria and the Sahara.

The time had come for the journey to Laghouat and thence to Ain Mahdi. Laghouat is over three hundred miles from Algiers and in 1872 there was no road worthy of the name. To reach the desert one had to travel by caravan, crossing the Atlas where the watershed rises to nine thousand feet above sea level, and then over the seemingly endless plains of sagebrush and alfa grass, running down to the Sahara Desert itself. Aurélie had to undertake this long journey on horseback with her husband riding beside her. This was already a departure from the native custom of women travelling in a kind of curtained litter roped to the back of a camel, but then Aurélie did not wish to be in any way identified as a native of Algeria in custom or in dress. She slept at night on a carpet in one of those black blanket shelters which the nomads call tents.

When Aurélie suddenly saw the desert country rolling away from her from the top of the Atlas, she felt an unexpected ecstasy. The warnings of the French people in Algiers who said that no Occidental could adapt himself to living in these waterless wildernesses she put out of her mind. She was captivated by the Sahara from the start. She never became bored with what some people call the monotony of the landscape and never blasé over the blood-red sunsets and the golden sunrises.

Finally Laghouat was reached and Aurélie, who had little riding experience, had to admit that she was exhausted. Si Ahmed took her to his house in the oasis where she could eat a hot meal from a table and sleep in a comfortable bed. The next day the caravan set out soon after dawn for the last stages of the journey to Ain Mahdi.

All along the road faithful adherents to the Tidjanis almost fought their way to kiss the feet or the robes of their marabout, whom they had not seen for so long. At the entrance of the oasis one of those famous "fantasias" of the Bedouins was put on as a welcome. Aurélie witnessed for the first time that rather terrifying charge of mounted men firing their flintlocks as they came, or throwing them into the air and catching them again while the women, crouching on the flat roofs of their houses, uttered those wild "you-yous", once the battle cry of wives urging their men to destroy the enemy.

It was here that Aurélie had her first disillusioning experience. Both in Algiers and in Laghouat her husband's houses had been miniature palaces, but at Ain Mahdi she found herself in a tumbledown old building which had obviously been neglected for years.

Her first action was to make sure that her husband got rid of his two wives. This Si Ahmed did by the simple method of repudiating them, and banishing them to their own homes in Ain Mahdi. Aurélie discovered that one of the ladies had a son called Si Ali, and rather ruthlessly decreed that he should live with her and his father.

Aurélie could not do much more for the moment, as according to Moslem custom the wedding celebrations went on for several days, which included hunting with falcons in the desert, and feasts at the houses of other noble Tidjanis and more wild and merry fantasias.

Once the feasting was over Aurélie began to see about putting her house in order. She had an Occidental bed made up with sheets and white blankets which she had brought from Algiers; she began teaching the cooks to prepare European dishes, appreciating that this highly spiced Arab food would soon play havoc with her digestion. She did all this with tact and gentleness so that she soon had every member of the marabout's household running to do her least bidding. Luckily, too, Si Ahmed had learned to enjoy French food and French habits so that he backed her up in all her innovations. He preferred also to eat at a table rather than on a carpet, and to sleep in a European bed.

Unfortunately Si Ahmed had grown to like champagne and had brought many cases of it with him from Algiers. At first the members of his *zaouia* looked with disapproval on this beverage forbidden by their religious laws. However, Si Ahmed had an astute mind and he convinced his followers that he changed the sparkling wine into water before a drop had touched his lips. Everyone seemed to believe this as they believed him when he told them that his new teeth had sprouted from his one time, almost toothless gums. The fact that Aurélie backed up her husband in these assertions enhanced her prestige with the Tidjanis, who had feared that she would be an evil influence on the man they so revered.

Aurélie also put her husband's financial affairs in order. These were in a terrible state, owing to the mismanagement by the Caid who had been appointed by the French to attend to them during the marabout's absence. She found that the millions representing the offerings which the Tidjanis brought yearly as tribute had been almost dissipated. That the marabout could live at all comfortably was due to the moneys, which normally went to the *zaouia*, being handed over to him.

But of this Aurélie did not approve, and explained that all he needed now was a capable accountant and manager to look after his business affairs. The marabout agreed, but who among these holy men could take over such a task? Aurélie suggested that she do it, and he gladly accepted her offer.

Little by little, and by observing the rules of thrift to which she had always been accustomed in her home, a financially balanced situation began to appear in these muddled accounts. This, as well as the work she did in caring for the women and children, was noticed and approved by the elders of the *zaouia*. Aurélie felt that she had gone a long way towards establishing herself in the confidence of these desert people.

The only antipathy towards Aurélie came from the wives whom Si Ahmed had put away. They detested her and were prepared to go to any lengths to get rid of her. While the men settled their differences with a sword or a musket, the women had subtler means, such as poisoned food. Aurélie, for the first time since leaving France, felt afraid. She accordingly persuaded her husband to take her to Laghouat for a rest and a change. From now on, she made this a practice and spent some months at her husband's home in the oasis while his brother, Si Bachir, carried on for the marabout at Ain Mahdi. The danger of revenge by the jealous wives continued, and she knew that she must deal with this drastically if she wanted to remain alive.

Her method of achieving this deserves praise. She had the marabout appoint one wife, Zorah, who was the mother of the only son, to be head of the Tidjani *zaouia* at Tlemcen on the Moroccan border, and in order to make certain that this woman got there safely, she escorted her to Tlemcen herself. Their journey on horseback was through some of the most desolate country of the desert land above the Sahara and took nearly three months of continual riding. Besides the woman who wanted only her death she took a small retinue, but all went well and she returned refreshed.

Once home Aurélie decided that it was time she took some part in the political doings of the Tidjanis who, she now appreciated, were not too intelligent or tactful in handling such matters. What actually brought about this decision was France's feelings of uncertainty over the future behaviour of Algeria's neighbour, Tunisia. The Tunisians were being flattered by the Italians, who wanted another foothold in North Africa besides Tripoli and had, that year, refused to give the French their usual guarantees of non-aggression, which were essential if Algeria was to remain peaceful.

There were a great many Tidjanis in Tunisia, including the Bey of Tunis himself, who had a great influence in the political leanings of that country. Aurélie thus saw a chance of enhancing her husband's reputation with the French government by having him use his authority on behalf of France. Si Ahmed, who fundamentally was a lazy man with few original ideas, accepted his wife's suggestions and authorized her to act as she felt would be best. She went to Algiers and called on the Governor-General who showed great interest in this idea and authorized Aurélie to put the plan into execution. It was decided that Si Bachir would go as emissary to the Bey of Tunis. This mission he carried out so successfully that the Italians were, thenceforward, cold-shouldered, and when the French occupied Tunisia two years later they were not opposed and were treated as friends.

Unfortunately, this wise diplomacy of Aurélie was counter-balanced by the revolt in the desert, south of Oran, instigated and led by the famous Bou Amama, which was to bring Charles de Foucauld back into the army and, eventually, into the Church. Unfortunately, too, Bou Amama was on friendly terms with Si Ahmed, which, since Si Ahmed was of a religious nature, made the French feel that he might give sanctuary to this dissident chieftain, or help him in some way.

Thus, most unjustly, since Ahmed had to all intents and purposes given Tunisia to France, he was ordered to leave Ain Mahdi and live under military supervision at Medea.

Aurélie does not seem to have been too distressed over this exile, as Medea was comparatively close to Algiers where she had installed her family. Thus, in 1876, Aurélie, the gendarme and her mother were once more living an essentially French bourgeois life where they were later joined by Si Ahmed, who was delighted to find himself again in a French atmosphere, where he no longer had to pretend that he was performing miracles with the wine. He was happy with the Picard family and made over some valuable property to his father-in-law.

The Bou Amama rebellion had been put down by the drastic action of General Lyautey, and Si Ahmed was allowed to return to Ain Mahdi, which he did, accompanied by his wife. When the party reached Ain Mahdi they found other troubles awaiting them. Si Bachir, who resented the subordinate role which he now played at the *zaouia*, chiefly because of the ascendancy of Aurélie, not only over her husband's domestic affairs but also over those which were political and religious, met them in a surly mood, and was as rude as circumstances permitted to his sister-in-law.

The next day Si Bachir drank a great deal too much champagne, until he was in such a state of frenzy that he beat one of his wives almost to death. She came screaming to Aurélie who was taking coffee with her husband. Si Ahmed summoned his brother and rebuked him, whereon Si Bachir flew into an even greater rage and broke down the door of the room where the marabout kept his sporting guns. Finding a double-barrelled shotgun which was loaded, he returned and fired at his brother. Possibly because he was drunk, he missed him and only a few pellets broke the skin of the marabout's thigh. The marabout sent for the sergeant of the Zouave guard, which was always on duty at Ain Mahdi, and had Si Bachir handcuffed and locked up in the guardroom.

Si Bachir showed no repentance when he came to his senses and was consequently dispatched to take care of one of the minor fraternities of the Tidjanis at Temacine near Touggourt. Simultaneously Si Ahmed and Aurélie had an unexpected windfall. Aurélie had sued the delinquent Caid who had embezzled her husband's Tidjani revenues. The case involved the French government, since they had appointed the man to take care of the marabout's interests. To her surprise and delight Aurélie now heard that this very large sum of money would be refunded. The marabout was finding it difficult to meet the grasping demands of his numerous relatives and relatives-in-law, who had always regarded him as a source of revenue and now blamed his French wife for the lack of resources.

Si Ahmed was equally pleased at this news and told Aurélie that she could do as she wished with the money. This she did, and found that there were literally millions of francs left over after paying off the relatives which, together with the gifts from the many Tidjani sects, would make it impossible for her ever to be in need again. She decided to build a house worthy of the position which her husband held in the Moslem world—a wish she had long had in mind. Si Ahmed was in favour of this, and it only remained to select a site for the house. About three miles from Ain Mahdi was a limpid spring which, as is rarely the case even in the northern Sahara, gave a seemingly unending stream of water. Near this spring the palace was constructed and called "Kourdane" after the name of the spring.

Before making any start on the building Aurélie had the gardens laid out, planting flower seeds from France and grass which, with the spring so near, would stand the dry, hot climate of the Sahara. She also had sent down from Algiers shrubs other than the interminable orange and lemon and pomegranates, which were all that grew in oases gardens outside the date palms. As soon as thirty or so acres of grass and flower beds and European trees had been planted, she turned her attention to the house.

Aurélie Picard was now thirty-five and maturing into a dignified, handsome woman who looked much more like a ruling sovereign than her rather dumpy husband, who was lazy and sensual, and still lived on the doctrine of *In Sha Allah*. Nothing seemed impossible for her energy to accomplish.

She decided that building materials must be of the best and from Europe. So she set out with a huge caravan of camels for Algiers and obtained from there wrought-iron work, and lovely tiles, and stained-glass windows. Italian marble as well as superb carpets and curtains and fine furniture were also purchased. All these things were loaded on to the camels and were transported over those arduous three hundred miles back to Ain Mahdi.

By the time she arrived the foundations of the palace had been laid, under the direction of an able Berber foreman, who had lived in France and understood what his lady wanted. He had previously made use of those Sahara mud bricks which, when plastered over, did not disintegrate.

Aurélie was pleased with all she saw, but it took two years more to complete this residence for the Lord of the Tidjanis. When ready for occupation it was furnished with a mixture of French and Oriental *objets d'art*, each room having its own style. The gardens had rivulets and marble fountains, which flowed among mimosa and jasmine and peach and apricot trees growing out of grass, rarely seen south of Algiers. It was a remarkable achievement and today it remains to show what someone of imagination and energy can do in a country where nothing new had been produced for centuries.

As for the marabout, he was delighted and fell more and more under the influence of his wife, though this did not mean that he had completely given up his Moslem habits, and, in return for what Si Ahmed had given her so freely, Aurélie had to close her eyes to his infidelities.

Si Bachir had also come back from his *zaouia* in Temacine. While outwardly cordial, he maintained his jealous hatred for his sister-in-law. She herself had become rather self-important and insisted that everyone at Ain Mahdi show her the same reverence as her husband. There were occasions when she would personally whip a servant who had neglected his duty. She continued to be extremely generous and helpful to the poor of Ain Mahdi, but neglected her mother who, since the death of the gendarme, was living penuriously on his pension in Algiers.

Aurélie was lavish in her entertaining, and had some of the most famous painters, writers, and explorers visit her at Kourdane. The Governor-General even took the time to spend a few days with the gendarme's daughter, who received him looking like an empress in the latest-styled gown from Paris.

I have seen a portrait of her, probably a coloured photograph, when she was at the zenith of her power. In this picture there is nothing to suggest an Algerian or even a Frenchwoman married to a Moslem, living in a lost city of the Sahara. Her hair is beautifully done after the manner of Parisians at the end of the nineteenth century. Her dress is that of a dowager duchess, over which is draped a lace shawl. She wears a diamond necklace and pearl earrings and in her hand she carries a fan.

At about this time Colonel Paul Flatters appeared in Laghouat with his nondescript caravan of cameleers, soldiers and engineers. He was going to try and penetrate into the forbidding mountains of the Hoggar and make contact with the Twareg, who certainly did not want him there. Aurélie Picard gave a dinner at Kourdane for the Colonel and the senior members of his staff, all of whom were to lose their lives less than six weeks later. While the Colonel was optimistic about forcing his way into the Twareg country, most of his subordinates were not. They declared that they had too few armed soldiers as it was quite clear that these veiled men would do all in their power to hold up and destroy the caravan. Aurélie Picard took the Colonel's side and said that if someone did not penetrate into this almost legendary country,

The corsair palace in Algiers which belonged to the author's grandfather

Before the toothache-curing episode: patient and dentist to the right of
the tent and Caid Isa inside

Laghouat, where Aurélie Picard had her "town" residence and where the author lived for many years

Si Ahmed Tidjani   Aurélie Picard

soon it would remain for ever closed to the French. She had more champagne opened and toasted the expedition. She also promised to attach to Colonel Flatters' staff a *mohkadem*, a holy man of the Tidjani fraternity whose presence would ensure the safety of the Moslem members of the expedition as well as those who were infidels. She added that not even a Targui would dare to molest an official of the Tidjanis whose influence covered the entire Sahara as far as the Niger. These words, together with the champagne, revived the morale of Colonel Flatters' staff officers and the next morning they led their motley caravan out of Laghouat and south towards the menacing Hoggar mountains. Thus did Aurélie Picard's infinite belief in herself and in France cause almost every one of the ninety men who followed Colonel Flatters into the Sahara to die the most hideous deaths.

Aurélie Picard was not entirely responsible for the Flatters' disaster as the fault came from higher up in the French government. She could have avoided giving such an optimistic view of the situation, especially knowing the Sahara as well as she did, and should have realized that the Twareg, being lax Moslems, had no reverence for the Tidjanis or any other religious brotherhoods. The fact was that she had become so rich and so powerful that she could not imagine a wretched veiled man defying her envoy.

Money seemed to pour in unceasingly from the unquenchable source, the Tidjani faithful, who still had this fanatic reverence for their rather unworthy marabout. Although money might have tempted her to be lazy, Aurélie never forgot her childhood's instinct to work. She established a French school in Ain Mahdi, in which she took a personal interest. She loved children and one of her greatest disappointments during her successful life was that she had none of her own. She also continued her education by having books sent to her regularly from France from which she could add to her knowledge of history, which she had had little time to study when she was a girl.

In 1897 Madame Aurélie had Commandants Lamy and Foureau visit her as her guests. Their crossing of the Sahara was one of the greatest penetrations towards Central Africa made in this era. Savorgnan de Brazza also stayed at Kourdane on his way to explore the Congo.

On 20th April, 1897 Si Ahmed died suddenly at a Tidjani *zaouia* in Guemar, near El Oued. Madame Aurélie was deeply distressed by the death of her husband, for in spite of his infidelities she had lived happily and prosperously with him for twenty-five years. Madame Aurélie and her stepson quarrelled over what belonged to her at Kourdane; in this she behaved much as a Frenchwoman of that class might under similar circumstances, while Ali, who had become more temperate, merely asked to keep some personal mementoes of his father. She declared that everything at Kourdane belonged to her. She was also most exacting about the Tidjani revenues which she felt were still due to her. No one seems to have appreciated what it meant to Madame Aurélie to leave this palace which she had built and the gardens which she had created, and where she should have been allowed to die in peace.

On 18th June, 1911 Aurélie went to Laghouat, where she established herself in the marabout's house which she had first visited as a bride nearly forty years before.

Life with nothing to do in this semi-French oasis distressed her and one day she ordered her mule-drawn carriage and drove back to Ain Mahdi on the pretext that she wanted to see how her flocks of sheep were being cared for. To her surprise, Ali received her most cordially and asked her if she would stay and help him with the management of the estate, which he was finding a difficult job. She accepted gladly and reinstated herself at Kourdane.

The outbreak of the First World War in 1914 galvanized Madame Aurélie into action on behalf of France. She became indefatigable in making tours of the nomadic tribes encouraging them to join up and fight in the French army. As soon as the Armistice had been signed she decided that, after fifty years' absence from her native land, she should return to France. In 1920 she went back to her village in the Haute Marne. Apart from the fact that all her contemporaries were dead, she felt that lack of colour and warmth which makes so many Sahara veterans return to the desert. She remained in France for two years trying to fit herself into a life which was strange to her and then set off once more for Algeria. Like the original house to which Aurélie had been brought as a bride, she found Kourdane neglected and much of its splendor had vanished. The gardens which she had so carefully planted were overgrown with weeds. Nor did her stepson or his relatives seem to feel that anything was amiss. Like most Bedouins, with the exception of those who built the magnificent buildings in Spain and Syria, anything permanent meant little to them. A shelter in which to sleep, sufficient food to eat and Allah to take care of the rest, was their philosophy. But to Aurélie this slow death of all she had created was heartbreaking. She was also in a bad way financially. All the wise counsels which she had given for the administration of the estate and the handling of the Tidjani money had been forgotten. All that Ali, the young marabout, cared about was cash for his dissipated life, and in this he was eagerly abetted by the Tidjanis of his own generation.

Gradually, Aurélie began to sell her belongings and her jewellery while she established herself at Laghouat in the marabout's house. She was now over seventy, and the energetic life which she had led was beginning to take its toll. She was no longer physically active, and her mind no longer functioned with its accustomed clarity. Then, one day, she had an urgent call from the young marabout urging her to come to Kourdane and save the place from falling down altogether. Gathering together her ebbing strength she set out eagerly for Ain Mahdi, but there was little which she could do to restore what neglect had done to her beloved palace. Soon she was back at Laghouat being nursed by the White Sisters. She realized, too, that she was dying and she sent for Father Py, who was the head of the White Fathers in Laghouat.

This gesture definitely cleared up the question as to whether or not she had adopted her husband's religion as the Tidjanis claimed. To Father Py she made her general confession and took communion, after assuring the priest that she had never had anything to do with Islam. Then she called her physician and asked him to allow her to return to Kourdane where she wished to die and be buried beside her husband. The doctor was opposed to such a move, but she insisted and had herself transported there in the carriage drawn by her four mules.

On 28th August, 1933 Madame Aurélie died and her burial was arranged for the 29th. She had expressed the wish to be buried beside Si Ahmed outside the Tidjani mosque at Ain Mahdi, which was on Moslem soil, but Father Py was not permitted to bless the body once it had left Kourdane. In fact, the elders assured the White Father that Madame Aurélie had been converted to Islam on her death-bed.

The truth of this we shall never know, although on her

property was found a small shrine with a statue of the Blessed Virgin, which suggests that she was always a staunch Catholic. As the body of this great old lady, wrapped in its shroud, was lowered into the grave, the commanding officer of the military territory of Laghouat placed on it the medal of the Legion of Honour and spoke as follows: "Madame Aurélie Tidjani re-organized and managed for forty years the *zaouia* of Kourdane, where she took care of all those who came to her when ill, or in need of help. In addition to the Legion of Honour, she was awarded during her lifetime, the medal of the Mérite Agricole in recognition of what she did for agriculture at Ain Mahdi, the medal of the Academy in recognition of the founding of a French School at this same place, and the order of the Nicham Iftikhar, with which the Bey of Tunis in person decorated her."

He then spoke of what Madame Aurélie had done in the promoting of better relationships between the Berbers and the French.

A few days later, a memorial service was held by the Bishop of the Sahara at the church at Laghouat and attended by the officers of the garrison. Spahis lined the church steps while those officers who were members of the Legion of Honour acted as pallbearers.

At Ain Mahdi she rested for a while under the traditional Moslem grave, consisting of three unmarked stones. Later, after the Tidjanis had raised her to the unheard of rank, for an Occidental, of "Maraboute", they erected a formal gravestone for her on which was carved in French:

Here lies Madame Aurélie Tidjani
died August 1933
at the age of 84

Thus ended in glory the life of the seamstress daughter of the French gendarme who did more for her country in Algeria than most of the governors and generals and administrators of North Africa. What remains of her house is still there as a memorial of the days when she had at her disposal more money than many millionaires in France and wisely spent it to beautify Ain Mahdi and to help the poor and the needy and the persecuted.

Although I had known Madame Aurélie in Laghouat and had dined with her once or twice there, I had never had occasion to

visit Ain Mahdi or Kourdane, of which she had told me a great
deal as well as many details of her life before she had become a
maraboute.

Ali was still head of the Tidjanis. He had matured and acted
more in a manner befitting his position, maintaining outward
behaviour in keeping with his holy attributes. However, his moral
instincts had changed little. In fact, in spite of his religious
responsibilities, he still liked having a good time and, with all that
money, could indulge in whatever backsliding he fancied.

One day I was invited by my friend, a curio dealer in the oasis,
Atalla Bouameur, and some local merchants who in their spare
time formed a kind of joyous orchestra of guitars and mandolins
and drums, to accompany them to Ain Mahdi. The marabout was
feeling the tedium of his maraboutic duties and had invited these
musical Arabs to cheer him up. They assured me that my presence
would aid to their host's pleasure, so I eagerly accepted the
invitation to visit this fantastic place which was forbidden
territory to both the French military and civil authorities, except
on matters of official duty.

The journey from Ain Mahdi to Laghouat, and vice versa, was
by an antiquated bus which did the round trip three times a week.
There was practically no road and it took two hours of shaking
and bumping to reach our destination, which made me wonder
how Madame Aurélie had been able to stand those drives in the
mule carriage. But the members of the orchestra were young and
they did not care. They were going on a holiday and everyone
sang all the way.

Ever since I had come to live with the nomads they were always
springing surprises on me, so that I was always braced for the
unexpected. Lately, the shocks had been less frequent, and I was
beginning to think that the Sahara had nothing more to teach me.
This trip proved that the Sahara always has something new to
offer.

Kourdane, which at that time I had heard of only from Madame
Aurélie, turned out to be a good imitation of a palazzo of the
Italian Renaissance. The effect of this noble building rising out the
desert was more fantastic than any mirage. In fact, until the bus
stopped before a landscaped garden, flagged with white marble
and interspersed with flower beds and fountains and tall cypresses,
I thought it was a mirage. As my friends did not seem to be

overcome by the sight of the several storied house and the water which was being "wasted" on flowers, I followed them up a horseshoe stairway with wrought-iron balustrades which led up to the front door.

At the top of these stairs, reminiscent of Fontainebleau, stood the marabout. Although I knew his origin I was surprised to find him quite black—not a strong negro type, though, as was his father, but with finely sculptured features as though carved from jet or ebony. He must have resembled his Sudanese mother, Zorah, whom Madame Aurélie had so summarily banished to the *zaouia* at Tlemcen. His only ornament was a large turquoise set in an old silver ring on the middle finger of his right hand, which my companions kissed.

The marabout greeted me by touching my hand and then carrying his own to his lips. He added a few words of welcome in educated French, which would have passed in the Faubourg St. Germain. He then led the way into a vast drawing-room which was in proportion to the rest of the place. The furnishing was Occidental and in the best taste, with some Oriental pieces which one no longer sees outside museums.

Servants brought in glasses of sugary mint tea, while the marabout made the traditional and often repeated inquiries as to our health. When he was satisfied we were well, had been well for some time and expected to remain well in the future, he excused himself and a steward took his guests to their quarters. These opened on to a long outside gallery with marble pillars which overlooked another decorative garden, landscaped in the style associated with an estate in France. Again I noticed the richness of the furnishings of the room—the four-poster beds with their brocade curtains and the carpets into which my feet sank.

Then I saw that my quarters were not just a bedroom but a suite. I thought that one of my companions would be sharing this with me, but the steward shook his head. Every guest had a bedroom, sitting-room and dining-room. In the case of the present marabout's father and grandfather meals were served separately and privately to each guest, regardless of his social position.

After half an hour's rest I was summoned to dinner, which was served in a high-ceilinged banqueting hall. The places were not, as is usual at Arab feasts, laid on the carpet, but at a long polished table which looked as if it might be loot from some Spanish palace when the Almoravid Caliphs ruled in Cordova. The *mechoui*, the lamb roasted and presented whole, as well as the couscous and other dishes, were Arab, but they were served occidentally on platters and plates. Some of these were made of gold and others were Sèvres porcelain. Everything else, with the exception of the knives and forks, also quite unusual in a Sahara household, seemed to be made of gold, while from golden pitchers champagne, properly cooled and of an obviously first-class brand, was poured into golden goblets.

This departure from Islamic convention surprised me more than anything else. While there were Bedouins who sipped anisette in the French café of the oasis, they were not approved of by the orthodox Moslems who obeyed the precepts of the Koran. However, this appeared to be an exceptional occasion, as I noticed that Atalla and another of the musicians, who normally practised their religion, were not refusing the champagne. Perhaps they believed in those magic powers of the Tidjanis, who turned wine into water.

The other diners I could not see, but there were about fifty men sitting at the polished table, and the flickering candles in their golden candelabra did not give much light. Nor could I see our host. When I remarked on this to Atalla, he replied that he was not there. This was one of the few remaining traditions of Aurélie Picard. She had felt that it made a holy man much more important and mysterious if no one saw him going through the mortal procedure of eating and drinking, especially as he enjoyed the wines forbidden by the Koran. Later, the tradition was broken, for when we moved into the drawing-room for our coffee, the marabout joined us.

For a while he graciously kept up his part. He made appropriate conversation with me. He had our solo guitarist play traditional Arab music. He called on Atalla to sing to the accompaniment of that essentially Saharan drum, the *Debourca*. In fact, it was all most Moslem and formal and not in keeping with the vintage champagne.

I do not remember what actually changed the atmosphere, or whether anything in particular did change it. It was as if someone had heaved a huge sigh and cried, "For the love of Allah, let's have some fun!"

In a moment, the marabout and his retainers had shed their stately holiness. A couple of Ouled Nail girls who had been sitting discreetly in a corner, began to dance. A few more appeared at the doorway. Our guitarist picked up the mood and the classic melodies became an exhilarating mixture of *danse du ventre* and the Spanish fandango. Another orchestra materialized as if a djennoun had whisked it there. In less than half an hour all relationship with the semi-occidental world of the oasis, barely twenty miles away, had been severed.

Sudanese, with faces like polished jet, circulated among the guests carrying golden platters of perfumed cakes and golden trays on which were golden goblets of champagne and golden cups of sweet, thick coffee. From tall candelabra and chandeliers hundreds of wax candles enhanced the golden effect. Their soft light fell on the men and the dancing girls who rested on the damask-covered divans. The air was filled with incense and music. The conversation rose and fell. There was a kind of abandoned atmosphere, but it was not jarring and it was full of colour. There was movement, but it was rhythmical and graceful.

I have seen many performances of Rimsky-Korsakov's *Scheherazade*, but the most elaborate of these productions has seemed almost amateurish in comparison to the performance that night in the setting which the daughter of a French gendarme had created in the Sahara Desert.

The next morning after the party I visited the tombs of Aurélie Picard and her husband. They were in a garden outside the mosque surrounded by Italian cypresses. Both of them had the domes and trappings of the holy men of Islam. They were carefully tended, and evidently held in reverence. As I stood silently before the last resting place of this incongruous couple, I wondered what Madame Aurélie would have thought of the goings-on of the night before—being a level-headed Frenchwoman, she would probably have approved. Whatever may be the rights and wrongs of a marabout drinking champagne, my host never ceased to behave in a princely and dignified fashion. Nor did his guests show the foolish excitement which is often promoted by too much alcohol among Occidentals. Their exhilaration was that of well-bred gentlemen enjoying themselves.

4

THE TWAREG

~~~~~~

A NUMBER of books and articles have been written about the Twareg, yet what follows may come as new information on these veiled men who live in and about inaccessible mountains in the centre of the Sahara. This fresh information came to me directly from the greatest authority on the subject, Father Viscount Charles de Foucauld, who lived the last ten years of his life among the Twareg and was murdered in their territory in 1916.

In view of the fact that these tribesmen play a large role in the story of the Soundless Sahara, it has been thought necessary to explain exactly who they are or, rather, were. I say *were* because since Algeria became independent of France, the native government in Algiers has deprived these tribal warriors of their arms and put an end to their raiding of peaceful caravans and the massacres of any alien elements, such as Colonel Flatters and the White Fathers who penetrated into the dark boundaries of their hideous country.

To speak of "Twareg" is not correct, Twareg being the plural of the word "Targui"—one Targui, two Twareg. Most people spell the word "Touareg"; some "Tuareg". The nearest orthography in relation to the pronunciation is "Twareg", which I prefer to use. The female of the species is known as a "Targuia".

"Twareg" is, incidentally, a Shamba tribesman's name for these people, meaning "the veiled men". These men of the Hoggar refer to themselves as *Imouchar* which roughly translated means "those who are free and independent warriors". In Shamba talk the word *twareg*, in addition to meaning "veiled", suggests either abandoned by God", probably due to their being lax Moslems, or else "people of the sand" from the Arabic *areg* which denotes "sand".

Whatever the true appellation of these tribesmen, no two anthropologists tell the same story about the origin of the Targui Tribal Federation. The majority of people who have studied this subject declare them to be Berbers, as does Cabot Briggs, who writes in one of his pamphlets on the Twareg, "they are primitive Berbers of the Mediterranean classification of pure origins which have been modified through the ages by marriage with Shambi nomads, Arabs and negroes, as well as by the geographic nature of the country".

Others suggest that they came from the east as part of that Himyaritic migration during the centuries which preceded the birth of Christ. There are also those who regard the Garamantes who lived in the Sahara about 500 B.C. as the ancestors of the Twareg.

Some of those scholars who favour the eastern origin of the Twareg suggest that they belonged to those tribes of the Hyksos, the shepherd kings who probably originated in ancient Chaldea, today incorporated in Irak, and that they invaded Egypt about 2000 B.C. and later established their capital at Memphis a little south of present day Cairo. They were, however, soon expelled by the Egyptian kings who had taken refuge in the upper Nile regions, but were able to defeat these Hyksos nomads who removed themselves into Libya, crossing the desert on horses, which, up to that time, were unknown in Africa.

There is also the Carthaginian theory. This does not seem to apply to the Twareg tribesmen, who have (or had) all the characteristics of the warrior Berbers, living chiefly on the spoils of war and raids.

I have heard it said also that the Twareg were once Christians who may have been the survivors of the Donatist converts who met their end on the Mediterranean coast of Northwest Africa, first of all, at the hands of the Vandals in A.D. 428 and then by those of the Hilal Arabs in A.D. 1150.

To support this theory there is the fact that the Twareg are unenthusiastic Moslem converts; many of them do not know enough Arabic to understand the meaning of the prayers which they recite mechanically five times a day, or of the Koran, which, according to the Islamic faith, they are supposed to know by heart and which can only be read by a "Believer" in its original tongue. Other supporters of this notion suggest that these people were once Christian and cite as evidence the cross used to ornament the Targui shield, as well as the great two-bladed swords with cross-hilted pommels after the manner of the Crusaders.

As a matter of fact, while Christianity may have been practised by the Twareg, as suggested by their words *mesi* which in their language means "God", and *andjelous* meaning "messenger"—neither of which appears in Arabic—the cross has no bearing on the argument as it did not become a Christian emblem until three and a half centuries after Christ's death, while the Targui cross is of much older origin.

Whoever these Twareg may be, or where they came from, their story is extremely old. Many of their adornments, bracelets and the like, which they cut and polish today, belong definitely to the Stone Age, which, if that of the Neolithic or latest Stone Era, makes the date about the thousand years before Christ and, if of the Paleolithic, at least five thousand years older. Where investigators meet a blank wall when trying to elucidate the Targui mystery is the lack of contemporary written information, which is as deficient here as it is with the Phoenicians.

Professor Gautier, that trustworthy authority on matters North African, on whose declarations one can rely, says in his *Passé de l'Afrique du Nord*, "There is not one existing Berber book; nor is there, to any intent or purpose, any real caligraphy or even a language with grammatical rules. Nor is there any true Berber architecture. A few ancient tombs are found here and there which suggest small and extremely poor copies of the pyramids."

So, if we accept that the Twareg are Berbers, we can make no research among their archives, because they do not exist.

There is, however, a contradition here. The Twareg speak a language called Tamahchek[1] which is a Berber dialect, and use an alphabet called Tifinagh or Tifinar, which consists of about fifty symbols and is said to be derived from Libyan. This script

---

[1] Here is another spelling problem. E. W. Bovill writes "Temajegh", while in the latest book published about the Maghreb by Nevill Barbour, "Tamahagg" is the lettering. My own version is that of Father de Foucauld who, having lived for over ten years with the Twareg and learnt their language, should know, at least, the phonetic sound of the word.

is used to write messages on rocks and to record love poems and ballads. Sometimes the sentences are written right to left as by the Arabs, sometimes in Occidental fashion from left to right, and occasionally up and down in the manner of the Chinese or Japanese. In fact, all their inscriptions suggest an ideographic origin. However, little of interest is recorded by this script and it often consists of childish love messages from boys to girls such as we see today written on the walls of Occidental village schools.

All we know for certain is that the Twareg belong to a light-skinned race, and there are instances of some of the tribesmen having blue eyes, which are also found among the Berbers of the Atlas and the Aures. The dark skin of the Twareg is due to the rays of the sun. A baby is born white, but he is not clothed for such a long time after his birth that his body becomes tanned to a mahogany hue, and never regains its birth colour.

To add to the difficulty of obtaining information about the Twareg past, is their inability or merely obstinate refusal to tell investigators anything. In spite of their Paleolithic or Neolithic work, there does not seem to be even an inkling of memory among the oldest or wisest of these men, or among any of their scholars, concerning these implements made of stone. If a Targui is asked a direct question about a custom which must have come down from a far-off generation, his reply will be, "It has always been so."

For example, in this matter of the veiling of the men which characterizes the warriors of the Hoggar and has caused them to be regarded as a mysterious people, no one knows when or how it started, or why. It is all a matter of conjecture. Some of these conjectures are as follows—to protect the wearer of the veil from the ever blowing desert wind which is always charged with sand and dust. This argument loses its value when one recollects that the Targuia, who travel over the Sahara as much as their men, do not seem to need this protection for their throats or noses. Furthermore, a Targui wears his veil whether riding his drome-dary across the desert or sleeping in his tent or hut. In fact, Father de Foucauld declared that no one, not even a Targui's wife, had ever seen a man's mouth. In order to eat and drink the Targui skilfully passes his food or beverage (usually a glass of mint tea), under the veil.

Father de Foucauld further states that a Targui would no more think of removing his veil in public than would a European take off his trousers under similar conditions. Philippe Diolé, the traveller and writer, who was frequently a guest of a Targui family, one day caught his host adjusting his veil and was able to see the man's face, which he found had none of the nobility suggested by the bright eyes and high forehead appearing above the veil. In fact, Diolé said that the face of this particular Targui was narrow and rather rat-like, so that it might be that the veil is merely used to cover ugliness.

The rest of the Targui's costume consists of blue linen trousers which reach to the middle of the calf of the man's leg, a blue *gandourah*, that nightgown-like garment worn in most parts of the Sahara (the burnous cloak, which is an essential part of a bedouin's dress, is rarely worn except by chiefs and only on ceremonial occasions). On the head is a blue linen hood from which hangs the veil. Finally, while the Twareg possess sandals, they rarely wear them as, like most nomadic peoples, they walk as little as possible, and bare feet are all that a dromedary will tolerate on his neck.

The Targuia are slightly built and often beautiful. Dacine, the poetess of Tamanrasset who did so much to help Father de Foucauld with his research among the Twareg of the Hoggar mountains, had the kind of looks which would have been admired in any community. As a general rule the Targuia can thus be rated as a physically attractive woman, which may be one of the reasons for not concealing her face. They sometimes wear sarongs and expose their shapely breasts, and when they do wrap mantles about their bodies it is more from coquetry than anything else.

All Twareg weapons belonged to another age than today, and to another part of the world. They had lances used as javelins and so barbed that removing them from a wound tore the flesh. They carried this huge, double-bladed cutting sword, and in addition had a long dagger strapped to the left forearm, with the handle at the wrist and the point at the elbow joint. They used firearms when they could get them,[1] although until comparatively recently they despised enemies who fought from a distance and avoided the hand-to-hand encounter. While they are excellent

---

[1] Since the independence of Algeria, Colonel Boumediene's government has made it a punishable crime to sell any arms to the Twareg.

horsemen, the Twareg prefer to ride the tall, light beige, trotting dromedary.

None of these customs is characteristic of the Sahara nomads, who are no longer warlike, carrying weapons only for hunting purposes, and travelling only to find pastures for their sheep. In fact, the Twareg represent a distinct people whose territory has established political boundaries respected by the various Twareg tribal Federations, although not definitely separated by geographical or political frontiers.

That these veiled warriors have established political areas of sovereignty does not mean that they are by any means sedentary— they are no more so than any nomads within their tribal areas.

The census of the various tribes, that of all nomadic people, is calculated on the basis of the number of tents or families within the area, and does not, therefore, give us any definite figure, except for the purposes of local taxation which is paid in kind, that is to say, with livestock, usually lambs.

The home of the Twareg, unlike that of most Sahara inhabitants, is a country of high, rocky, precipitous mountains, impossible to scale and accessible only through narrow canyons. Although there is some doubt on the subject, these highlands are probably of volcanic origin. The volcanoes must have been extinct for centuries as Herodotus describes the Hoggar mountains much as they are today. Travelling through one of these narrow canyons, which are the only means of access to the interior of this country, makes one appreciate the expression used by other Bedouin Tribal Federations—"the land of fear and the *djnoun* [demons]". The only good which can be attributed to these dark chasms is that, through their protection from the sun and cold, they form reservoirs of rainwater, around which grow a few tamarisks and oleanders. This holding of any water at all is quite astonishing as the total rainfall over a period of twenty years has been estimated at under twenty inches.

In fact, so precious is water to keep human beings alive that few Twaregs of either sex can ever afford enough with which to wash; they are probably one of the most uncleansed nations of the world.

The name usually employed by the historians and geographers for this country is "The Hoggar" or "Ahaggar". The other desert Berber tribes, however, call it *Blad el Khouf* meaning "the

Land of Fear", which is easy to understand when one leaves the sun-drenched desert to enter those dark, narrow passages with cliff sides six hundred feet high. The sun never reaches the floors of these canyons except when at its zenith. When one has navigated these chasm-like corridors, there is no relief in the hideously uninviting land which is inhabited by even less inviting peoples who are nearly as inhospitable as the puritan M'zabites, although some have been forced to learn better manners (by their new native rulers in Algiers) than their forebears whose only joy was killing of aliens who came their way. The Twareg peoples as a whole detest foreigners, more so than they do Shamba Bedouins and even their cousins, the nomadic Berbers, whom they despise for having accepted the European customs.

To sum up, then, the whole aspect of the Hoggar is one of harsh, frightening desolation, and reminds one of Gustave Doré's illustrations of Dante's *Inferno* and *Purgatorio*. It is an appropriate setting for these proud, savage creatures who have, until comparatively recently, lived on the plunder of caravans which entailed the killing and mutilating of the caravaneers when they refused to surrender; or who when they did not need camels or money to buy groceries and dates or anything else which their flocks could not supply, killed and stole just for the sake of so doing.

However, although the Twareg are instinctively the cruellest of peoples in the Sahara, they regard murder and suicide as mortal sins. These men and women are not afraid of dying, yet the name of someone deceased is never mentioned, and the camp-site where the death occurred is never occupied again. The fundamental reason for this is the fear of ghosts or the return of the dead man's spirit to live again invisibly with the tribe. This is further evidence of how far the Twareg are separated from the beliefs of Islam which, as does the Christian belief, reserves a residence in a heaven, and a hell, for the dead departed, from which no return is possible. Yet while murder is condemned, these veiled men will slaughter mercilessly for plunder and especially for revenge, when their sadistic cruelty has no equal.

I heard the following story of vengeance from the Targui perpetrator himself. It appears that this man was courting a Targuia belle who reciprocated his attentions. However, there was a rival who thought that he should have first place. One evening he came to the lady's tent and insulted her favourite. This led to the quick drawing of those daggers always worn on the Targui forearm. The rival was faster than the other man, and landed the point of his dagger in his adversary's head, which caused the blood to flow so freely over his face that it obscured his sight and made it impossible to fight back.

The rival, seeing the man howling with rage as he staggered about trying to find his would-be assassin, rushed from the tent and, mounting his dromedary, fled. The Targuia washed and dressed her lover's wounds and next day he recovered sufficiently to avenge his honour. There was no question of his convalescing as, having been defeated in a fight in front of his loved one, immediate redress was imperative. He, accordingly, saddled his dromedary and, arming himself with his great sword and lance and shield, set out on the tracks of his rival who, believing that his blow had been sufficiently severe to keep his enemy inactive for some time, had not hurried on his way.

However, on the morning of the fifth day after the fight, he suddenly noticed a Targui who was evidently coming after him. He tried to urge his camel into a trot, but the animal was tired, while the pursuing dromedary seemed to have wings attached to its feet. Soon the two men were within hailing distance and the lover began insulting the rival and daring him to dismount and fight it out after the approved Targui fashion, with broadsword and shield.

However, the rival paid no heed and vainly tried to make his camel trot faster than the mount of his pursuer who, nevertheless, continued to gain on him. When he found himself within range of his enemy, he took his javelin lance, balanced it carefully in the palm of his hand, raised it to the level of his shoulder, and then, aiming at the back of his enemy, let fly with that astonishing strength which I have seen these men display when giving a demonstration of javelin throwing.

The lance flew straight to its mark and transfixed the small of the back of the fleeing Targui, who fell from his camel mortally wounded, but not quite dead. The man who had been offended then dismounted, and roughly pulled the lance out of his rival's back, thereby mutilating his intestines and stomach with the cruel barbs. Seeing that his enemy still breathed, he drew his dagger and cut the man's throat, leaving the body to be "cared for", as he said, "by the vultures and the jackals". Afterwards, he took the dead man's weapons and his camel back to the camp to prove to his lady that he had avenged his honour.

"And was she pleased?" I asked.

"Of course," replied the Targui. "Later on we were married."

"But," I insisted, "I thought that murder was considered a crime among your people?"

The Targui looked at me askance, "But that wasn't murder, it was revenge which could only have been settled by fighting it out. I would never have killed the man from behind if he had not run away and given me no other alternative."

And that seemed to settle that. For a moment there was silence and then the Targui spoke again: "In any case, I gave the man a merciful death and did not leave him to die of thirst, or acted as did another of our tribesmen who had to settle a question of honour. He also had to pursue his enemy and when he caught and overpowered him, proceeded to bury him alive and up to his neck beside an ant heap. The next morning, all that could be seen sticking out of the earth was a clean white skull from which every bit of flesh and skin had been eaten by the ants!"

I looked at my companions, who had been listening to this gruesome conversation, but no one seemed particularly impressed. It was the law of the Targui Sahara which caught the French unawares when their military expedition and religious missions began to penetrate into the Hoggar regions where they met violent and cruel deaths at the hands of the treacherous and cruel Twareg inhabitants.

But, if the Twareg are cruel, they are also brave and they showed this on many occasions when the French (when still rulers of the country) began to tame them with magazine rifles, weapons which did not, at first, deter these warriors from attacking the invaders with their lances until their bodies were piled in heaps a long way out of range of the javelin throwers. They seem also to be insensitive to pain or else can suffer it without complaint.

Father de Foucauld used to tell a story in connection with Dacine, the beauteous Targuia of Tamanrasset who had never found a man whom she felt was worthy of her spiritual or physical love. One evening she was having a musical party outside her tent. Reclining beside her was a Targui chief who vainly believed he was making progress in the courting of this woman

6

who was virtually queen of that district of the Hoggar. As the party went on other veiled chiefs rode up to Dacine's tent and, dismounting, planted their lances in the ground as evidence of their peaceful intentions. One of the warriors, in planting his lance, accidentally transfixed the thigh of the chief who reclined beside Dacine. The chief uttered no complaint and remained pinned to the earth rather than move from his favoured position near his hostess, and waited patiently until the party broke up and the other chief, without any idea of the suffering of his fellow suitor, had torn the lance from his leg.

These musical evenings play an important part in Targui life, for, in spite of the bloodthirsty lustings of the veiled men, they are ardent lovers and their love affairs are almost as important as their fighting. Father de Foucauld, strangely enough, brought to light this erotic side of the Twareg customs, probably because almost all Targui literature is of an amorous nature.

Father de Foucauld in his notes about the Twareg, tells us that, unlike the desert Berbers, the Twareg are monogamous and marry comparatively late in life when the girl is free to accept or refuse her suitor. She may even propose to a man herself! The woman alone has the right to divorce and needs no stronger grounds than that she prefers someone else. She can also be unfaithful to her husband without the risk of being killed, as she would be in most Moslem households and especially among the Berbers of Kabylie. Few Targui girls are virgins when they wed, a thing also unheard of in orthodox Moslem families, where the bride's virginity has to be proven before the bridegroom will accept her as his wife.

Nevertheless, the women have little to do officially with the politics of their men. Their influence is great, however, and by counselling their husbands or lovers they can have matters arranged as they wish without the men being quite aware that what they are deciding really came from their ladies behind the scenes.

In 1917, after the murder of Father de Foucauld, the Senussi, taking advantage of the desperate plight of the French army on the western front, had decided to take over the whole of France's Sahara dominions. Dacine had so much influence over the men of the tribe and was so respected that she caused the majority of the Twareg, and especially the followers of Moussa ag Amastane, the paramount chief of the tribal Federation of the Targui territory where Father de Foucauld had lived and died, to have nothing to do with the Senussi plottings.

It was in vain that these fanatics argued that, with the French apparently defeated by the Germans, there could be no question of reprisals against the rebels, who should, in any case, fight as one for Islam.

Then there is the case of that strange Targuia queen, Tin-Hinan, whose skeleton and jewellery were found in the sepulchre which Byron de Prorok excavated at Tafarist, southwest of Tamanrasset. Pierre Benoit's story of Antinea, the white queen of Atlantis, was based on this lady's legend, and there is no reason to believe that it was not all founded on historic data in spite of the fact that the novel was published before de Prorok's discovery.

Professor R. Chudeau, who travelled extensively in the Sahara and has written about the country from a geological and historical point of view, is convinced of the existence of this white queen, who probably lived at the beginning of the Christian era. According to Benoit, she had the gift of perpetual youth, as did Ayesha in Rider Haggard's novel *She*. In fact, so much did the two books have in common that Haggard brought an action against Benoit for plagiarism, although the latter was able to prove that he had never read *She*.

Those Twareg who revealed the secret of the location of this tomb to Byron de Prorok claimed that Tin-Hinan lived at the time when their realms extended from the Atlantic to the Nile. The tomb itself resembled those two Berber pyramids in Algeria in one of which was buried Juba II, King of Numidia, during the middle of the last century, before the birth of Christ. His son, who was married to Cleopatra Selene, the daughter of Antony and Cleopatra, and was restored by the Romans to rule his country, was buried in the other one. In fact, some writers suggest that this Tin-Hinan or Antinea may have been the daughter of Cleopatra Selene. According to the historical data available, however, a pyramid was piled up on the Mediterranean coast by her grieving husband as the last resting-place of Cleopatra Selene.

The opening of the Targuia queen's sepulchre must have been one of the most rewarding achievements in the history of excavation. Here de Prorok found the legendary lady wrapped in a crumbling painted leather shroud which must have once been covered with gold leaf. Inside it lay the queen's skeleton and beside her the most remarkable collection of ornaments made of gold studded with precious stones. Near her skull was a tiara or crown set with emeralds. The skeleton itself lay on a splendid bed carved from a wood which had nothing in common with the Sahara. Everything from the actual funeral room, which had been hewn out of rock—a task which neither a Targui nor a Shambi would or could have undertaken for the body of a deceased person—to the jewellery and toilet articles of the dead beauty, had a much closer connection with the excavated tombs of ancient Egypt, than with anything Saharan. Nothing discovered in the tomb other than a few gold coins seemed to belong to that Roman period of history suggested by the archaeologists. Experts on these subjects who later examined the findings could never come to an agreement on the definite or even approximate date of the burial of Tin-Hinan: some set it in early Carthaginian times, 800 B.C. or even before that—back into prehistoric times; while others declared that it could not be earlier than the reign of Constantine the Great during the sixth century A.D.

However, we must not imagine the Targuia as Amazon-type women or even javelin-throwing queens such as ancient Britain's Boadecia or the Berber Jewish warrior queen la Kahena. They were, and are, essentially feminine and voluptuaries, as is shown by the importance which they place on sexual pleasures.

The only historic link between this queen of a remote past and the present-day Twareg is that the succession to chief does not pass from father to son, but to the eldest son of the paramount chief's eldest sister. This gives more credence to the legend of Antinea, or Tin-Hinan, the queen, and adds even more importance to women than they already have by their own insistence on a matriarchal society.

Now that opportunist politicians like Colonel Houari Boume-diene and Abdelaziz Bouteflike rule Northwest Africa it may be easier for Occidental explorers and archaeologists to investigate the Hoggar. Under this new government the Twareg have ceased to be a warrior race menacing the existence of any outsiders, be they native inhabitants or Occidentals, and must therefore accept archaeologists and scientists whom the Algerian government permits to visit their forbidding land.

5

THE FLATTERS DISASTER

As already stated, it was Aurélie Picard who had inadvertently encouraged the justifiably nervous members of Colonel Flatters' staff to go boldly against the antagonistic Twareg and force them to allow the expedition into the Hoggar. The belief that the holy Mohkadem would guarantee a safe passage was another proof of how little anyone knows about the Sahara and its people even when one has lived there for years. It demonstrates also that the gendarme's daughter had an unwarranted reverence for the Tidjani fraternity and having conquered the antagonism of their elders, felt herself to be an all-powerful influence in the Sahara.

However, the main cause for this hideous adventure was the political aspirations of the French government in France and in Algeria. At that time Louis Tirman, a politician of sound judgment, was Governor-General of Algeria. He had the interests of Northwest Africa at heart and it was in no way his fault that this gruesome catastrophe was to take place. In fact, it was the fault of this system whereby the Ministry of the Interior (the Home Office) was responsible for the administration of millions of square miles of African territory without much knowledge of conditions in Northwest Africa, and none whatsoever of those of the Sahara.

What led to this needless disaster was primarily the doings of a French engineer, called Duponchel, who felt that Algeria could and must be linked to the Sudan by a railway running across the Sahara which would save endless time in the transporting of merchandise which still had to be carried by camel. There were three potential routes for this impractical scheme. The first, which was partially put into effect some years later, was to run along the borders of eastern Morocco and then follow, more or less, the route of René Caillé during his march from Timbuktu to the Moroccan Atlas. In fact, it was Caillé's detailed report on the flatness of the country which influenced the engineers who were consulted.

The second line suggested would pass through Laghouat and thence to Ouargla where it would not only have to negotiate some dangerous tracts of sand desert, but also the precipitous and quite unknown Hoggar Mountain system, the home of the veiled Twareg. The reason for even contemplating such a hazardous route was due to that encouraging and optimistic view of the Targui friendliness and good nature towards the French spread abroad by an explorer called Henri Duveyrier who lived with the Twareg as an honoured guest in 1862.

The third route proposed followed the ancient caravan tracks of the Garamantes, the Phoenicians and the Romans across the Fezzan desert from Tripoli and on past Djerma to Lake Chad.

The Minister of Public Works, Monsieur de Freycinet, later to be Prime Minister of France, had decided that the most advantageous route from all points of view would be that one which ran through the barren rocky mountains of the Twareg Hoggar. The reasons he gave for this clearly unsound choice were that, in the first place, French territory extended as far as Ouargla where supplies could be obtained and help sent, if required, more rapidly than from any other outpost of the Sahara. In the second place, he felt that the Twareg tribes would welcome having more facilities than heretofore, for sending merchandise to Senegal and receiving other goods which they needed from the south.

Nor would the Minister listen to French officers of the Bureaux des Affaires Indigènes who tried to explain that the Twareg did not trade in that way. When they were in need of some commodity, they sent out a raiding party to hold up a caravan, or else attack a camp, or even an oasis.

Furthermore, Monsieur de Freycinet paid no heed whatever to the counsels of a commission which had almost unanimously declared itself opposed to any railway scheme of thousands of miles over an unknown desert where there was just sufficient pasture and enough water for camels, but not enough to fill the boiler of a locomotive, to say nothing of coal or even wood to generate steam.

As if to make the whole expedition more perilous than it seemed at first sight, Monsieur de Freycinet was opposed to having this caravan of peaceful engineers escorted by soldiers, which might give the impression to these "friendly" Twareg of Duveyrier that France was setting out to conquer a land which had, so far, defied all invaders. In fact, no one, except Monsieur de Freycinet, believed that, with or without soldiers, the right people could be found to undertake the surveying of a country larger than Europe and with none of its amenities, and inhabited by men who were averse to any form of foreign penetration, especially when it was Christian.

Moreover, when the French government decided to support Monsieur de Freycinet and Monsieur Duponchel's scatter-brained scheme, it chose the most unsuitable type of man to lead the expedition. His name was Colonel Paul Flatters, a man of forty-seven who had occupied various military positions in southern Algeria and had taken part in the Franco-Prussian War during which he had been taken prisoner with the Emperor at Sedan. He knew a good deal about the Sahara as he had spent some years in command of the military territory of Laghouat, but he believed in the old school idea of European soldiering where discipline must be as rigid as on a parade ground and army regulations enforced regardless of how applicable they might be to actual circumstances. He was also a nervous, quick-tempered person who could not adapt himself to the intimate relationship between officers and the rank and file so essential for this kind of expedition. This relationship would eventually, he declared, be the *only* system for a group of Frenchmen and nomads bent on venturing into an unknown desert seething with enemies.

Nor did Colonel Flatters understand how to handle the native inhabitants or earn their friendship and respect. In fact, from the very start, he and his followers seem to have been doomed. As one follows the development of the dramatic happenings, one is overwhelmed by the same feelings of impending disaster, as created in a Greek tragedy where everything appears to be settled beforehand by an inexorable fate which must follow its course until the disastrous climax is reached.

The other members of what was to be known as the Flatters

mission were appointed at the end of 1880 as follows: in com-
mand, Colonel Flatters; chief of staff, Captain Masson; Monsieur
Beringes, an engineer from the public works department;
Monsieur Roche, mining engineer; Lieutenants Le Chatelier,
Brosselard and Lieutenant Dianoux of French Infantry regiments
raised in North Africa consisting of Berberized Arab soldiers;
Monsieur Cabaillot and Rabourdin, railway engineers.

This expedition reached Algiers in January of 1880, where a
military doctor, Captain Guiard, joined the party, which then, by
devious routes and methods, made its way to Biskra where the
principal guides awaited the Frenchmen.

The Colonel then thought it a good idea to write to the
Amenokal, paramount chief of the Hoggar territory through
which the expedition was to pass. He did this clumsily, suggesting
that it was his intention to enter the Hoggar Mountains regardless
of Twareg feelings. The paramount chief, or Amenokal, whose
name was Ahitagel, replied ceremoniously and somewhat in the
tone of a superior addressing a person of inferior rank. It was a
lengthy document which began significantly as follows:

"We have received your letter; we have read it and understood
it. You have asked us to open the road to the south to you. *We
will not open it!*"

This statement was followed by fairly logical reasons why the
French should take the easier and more westerly route to the
Niger. However, whatever the reasons, the refusal to let anyone
into the Hoggar country was formal and conclusive.

When the politicians in Paris were shown this ill-omened
message, they made fun of it. How could a group of uncivilized
tribesmen armed with lances and a few muskets, they asked, bar
the way to a Franco-Berber force which carried the latest firearms? What a lesson they would learn when they came face to
face with disciplined troops! It was almost worthwhile sending
this mission to the Hoggar to show this impertinent "native"
what modern civilization represented.

What these bureaucrats had forgotten, or did not know about,
was the *Sahara itself*! The desolate Sahara between Ouargla and
Tamanrasset, waterless and trackless, was a redoubtable enemy
even without the addition of hostile warriors. They had not taken
into consideration the mobility of these camel-riding veiled men
who knew every kilometre of their country and every water hole,

and accepted heat and thirst and hunger as a matter of course. They could not visualize the isolated plight of a caravan dependent on the food and water and ammunition it carried if anything went wrong with plans. They could not imagine the resentment which the Twareg felt towards any kind of foreign encroachment on their territory, whether or not it was of French or Moslem origin. They had no conception of how little the life of a Christian counted in the minds of these converts to Islam. In fact, they knew as little about what the Flatters' mission was undertaking as the Twareg knew about an ocean voyage on the sea, which none of them had ever seen.

The surveying column was, accordingly, ordered to assemble at Laghouat during the first half of November of 1880. This it did, and set out from there on its fatal journey on the eighteenth, and while far from adequate for this undertaking, the expedition was better organized than that which the government in Paris had suggested. In addition to the army officers and engineers previously mentioned, there were also forty-seven Arab soldiers of the Algerian Tirailleurs, with two French N.C.O.s and two orderlies. As well as these men, there were thirty-one Shambi cameleers and guides in charge of 183 pack camels, carrying tents, ammunition, food and enough spare water to meet emergencies in the event of a well not being found from which to replenish their supply.

Most of the men were mounted on *mehara*, those essentially riding dromedaries, and the rest on transport camels. There were also three horses to be used primarily as gifts to the Twareg chiefs, and usually ridden by the colonel and his chief staff officers.

There was also the *mohkaden*, holy man of the Tidjani religious fraternity at Ain Mahdi near Laghouat, whom Madame Aurélie, as promised, had attached to Colonel Flatters' staff.

In addition to this, a letter had also been sent by the then head of the Tidjani fraternity to Ahitagel himself, asking him to be a good host to the French mission. But even this was to have no effect on the xenophobic veiled men of the Hoggar. The reels of the tragedy were spinning out to their inevitable conclusion.

On 4th December, 1880, the column passed through Ouargla, which none of the Frenchmen and few of the Shambi would ever see again. It moved slowly in a southeasterly course towards Tuat.

The news that the French were *en route* had brought a rather more encouraging message from Ahitagel than before, suggesting that if Colonel Flatters offered rich gifts, a safe passage might be arranged. However, nothing was promised regarding the journey through the Hoggar and no representatives of the Amenokal or Twareg guides came to meet Colonel Flatters.

In fact, the Shamba guides soon began to show their misgivings and urged their leader to halt until something more definite had been heard from Ahitagel. However, the Colonel would not listen to this advice.

On 10th January further warnings were disregarded when members of a small Shamba caravan moving north told the Frenchmen that Ahitagel was making no secret of his hostility towards these invading infidels.

The officers and engineers now joined the guides in begging Flatters to show caution, but to no avail. The Colonel had made up his mind to go on until he met the Amenokal in person.

The situation also became more hazardous, for the column now found itself in the most terrifying and desolate desert with little pasture for the camels, and wells which had to be cleared of sand before any but brackish water could be found. By day, the sun made the stony landscape reverberate with shimmering heat; by night the men shivered in their tents with temperatures close to freezing. The infernal aspect of the landscape was now enhanced by black crags on the horizon, which marked the boundaries of the Hoggar.

A feeling of apprehension spread over the members of the mission as they gazed at this hideous, inhospitable country where lizards seemed to be the only living creatures. Then out of this glittering wilderness a Targui on a white dromedary suddenly materialized bearing a letter from Ahitagel in which he stated that he had been trying to find the Colonel in order that he might furnish him with competent guides to lead him into the Hoggar highlands. In token of this, he was dispatching his brother-in-law, Ag Chikkat Attici, to lead the way.

On 25th January Ag Chikkat arrived in person and showed what, for a Targui, seemed to amount to the friendliest of feelings. The Colonel, with his strangely trusting nature when dealing with people to whom knavery was second nature, accepted the Targui's overtures with smiles and gifts. From then on, too, he handed over the leading of his caravan to these veiled men about whom he knew nothing, refusing even to have his Shamba scouts out in front to warn him of any signs of treachery.

For the moment, this confidence did not seem misplaced. Furthermore, as the column advanced towards those black mountains, groups of Twareg appeared out of the haze, bringing with them words of welcome from the Amenokal. The French officers began to feel that their fears had been unfounded. Only the Shamba remained anxious and suspicious of this unusual friendliness on the part of a people to whom xenophobia was their creed. What especially dismayed them was the familiarity with which the veiled visitors treated the Colonel, which almost amounted to condescension and an attitude that his gifts were theirs by right. In fact, some of the guides begged the Colonel to release them from their duties and allow them to return to their homes before it was too late.

So genuine, too, was their terror that while Flatters refused to grant their request, he did make the gesture of doubling his sentries around the camp at night. This reassured no one, as it was evident even to the simplest-minded cameleer that the Twareg would not deliberately attack a disciplined group of soldiers armed with magazine rifles. If they did have murderous plans, which every Shambi believed, they would leave nothing to the hazard of battle.

Early on 16th February the caravan was made to change its course towards the southeast over a stony plain interspersed with large patches of sand. At about 10 a.m. it reached a place where there were a few pools of water left by a rainstorm, but not enough for all the animals. It was suggested, therefore, by the Twareg guides that the main camp be established there while the Colonel and some of his officers accompanied the camels and their cameleers to Bir el Gharama (Wells of Gharama), at a place called Tadjemout, which has the ominous meaning of "Crown of Death", a couple of hours' march away. There they would find plenty of water for the animals as well as for the filling of water skins.

To this suggestion the Colonel agreed, and leaving one officer in charge of the camp set out for the well, taking with him the doctor and two other officers, with guides and camels. The only precaution which he maintained for his own safety was to have himself followed by a small rearguard of twenty Algerian Tirailleurs under an N.C.O.

As the little party moved away from the main body, Bou Djemma, the Targui guide who had been the first to join the expedition and proved himself to be the only reliable person of the group accompanying that mission, drew his camel alongside the Colonel's horse, and, bending down, said:

"Colonel, you have been betrayed. These men have separated you from your camp and your men. Take care, you are betrayed!"

However, the Colonel merely shrugged his shoulders and when Bou Djemma begged him to go back to the camp, told him sharply to mind his own business. Nevertheless when after two hours of travelling there was no sign of a well, the Colonel became impatient and demanded of the Twareg guides where they were headed. The Twareg replied by pointing towards a kind of ravine where, sure enough, Colonel Flatters saw tamarind trees growing near what were, obviously, wells.

When they arrived at the wells the Colonel and his companions, two of whom, in addition to himself, were on horseback, were invited to dismount. This they did, and sat under the welcome shade of a tamarind while the watering of the camels proceeded. It was a peaceful scene and the Colonel was in excellent spirits, which was due to his lately having had a message from Ahitagel in which he promised to supply competent men to lead the French from the Hoggar to the Niger. The Colonel's happy thoughts were interrupted by savage yells from the valley which ran down from the hills surrounding the well. The cries were followed by an avalanche of blue-veiled, screaming men on camels, brandishing lances and swords.

Colonel Flatters and his officers leaped to their feet, looking for their horses, but these had been led away by the Twareg guides under the pretext of watering them. They, therefore, turned and, drawing their revolvers, faced the waves of veiled warriors who bore down on them like a river in flood. Monsieur Beringer was cloven in two by one of the Targui broadswords, Monsieur Roche and the doctor, caught from behind, had their throats cut and died gurgling on the sand like two slaughtered sheep, and the remaining two Frenchmen, Colonel Flatters and Captain Masson, emptied their revolvers into the swirling avalanche of veiled men, bringing to account great numbers of their attackers and their camels before they were mercilessly hacked to pieces by the great double-edged broadswords. A few minutes later the precious camels had been driven off into the mountains by the Twareg, leaving a hundred or so of their companions to guard the well, lest any survivors of the French expedition venture near the life-saving water.

In the meanwhile the Tirailleur rearguard had reached the crest of the hill which looked down on the well. The N.C.O. and his men had just time enough to witness the massacre of their leader, and, while too late to save him, unhesitatingly advanced against the enemy. They were, however, held up by the fire from the French rifles which the Twareg had captured from the Arab cameleers who had been killed. In spite of this the N.C.O. in command of the rearguard continued to hold his ground, hoping to drive off the guards at the well and round up their camels.

But while numbers of Twareg were killed by the accurate fire of the soldiers, the latter also were having casualties and the ammunition which they had brought with them was running low.

When it became evident that it would be suicidal to press the attack further, the N.C.O. led his men back to the base camp, harried all the way by the veiled men now reinforced by hundreds more who had come out of the hills at the sound of the firing. But these Algerian soldiers knew their business and, in spite of the tremendous odds against them, ten out of the original twenty who had set out that morning managed to reach their companions and told them of the tragedy which had taken place at the wells.

It was immediately appreciated that there was only one course open to the survivors—to trek back on foot to the nearest French outpost 750 miles away! As there was not one transport animal available, each man would have to carry a rifle, ammunition, all the water available and some rice.

Seven hundred and fifty miles represents about the distance between the English south coast to the Scottish north. To cover this on foot along a good road and in a temperate climate would be an ordeal. To do so across a trackless, stony desert with 100-degree temperatures by day and frost by night sounds like an impossible feat for human beings. Added to the exhaustion of marching under such conditions, there were the Twareg on their fleet camels hovering round the caravan ready to pounce on it and finish off the survivors of the original expedition. Nevertheless, Lieutenant Dianoux, with forty desperate men, set out to try and achieve what seemed impossible.

As the rice ration gave out, men began chewing their leather equipment. Two saluki dogs which had started out with Colonel Flatters were killed, but the Moslems would not eat their flesh. A wild ass was shot and devoured raw.

Some of the Tirailleurs wanted to commit suicide while they still had strength to do so, but the Frenchmen continued to maintain a bold front, assuring everyone that sooner or later a relief party would be sent out to search for them. This optimism was enhanced when four camels, probably belonging to some Twareg nomads' camp, were rounded up. On these were placed the ammunition and the remaining, still filled water skins, which permitted the weakened men to cease being beasts of burden.

In the meanwhile, the Twareg were growing bolder and actually sending emissaries to the French camp offering to sell them camels. As Dianoux still had the money belonging to the Flatters mission in his possession, and appreciating that, whatever might be the motives in the minds of these treacherous men, camels were camels, he paid the exhorbitant sums they were asking for a few skinny animals.

Eating the raw flesh of the wild ass had revived the men, who knew that they were approaching the gorge at Amguid where plenty of water had been found on the way out but which would undoubtedly be defended this time by Twareg. Sure enough, the following morning a band of veiled men appeared on the flank of the French column, but instead of attacking it, a messenger approached and dropped two bags of crushed dates and a promise of some sheep next day, if the price demanded was met.

Dianoux gladly accepted the dates and carefully divided them among his dwindling company. Hardly had the starving men swallowed the first mouthfuls of the oily fruit than they fell to the ground, foaming at the mouth and raving like maniacs. Lieutenant Dianoux and Sergeant Pobeguin began to tear off their clothing and fire their revolvers at their companions. Some of the Tirailleurs rushed off into the desert and were never seen again.

Luckily, however, most of the Shambi had been suspicious of this unbelievable Targui generosity and did not touch the poisoned dates. They were thus able to subdue their raving comrades and control them until they all fell into comatose stupors. What is surprising is that the Twareg did not immediately attack their victims. They knew the effects of the betthina grass which had been mixed with the date mash—and it would cause delirium followed by lethargy and an unbalanced state of mind. Perhaps the Twareg merely wanted to add to the slow agony of their enemies, feeling sure that none of them could, in any case, reach the end of their journey alive, and it would be simpler to rob them of their money they carried, as well as their arms, when everyone was dead.

As a matter of fact, the Twareg had planned further torments for their victims. This time they approached with offers to sell them some sheep with the understanding that responsible men would be sent to arrange the deal, and Dianoux, feeling that the holy Mohkadem would be a safeguard to the others, delegated him to accompany three men who had not been affected by the poisoned dates. What followed surpasses in savagery anything ever recorded in the dramatic annals of the Sahara.

The Twareg who said they had the sheep to sell were grouped on the edge of a cliff which dominated the Amguid gorge where water flowed so sweetly. As the Mohkadem and the three emissaries reached the veiled men, they were set upon by the Twareg who bound them with ropes and lined them along the edge of the cliff well in sight of their companions.

The veiled men then drew their great two-bladed swords and decapitated, one after the other, the three Shambi soldiers. When they reached him, the Mokhadem halted them with a cry that he was a marabout of the Tidjani fraternity and held up his rosary as evidence. This merely made the executioner pause but a moment and once more raising the heavy sword, he split the holy man from his skull to his hips so that he fell apart in two neatly carved halves.

This action proves what has already been suggested: that the Twareg fiercely resented strangers encroaching on their territory, regardless of their religion, and had no respect even for a marabout unless he was a Targui.

As the Twareg were keeping well out of range of rifle fire, nothing could be done to avenge the death of the Mokhadem and his companions, so that Lieutenant Dianoux, in spite of still being in a state of semicoma from the poisoned dates, ordered the men to resume their march towards that water which they so badly needed, and staggered on, followed by his tattered skeletons.

In a few hours the entry to the ravine was reached. As suspected, it was found to be strongly held by the veiled men. However, with great courage and discipline, an attack was carried out with the orderliness which might have suggested well-fed soldiers fighting under normal conditions of war. The shooting was cool and controlled and accurate, so much so that the Twareg had to give ground and then retreat, leaving many casualties. This, unfortunately, was at the expense of the lives of Lieutenant Dianoux and two other Frenchmen—Corporal Brame, Colonel Flatters' orderly, and Corporal Marjolet, his personal cook, who had bravely but recklessly exposed themselves when leading the attack. One Tirailleur had also been killed and six others wounded, but they had to continue the advance through the gorge as best they could to find the life-giving water.

The command of the survivors of the Flatters mission was now devolved on Sergeant Pobeguin, a cavalry N.C.O., like René Caillé from the Poitou in France. But Pobeguin was still suffering from the effects of the poisoned dates and had to be carried on one of the remaining overloaded camels. He was really incapable of giving orders or making sensible decisions.

The condition of the other men was nearly as bad as Pobeguin's and only the knowledge of what would happen to them at the hands of the Twareg made them stagger on.

On 18th March, after nearly five weeks of this terrifying trekking, one of the old camps which had been occupied in January was reached. Here the ravenous men found a dead camel dried up by the sun, which they tore apart and cooked the skin and bones over a brush fire. Then, as if they had not been made to suffer enough, a sandstorm roared out of the desert causing the weakened men to lie on the burning ground until it cleared. Then on again they went, struggling towards the goal which, although comparatively close now, they knew they could never reach without food.

Now with no active leader, and the only Frenchman a dying invalid, discipline had vanished and each man was on his own, fighting for survival. What followed this new state of mind can best be described by quoting from the official account of the Flatters expedition published in Paris in 1884:

On March 22, several men left the camp under pretext of hunting gazelles of which quite a number had lately been seen. A little later on, shots were heard by those men who had remained in the camp and in the afternoon, one of the hunters returned carrying meat which he said was that of a moufflon. Pobeguin, however, recognized this to be human flesh and refused to touch any, realizing that it was the remains of one of the hunters who had been murdered by his ravenous companions.

Under the circumstances there was little that Pobeguin could say and the cannibal soldiers continued the trek towards some well, remembered during the march south. During the night several rifle shots were heard, and at daybreak two Tirailleurs went to investigate. They brought back news that a soldier had quarrelled with his two companions and killed them. Then he and the men who had come to find out what was going on had cut up their bodies and eaten them. What meat they could not use, they brought back for Sergeant Pobeguin who, during the past six days had been living on leaves and insects. So famished was he that he at last gave in to the aroma of the roasting human steaks and ravenously joined his men in sharing this ghastly food. By that time cannibalism had been accepted as a matter of course.

Private Bel Kacem, the mulatto cook, had now assumed the role of official executioner of the survivors of the Flatters expedition, while he likewise took care of the carving up and preparing of the human carcasses for roasting. The men dared not sleep and tried to keep themselves awake at night with their eyes on the butcher who now scanned the terrified soldiers with professional interest. Next day two more men were slaughtered, carved up and roasted.

Sergeant Pobeguin's condition was not improving in spite of now having regular "meals". He was, in fact, growing weaker every day. On 31st March it was evident that he had but a very short while to live and one of the soldiers suggested that it might be well to put him out of his misery and at the same time give his hardier companions something more to eat. There was a good deal of discussion over this suggestion. El Madani, the only surviving N.C.O. of the Tirailleurs, who still had respect for a Frenchman of superior rank to his, was opposed to such a measure. However, Bel Kacem put an end to all arguments by shooting Sergeant Pobeguin with his revolver and then slicing him up as he had the others with the sword which Colonel Flatters

7

had honourably carried through many campaigns in Europe as well as in Africa.

Ironically enough, the next day the surviving soldiers reached a nomads' camp, where the shepherds welcomed them with milk and mutton and couscous. For two days the wretched wanderers slept and were then able to hire camels which would take them to Ouargla, towards which they had marched over the desert for nearly two months. Here, on 4th April 1881, Corporal Madani with eleven shoeless, almost naked, corpse-like Shamba cameleers, reported himself and his men as the survivors of the well-equipped, well-nourished, well-armed trans-Saharan Railway surveying expedition which had set out on its fatal journey just over three months before. Of its original numbers, eighty had perished, some in battle, some from exhaustion and thirst and some to feed their starving companions. The Sahara had made one of its richest hauls in human lives. It had once more emphasized that no one could defy it, not even the French government, without paying heavy penalties.

It was not until several years later that any punitive force was sent to avenge the murder of those courageous European and Arab soldiers. The bureaucrats at the Ministries of War and Public Works were shocked to hear of the disastrous outcome of the expedition, but they filed the story as one of the natural risks which professional soldiers had to take. The public read the story rather in the same way, as they might the news of some railway accident in which no relatives were involved. In fact, it took considerable time for the detailed account of all that had happened to be published. By that time everyone was apathetic.

Several men who had been thought to have died at the massacre of Bir El Gharama reappeared to confirm the story of the fighting end of Colonel Flatters. Some of these men had been hidden and protected by less bloodthirsty Twareg than the vassals of Ahitagel, some had joined caravans moving north and had been accepted as stray Bedouins separated from their camps. One of them travelled as far as Tripolitania and inadvertently brought the curse of the Flatters Expedition to another group of brave men, members of the Order of Cardinal Lavigerie's White Fathers, who were to perish as had his late companions at the hands of those murderous, veiled men from the "enchanted mountains" of the Hoggar.

CARDINAL LAVIGERIE AND
THE WHITE FATHERS

In order to follow the story of the soldier who returned like a ghost from the Flatters mission, it is necessary to go back a few years to the appearance in North Africa of Charles Lavigerie, the Cardinal-to-be, and the founder of the order of White Fathers, since it was under his régime that the second and third catastrophes at the hands of the Twareg took place.

In 1886 a plague of locusts had destroyed almost all of what was growing in the cultivated areas of Algiers. A famine ensued which was, as it usually is, followed by a widespread epidemic of typhus, then cholera. A drought completed the disaster, so that men, women and children were dying by the roadside with no help available. The official death roll was estimated at three hundred thousand, although it is probable that the number was twice as great.

Marshal MacMahon was at that time Governor-General of Algeria, and to assist him controlling this catastrophe he had with him at the archbishopric of Algiers Cardinal Lavigerie. Lavigerie had been born on 31st October 1825 in Bayonne on the banks of the Adour in the Basses-Pyrénées, where he had shown himself to be an intelligent, hard-working boy. His father thought that he would make a good lawyer or doctor. Charles, however, had other ideas and, much against his family's wishes, entered the minor seminary of Laressore in the Pyrenean foothills not far from his home town. After a comparatively short novitiate which included a professorship at the Sorbonne he was then appointed Bishop of Nancy and after that Bishop of Lyon. In 1887 he was nominated Archbishop of Algiers.

He was now on the threshold of the land where Moslems out-numbered all other faiths by millions of people. It was a post where he could try and put into effect what had come into his mind when tending the persecuted Lebanese Christians among whom he had worked as a missionary.

Opposing the anti-clerical policies of the government of Napoleon III, he publicly declared:

> The sad blindness and impotence which we have seen for thirty years in Africa is only explained by the calculated absence of all Christian thought in the administration of Algeria. Instead of assimilating these Berber populations by leading them to our civilization, we encourage them in their barbarity and in their faith in the Koran.
>
> Algeria is the only door which is opened by providence to a barbarous continent of two hundred million souls. It is especially there that we must bring the Catholic apostolate. That is what I believe the clergy of Algeria will be called upon to carry out one day. And that is what they can attempt tomorrow, even at the risk of their lives.

The government at once guessed that, with a brilliant, energetic and fearless man like Lavigerie in the archbishop's palace, it would not be long before quite the wrong spirit, from its anti-clerical point of view, would be spread among the native population. These fears were well founded and this was shown the very day that Lavigerie took over his duties in Algiers.

To begin with, he showed members of the French military and civilian upper classes that he had not come to North Africa to make his official and sumptuous residence into a centre for social functions. Secondly, he declared that he would go to any extreme to defy any anti-clerical measure to limit his authority over his secular and monastic clergy. And thirdly, while he knew that adult Moslems could not be converted to Christianity, he would exert himself to help them to rise above the pitiable level at which most of them lived. Above all, and this distressed the government more than anything else, he would eventually try to better the lot of the women, who were treated like animals by all but the higher class Berbers.

Lavigerie established an orphanage for the many derelict children of Algeria. At the same time, he began to give demonstrations to Arab farmers on how to make good use of the modern implements supplied by France; for France had not furnished much guidance as to how these implements could be employed to better their crops. After that, he asked the Vatican to send him brothers and nuns to help fight the typhus which had taken a firm hold on the population, partly due to the famine, but chiefly to the unhygienic way in which the poorer natives lived. The Government and soon the Governor were outraged and threatened to have Lavigerie removed from Algiers. The Archbishop was not impressed by these remonstrances, and replied prophetically to the Governor's threat of expulsion: "Unless you help the native inhabitants now, they will one day rise up against you!"

In the meanwhile, a new idea had materialized in the Archbishop's mind—the creation of an order which must be exclusively North African in conception and eventually pan-African. To start this project, he must not only have priests who spoke Arabic fluently, but also had an intimate knowledge of the Koran. They must wear the same type of clothing as the Arabs and be prepared to live among them. Only in this conscientious assimilation of native customs could they ensure the trust of men who had been brought up to despise Christians as infidel dogs and resent the French as unwanted conquerors.

When Lavigerie had an idea, he did not allow it to remain dormant. A few months after his arrival in Algeria he discussed what he had in mind with Father Girard, who was head of the small seminary which had been established in a suburb of Algiers. Father Girard understood immediately what the Archbishop wanted to do and enthusiastically approved.

The next evening, Father Girard outlined the scheme to his seminarians. A few days later three young men came to see him and declared that they would like to be the first members of this Order. The Archbishop interviewed them and explained that the rules of the Order might be harsher than any others in the world as, apart from the religious angle, it would mean almost forgetting France and French nationality. The young men replied that they appreciated this fact and were determined to devote themselves to the end in view.

It was from this small beginning that the Order of the White Fathers came into being. Today this is an international body of men numbering 2,253 members who are drawn from fifteen different nations, including Canada and the United States, while many of these good monks are of African birth. Their missions extend across the Sahara to Central Africa with others in Tanganyika and Uganda, covering an area of over two million square miles. The headquarters of the White Fathers is at Maison Carrée, a suburb of Algiers, and, while accepting members from all over the globe, it is still essentially a French organization.

This expansion took a very long while and was fraught with difficulty, the greatest being the harsh conditions imposed by Lavigerie for the making of a White Father. As he had pointed out to the three original volunteers, there had to be a complete dissociation from anything to which a young Frenchman had been accustomed. There had to be such self-discipline that any hardship must be endured for the sake of the cause. None of this would be any good unless the aspirants had the ability to learn Arabic in all its forms and then the dialects which varied with different districts of North Africa. The Koran had then to be sufficiently well memorized for them to be able to discuss it with educated Arabs.

Although the order was officially named "The Society of Missionaries to Africa", it soon became known by the colloquial name of "White Fathers" because of the clothing which its members wore. This consisted of a white *gandourah*, that full-length nightgown-like garment made of cotton or wool according to the season; the burnous, which is a long white cape with a hood, and a *chechia*, the red fez. So as to show themselves to be Christians, the Fathers wore a rosary of black and white beads with a crucifix to distinguish it from the plain Moslem rosary. The only concession made to European dress were the black shoes and stockings which they wore.

As soon as Lavigerie felt that the White Fathers were progressing well, he decided that he would try and establish a similar group of nuns to be known as the "White Sisters".

This project was even more difficult than with the men. The nuns whom he had imported from France to take care of his Arab orphans were well-bred, educated women who could nurse and teach, but would be useless among Arab women in isolated Moslem communities or in Sahara oases. He, accordingly, experimented with French farm girls, but soon discovered that, while they were as hardy as plough horses, they were almost illiterate and could not even sew. In fact, a moment came when the Archbishop became discouraged and thought of abandoning the whole idea of establishing an order of nuns in Africa. That he persevered was due to the entreaties of the maturing Order of the White Fathers.

Yet once more it took time. It was due to Lavigerie's personal selection and training of the right kind of women to fulfil the duties of this new order that it succeeded at all. Today the White Sisters in Africa number more than twelve hundred.

The main difficulty encountered in the recruiting of members was the perfection which the Archbishop demanded. He had no patience with inefficiency of any kind, and when a novice arrived who had ideas about herself or how nunneries should be organized, he went to extremes to humiliate her. He was determined to have in these African Orders only men and women who were sufficiently disciplined and inspired to sacrifice their lives for the cause.

The women, like the men, had also to be linguists who could learn to speak colloquial Arabic, as well as the classical language of the Koran, and in addition be practical nurses and also able to teach Arab children to sew and to weave as well as to look after their homes hygienically. In all of these aims and ambitions, he was successful.

As soon as Lavigerie had his missions north of the Atlas running to his satisfaction, he turned his eyes boldly towards the Southern Sahara. In order to encourage this new venture, Pius IX had appointed him to fill the newly created post of Missionary Prefect of the Sahara and the Sudan, which included the title of Bishop of Timbuktu, the diocese of which extended as far as East Africa and the Congo.

There were, at this time, no Christians in Timbuktu or the Sudan other than French soldiers and not very many of these in the Sahara. The White Fathers had barely reached the fringes of the desert. They had gone in groups of three with strict instructions from the Archbishop to assimilate the oasis life, but make no attempt to convert or even discuss Christianity with the Arab inhabitants. At the same time, they must openly declare themselves Christians and pray in public as did the Moslems.

This was the only way to win the confidence of these desert

people who needed physical help more than spiritual. In fact, where the Jesuit missions had failed by their aggressive intransigence, the White Fathers would succeed by their tolerant understanding.

Lavigerie first sent a group of White Sisters to Laghouat, the lately conquered oasis. At first the mayor of this town, who was a Moslem, would not permit them to remain. He knew how to deal with interfering priests like the Jesuits, but he feared these women dressed more like Moslems without veils who could go into the harems and talk to the occupants without any male supervision.

However, these White Sisters had not been trained in vain. They were tactful and kind and when the mayor fell ill, they nursed him so skilfully that he decided that they were not as dangerous as they had seemed at first. Thus, the White Sisters remained, built a convent in the oasis and started to recruit Arab girls to whom they taught hygiene, baby care, needlework and weaving.

While I lived in Laghouat, the successors of these original White Sisters lived in a comparatively large convent in the oasis. It was overcrowded by Arab pupils whose parents felt that their girls were not worthy of good marriages until they had worked under the Sisters. Housekeeping and cooking were no longer a haphazard craft, and the weaving and sewing which they were taught were so superior to anything of this kind made in the oases or camps that the Sisters earned a worthwhile income selling carpets and curtains and table linen to French officers' wives and to tourists.

By the time that I came to live in the desert, the White Order had penetrated far into the Sahara and beyond the Niger into Central Africa. There were three White Fathers in Laghouat under the saintly supervision of le Père David, who was still there in 1950. A fine church had been built whose exterior resembled a domed mosque with minarets surmounted by unobtrusive crosses. This was another of Lavigerie's principles—to have nothing too obviously Christian to offend Moslem eyes.

In those days Christians and Moslems mingled on the best of terms. While neither the White Fathers nor the White Sisters had made any converts, except with occasional orphans, they had done so much good to the Moslem communities that they were treated with as much respect as the Aghas and Caids, and with a great deal more affection.

In spite of what Lavigerie told his men: "Do not try to Europeanize these people, rather make yourselves what they are, adopt their customs, etc. . . ." no nomad or oasis dweller could completely dissociate a Frenchman from the French soldiers who had occupied their land. The infidel had proved himself worse than depicted by Islam and his presence was to be discouraged whenever possible. Nevertheless, Lavigerie had his priests move south behind the gradual military penetration. Soon there were posts as far south as Metlili and Ouargla, five to seven hundred miles south of Algiers.

Then, in 1874, a French explorer called Doumeau Duperé was attacked on his way to Ghadames and murdered with two other Frenchmen. The murderers belonged to a well-known gang of raiders and were shortly afterwards rounded up by the French army and locked up in Metlili not far from Ghardaia. Among these bandits were five Twareg, and to these in their prison went Father Charbonnier, an eager young priest and a member of Cardinal Lavigerie's White Fathers Order. He felt that these savage veiled men could tell him much about their so far unknown and unexplored part of the desert.

While at first suspicious and hostile, the Twareg gradually unbent before Charbonnier's obvious goodwill. Soon they were giving him much information about tribes and tracks and wells in these unmapped, arid territories of the Hoggar. When their trial took place, Lavigerie suggested that it would be much better for France's future in the Sahara if, instead of being punished, the Twareg were brought to Algeria where they would have a glimpse of French civilization and then go back to their people with word that France meant them no harm.

What the good Archbishop failed to realize was that it was not merely a question of French, but of *any* encroachment by *any* foreigners into Targui country, especially Christians. These veiled men wanted to live their own lives as did the Shamba in much the same area and the Negroes further south. True, colonization would, eventually, give the native inhabitants many advantages which they then lacked, but that did not make alien occupation any more acceptable.

The Archbishop's suggestion was followed and the veiled

warriors were taken to the coast where, instead of being treated as criminals, they were entertained as distinguished guests. The Civil Service, the Army and the Church, especially the Church, gave parties for these bandits as if they were visiting monarchs.

When eventually and unconditionally pardoned, and given every facility to return to their homes, the Twareg invited Lavigerie to accompany them. They had seen a great deal of him and he had frankly explained his ambitious plan to link up Algeria and Central Africa with a chain of missions from Algiers to Timbuktu.

Lavigerie could not, of course, accept this invitation but he felt that here was a God-sent opportunity really to find out what prospects for missionary penetration existed south of Metlili and Ouargla. The Twareg had assured him that any White Father would be as safe in their care as in the streets of Algiers.

The Archbishop delegated Fathers Alfred Paulnier, Pierre Bouchard and Philippe Menoret to join the five veiled men. Everything went smoothly as far as Metlili where the unknown desert began. Here the French military commander warned the priests that a Targui was always a Targui, whose only instinct was to kill foreigners and more especially if they were French and priests of the Christian Church. In fact, he forbade the three Fathers to go any further south without signing a document absolving him from any responsibility. Even the native inhabitants of the oasis foretold treachery on the part of the Twareg. Only the Agha of the oasis seemed to feel that, under these particular circumstances, the Twareg would respect the unwritten law of Islam never to betray guests whose hospitality they had accepted.

However, to make sure that nothing unexpected would occur, he delegated his son, El Hadj Bou Bekher, with a small escort of mounted Bedouins to accompany the White Fathers. On 14th January, 1876, these three saintly priests, believing that it was God's wish that they should proceed to the Hoggar, where they might find guides who would take them on their way to bring Christianity to pagan Africa, set out on the then quite unknown and trackless desert which separated the land of the oases from the rocky highlands of the Hoggar. Their belief that they could accomplish their mission was as vain as that of Colonel Flatters a few years before.

The first week of the journey passed normally. The Twareg

were friendly and every evening dined with the White Fathers around the camp fire, telling stories of their country and its people which gave the missionaries the information they needed in order to establish missions in these unknown parts of the Sahara. Little did they appreciate the true nature of these talkative men who never uncovered their faces even when they ate.

The drama took place suddenly and quickly one morning when the caravan was crossing a rocky part of the desert which did not permit the whole group of camels to move in one body as in the sandy tracts. At the head of the procession, riding side by side, were Father Paulnier and the leader of the Twareg; a few yards behind were Father Bouchard with Ida Ag Gemmoum, who had been nursed back to health by the White Fathers and Sisters after his capture and wounding by the French the previous year; and still further behind Father Menoret with another of the Twareg, all of whom had been guests of Cardinal Lavigerie in Algiers. Quite a distance in the rear on horseback rode El Hadj Bou Beker with the small, mounted escort.

Father Paulnier's companion was explaining Targui customs and rites, especially as they concerned the great, two-bladed sword for which these veiled men had the same kind of respect which Japanese Samurai had had for their weapons. On the excuse that he wanted to illustrate something in connection with his sword, the Targui drew it from his scabbard and Father Paulnier, who already knew of the reverence of these warriors for their swords, leaned over towards his companion's camel, to examine the razor-like blade. As he did so, the Targui, with a sharp gesture, raised the sword and brought it down on the priest's skull, splitting it down to the eyes.

This was a prearranged signal for the massacre of the missionaries to begin. The second Targui in the procession drew a pistol from under his robes and fired it point-blank into the chest of Father Bouchard, who reeled from his camel dead, while simultaneously, Ida, whose life had been saved by these saintly men, drove his dagger, which every Targui wears strapped to his left forearm, into the back of Father Menoret, but without killing him outright. In fact, the wounded man managed to pick himself up when he fell from the camel and flee in the direction of El Hadj Bou Beker. Before he could reach the protection of his escort, Ida caught up with him and hacked him to pieces with his sword.

Then El Hadj Bou Beker, who had seen what was happening, made ready with his men to defend themselves. But the Twareg assassins called out: "Don't be afraid. We are only killing Christians. You, as a true Believer, will come to no harm!"

This was as treacherous as all the rest, for unknown to Bou Beker, the Twareg had been able to include in the escort an outlaw whose family had a blood-feud with Bou Beker's family. Without warning, this man now said to Bou Beker, who was no longer on his guard: "Last year one of your people killed my cousin. The day of reckoning has now come!"

With these words, he shot the young chief dead with his pistol. The rest of the Beker escort then fled.

In the meanwhile, the Twareg were ransacking the White Fathers' baggage and, discarding the papers, the missals and the breviaries, loaded the sacramental vessels and the vestments and the priests' changes of clothing on to the now spare camels, and rode on into the glittering, trackless wilderness of the desert. Before going, however, they decapitated Father Bouchard, the only one of their victims whose head had not been mutilated.

They left the bodies of the men on the blood-splashed rocks where they had fallen. They were later found by some Bedouin gazelle hunters who, recognizing the identities of the corpses and knowing that the French army had been alerted to catch the assassins, thought it safer not to become involved in a crime which might be laid to their door and so burned the three saintly men on a pyre of desert brush.

It later transpired that this assassination had been planned by the Twareg warriors in Algiers when they were the guests of the French government. In fact, they had hoped to have Cardinal Lavigerie as their victim, whose death, they believed, would have put an end to his project of linking North and Central Africa via the Hoggar.

This did not prevent the other White Fathers—Richard Morat and Pouplard—from setting out in 1881 to try and reach Timbuktu. It happened in this way.

Owing to the murder of Father Paulnier and his companions, the French government forbade Cardinal Lavigerie to make any further attempts to penetrate into the French Sahara and thereby reach Timbuktu and black Africa. But while the Cardinal had been deeply distressed by the death of his disciples, he was still determined to establish missions in the southern territories. As the routes to the French-occupied oases were barred to him by government orders, he decided to bypass them and delegated Father Louis Richard as head of the mission at Ouargla to proceed to Ghadames, in Tripoli, which was now under the rule of the Turks, and there establish a base from which it might be possible to start the longed-for journey to the Niger.

Father Richard went to Ghadames and was careful not to try any kind of proselytizing among the people, most of whom depended on the goodwill of the fanatical Senussi. On the contrary, he went to extremes to care for the weak and the needy, until the courtyard of the humble house which a friendly Moslem lent to him, was filled with hungry and sick men and women who had come to look on the priest as a kind of white marabout.

Still Father Richard was determined to carry his Christian influence further south, and urged Cardinal Lavigerie to allow him to make the attempt. Cardinal Lavigerie was also in favour of such a venture, but before authorizing it, he sent Father Richard instructions that he must first of all establish a mission house in Tripoli, which would be a base from which supplies could be sent to Timbuktu, and to the Senussi citadel of Ghat, which must be the jumping off place for the White Fathers in their trek to the Sudan.

While Father Richard agreed about Tripoli, he had grave doubts about Ghat, which was still the most fanatical centre of Islam in the Sahara. In any case, with only a few encounters with bandits, two abortive attempts to murder him and one bad sandstorm, the good father reached the city of Tripoli safely, where his plans were held up by the bureaucracy of the Turkish government. It was partly because of his faith and partly because of his nationality that the Turks did not wish the Frenchman to establish a foothold in this Turkish protectorate. He was thus frustrated every time he tried to buy headquarters for the new mission. There were many Tripolitanians ready and willing to sell, but every time the documents were taken to the Pasha for the official seal on the title deeds, it was refused for some unexplained regulation or other.

Every night Father Richard knelt in the miserable room which he had managed to rent and prayed for God's help and guidance. His prayers were answered in the form of a man who was being sued for debt and agreed to sell him a tumble-down house in the oasis in return for the payment of his debts. This sum was far above the value of the house but, because the creditors wanted their money, the sale was allowed to go through.

With the help of an old negro ex-slave, Father Richard set about repairing his mission house. Soon he was able to buy a few mats and a table and started planting vegetables in the garden. He had already turned one of the rooms into a chapel. A little later on he was joined by Fathers Morat and Pouplard from Algiers, and the mission was finally established.

Now the first step must be prepared for the dangerous journey south. Regardless of the frightening precedents, Father Richard behaved as recklessly as had Colonel Flatters and as trustingly as Father Paulnier in their dealings with the Twareg. What he did appreciate was that he must establish some kind of a friendly relationship with these veiled men who were such implacable adversaries of foreign encroachment, and hated the idea of interference with their looting of caravans from Timbuktu.

Father Richard had by now been accepted by the Turkish and other Moslem inhabitants of Tripoli as a good man who only wanted to help the sick and the needy of the town and the oases, and not only demanded nothing but gave according to his means.

Soon after the arrival of his colleagues, Father Richard heard that Twareg nomads were pasturing their flocks on the desert not far from Tripoli. To these he went, boldly carrying as his passport a kind of introduction which the Marabout of Temacine had given him. This document was well received and the White Fathers were accepted cordially by the encamped men. In addition to the document, his first-aid kit enhanced his prestige, particularly when he was able to cure old wounds and eye ailments which needed only a little antiseptic treatment.

Father Richard was warned, however, that things might not go so easily for him in Ghat, where the Senussi fanatics would be hard to convince that the White Fathers were saintly men. This news was forwarded to the Cardinal in Algiers. A postscript was added by the three priests to the effect that even if these Twareg nomads were not sincere, they were prepared to give their lives for the Christian cause as had Fathers Paulnier, Menoret and Bouchard on the road to the Hoggar Highlands.

In a few weeks, Father Richard received the authorization to organize the caravan, with the further news that three more priests would soon arrive to take over the mission and bring stores for the journey south. Unfortunately, the ship which carried the stores from Algiers was wrecked in a storm; though the three White Fathers, having come by land, arrived safely.

There was only one thing to be done now, they must purchase any stores available in Tripoli. This the six priests set about doing, but before they could get the caravan together a telegram was received from the Cardinal as follows: "Have just received official confirmation of the massacre of the Flatters mission. You cannot go beyond Ghadames until further orders."

It seemed that every obstacle was being put in the way of the three priests' fatal determination to trust their lives to this Twareg-infested part of the desert. Then one of the wounded Shambi guides of Flatters' caravan appeared at the mission and explained that he had been one of the cameleers accompanying the ill-fated expedition. He had escaped from the massacre at Bir el Gharama by pretending to be dead and then creeping away until he found a caravan of his own people moving north. He stated that there would have been no such disaster had Colonel Flatters kept his men together and not allowed the treacherous Targui chief, Attici, to separate him from the main body of his mission, on the excuse of watering the camels. With their modern magazine rifles, he added, the soldiers could have defied and defeated the Twareg and then made their way safely to the Niger, or back to Ouargla.

Father Richard nursed the soldier back to health. He then sent him to Algiers with a letter to the Cardinal, explaining that the Flatters massacre need not have occurred if Colonel Flatters had observed the elementary rules of precaution for a column operating among hostile people. He once more begged for permission to form his own caravan and start on its southern journey, insisting that what had happened to Father Paulnier and Colonel Flatters was due to necessary care not having been shown to protect their respective parties.

At last Father Richard's plea was granted, and the tragic destiny which had relentlessly led the Flatters mission to disaster and Fathers Paulnier, Bouchard and Menoret to their deaths, began to spread its shadow over the brave but reckless monks.

The first essential for the trek south was to secure competent and trustworthy guides. Accordingly, Father Richard sent a messenger to Ouargla to summon a Shamba nomad called Saiah Ben

Bou Said, with whom he had already made several expeditions in the neighbourhood of that oasis, to join him at Ghadames, which he had now made his advance headquarters. The good father must also obtain healthy camels with suitable cameleers, and so was put into contact by local people of whom he knew nothing with a Targui called El Khadjem, who owned property in Ghadames and was reputed to be honest. To him was left the hiring of the rest of the personnel, who, the Targui decided, could be confined to his son, Betika; his brother-in-law, Isa; and his black slave, Djaddour.

When the guide Saiah arrived from Ouargla he was very suspicious of this personnel, and reminded Father Richard that to a Targui all Christians were pigs or any low-bred animal. Father Richard laughed off this warning, telling Saiah that he was a pessimist and that no one wanted to kill poor priests with nothing worthwhile to steal. Saiah shrugged his shoulders and went into the village to collect his own stores.

In the market-place Saiah picked up a great deal of gossip. While many of the inhabitants were sincerely distressed at the thought of losing the kindly, holy men, the Senussi merchants were delighted at the prospect of seeing the last of these promoters of a detested religion who had established such a favourable position for themselves, not only at Ghadames, but in Tripoli itself.

The most violent antagonist of all was a certain Si Mohammed Bou Etteni, the richest merchant of the oasis and the leader of the Senussi there. Making friends with a slave of this local plutocrat and fanatic, to whom Father Richard had shown kindness, Saiah was warned to tell the priests to be on their guard as their caravan leader, El Khadjem, had not only been spreading rumours that these three White Fathers were spies of the French government sent to open up caravan routes to the Sudan which would then be protected by European soldiers, but also that this El Khadjem was in constant touch with a mysterious Targui whom no one in Ghadames had ever seen before. This man never let down his veil so that he could not be identified.

As the slave spoke, he nudged Saiah and whispered "Here he comes."

As reported, this man wore his veil so high that it was quite impossible to see anything but his eyes. Nevertheless, Saiah followed him through the market-place and as luck would have

The Hoggar country
in the region of Tam-
anrasset

A Twareg tribesman

Top: Father Richard (*left*) Father Pouplard (*right*)
Bottom: Father Pauliner (*left*) Father Bouchard (*right*)
Centre: Cardinal Lavigerie

it someone in the crowd bumped into the man so that for a moment the veil was lowered. On seeing his face, Saiah nearly let out a cry, for the man was Ida, the actual murderer of Father Menoret, one of Father Paulnier's companions on that fatal trek from Algiers to the south.

Before Saiah could get over his surprise and alarm, Ida had vanished into the house of Mohammed Bou Etteni. All Saiah could do was to run as fast as he could to Father Richard, and tell him what he had found out. The priest received the information calmly and without concern and assured Saiah that no harm could come from Ida, as his own Targui guide, El Khadjem, belonged to a tribe of Twareg which was on bad terms with the tribe to which Ida belonged.

This did not reassure Saiah, who declared that where the killing of Occidentals was concerned, tribal differences were set aside. Even so, Father Richard remained obstinate in his determination to set off with El Khadjem, of whom he knew nothing. Saiah then became impatient and demanded a signed and notarized statement from Father Richard and his two colleagues stating that he, Saiah, would not be held responsible if anything disastrous happened during the trip. To this Father Richard agreed and obtained the signatures of Fathers Morat and Pouplard, who had by now joined him in Ghadames.

The final and most urgent warning which the White Father had against their setting out on this march to Ghat, was El Khadjem's declaration that he would forego the usual money advance made to caravan leaders before starting out on a journey and would accept a settlement of accounts at the end of the expedition. To Saiah, this was irrefutable evidence that the Targui had been already well paid by Mohammed Bou Etteni or some other Senussi to lead the holy men into ambush. Father Richard regarded this situation as an answer to his prayers, as the necessary funds had not yet arrived from Algiers.

On 18th December 1881 the three White Fathers celebrated Mass before dawn. At the end of the service Father Richard prayed aloud: "Oh, God, Who caused the children of Israel to cross the Red Sea on dry land, Who by means of a star, guided the Magi towards Thee, Who protected Abraham during his wanderings after leaving Chaldea, help us as we depart, console us as we travel, give us shade when it is hot, protect us against cold and

8

rain, give us a staff to help us down steep slopes, so that like St. John, Thy Precursor, we may surely reach Him, whose coming he foretold."

After a moment's pause, the three priests said together: "Let us go in peace, in the name of our Lord, Amen."

Never were brave men more in need of divine protection, for in view of what had occurred to Colonel Flatters and Father Paulnier and their companions at the hands of the Twareg, Father Richard behaved without any sort of sense at all. In fact, even without Saiah's constant warnings and forebodings, he behaved like some amateur explorer, who knew nothing of the desert, nothing of its inhabitants, and deliberately forgot what he knew of the instinctive resentment of the Moslem towards any Christian who showed signs of interfering with his religion or brought to mind that a man who killed an infidel would automatically be eligible for eternal salvation. Even when the Turkish police commissioner advised the White Fathers to steer their course in the direction of Ouargla, where there would be Shambi and French protection available, no notice was taken. The priests wanted to reach Ghat by the shortest route, which ran through Senussi infested country.

And so they began their tragically predestined journey. Father Richard, who was a first-rate horseman, was mounted on a horse and sat his saddle as erectly as a cavalryman. Fathers Pouplard and Morat were on dromedaries, but being unused to desert travel or the right way of handling a camel, found that the wooden saddles chafed their legs and, by the end of the first stage, they were in great physical pain.

Father Richard had wanted to start at dawn but the Twareg could not be awakened. When they did come out of their tents, they worked at loading the camels so slowly that Saiah became angry and cursed and insulted the leader and the cameleers as only a Bedouin can when addressing a Targui. He then took Father Richard aside and warned him that these delays were deliberate and it was obvious to him that the Twareg guides had some kind of schedule arranged, probably to meet accomplices from the desert. Even so, the trusting priests refused to be convinced that anything was amiss. The journey, therefore, continued, with Fathers Pouplard and Morat suffering more and more from the discomforts of camel riding. It was also extremely hot, and water had to be rationed carefully.

As if to reassure Father Richard, the Twareg were now most co-operative and unlike most of their kind, talkative, telling the White Fathers all kinds of desert stories. Saiah, however, saw in this friendliness something quite unnatural and therefore suspicious. Soon a forced halt had to be made due to the fact that Fathers Pouplard and Morat developed some malarial type of fever which Father Richard treated from his medicine chest.

After a night's rest the two priests seemed better, and Father Richard was preparing to set off again when one of the Targui guides, Isa, came to his tent and told him that not far from where they were now camped was a well surrounded by trees. He thought that this might be a good place for the invalids to recuperate from their unaccustomed hardships. To this suggestion, Father Richard agreed and stated that the caravan would leave at once.

The guide replied that it would be better if he went first to see if there was water in the well. If there was none, it would be a waste of time to make the detour. The guide then mounted his dromedary, and promising to be back by noon, disappeared into the haze of the shimmering desert.

When Saiah heard about this decision, he threw up his arms in despair. "There was no necessity," he exclaimed, "for Isa to go alone! The wells are not much off the direct route, and less time would be wasted if we took the caravan along than waiting for Isa to go and return."

The place where the camp was now pitched was in a kind of gully of rocks which would become unbearably hot as the sun rose and where an attack by bandits could be made without warning. When Saiah pointed this out to the priest, he was rebuked for continuing to be so suspicious of his fellow men. When noon had passed and there was no sign of Isa, the White Fathers became anxious, especially the youngest of the trio, Father Pouplard, who was having strong premonitions of impending disaster. But it was now too late to make a move, and the furnace-like heat given off by the rocks of the gully became more and more unbearable.

The priests retired to their tents and tried to sleep. Towards evening, Isa returned. Saiah immediately began to cross-examine him—why had he taken all day to ride but a few miles to the wells? How had he found them?

"Dried up," came the reply.

Then, why had he not returned with the news immediately so that the caravan could be on its way?

"Because," he replied, "I had caught sight of several moufflons and had pursued one which I thought would make a welcome change from the daily diet of couscous and tinned food."

"Where is this moufflon now?" asked Saiah.

The reply was as glib as it was unconvincing. The animals had escaped into a dry river bed, and Isa, afraid of losing his bearings, had let it go and made his way back to the camp.

Sarcastically, Saiah exclaimed, "This is the first time I have ever heard of a Targui being afraid of losing his way in the desert."

Isa showed a certain amount of sulkiness over this remark but went out of his way to be pleasant to the White Fathers and had his men prepare a special Targui dinner in their honour.

Little did these holy men suspect that this moufflon had been, in reality, a "rendezvous" with eight of the most notorious bandits of the Sahara. The leader of which was Ida Ag Guemmoum, the murderer of Doumeau Duperé, the French explorer, whom he had killed on the way to Ghadames in 1874. This had led to his capture and to Cardinal Lavigerie's disastrous experiment of entertaining these veiled men which had later brought about the massacre of Fathers Paulnier, Bouchard and Menoret. In fact, it was this same Ida Ag Guemmoum, whom Saiah had seen in Ghadames, who had used the dagger which had ended the life of Father Menoret and who had now been delegated by Mohammed Bou Etteni, the fanatic Senussi merchant of Ghadames, to deal in the same way with Father Richard and his companions.

For the moment everything was serene around the camp fires where the treacherous Isa and his accomplice, caravan leader El Khadjem, were entertaining their trusting companions. After drinking the traditional cups of mint tea, the Twareg rose one by one for the last prayer of the evening.

Father Morat watched the strange spectacle of these veiled men bowing and prostrating themselves on the stony ground as they praised God and thanked him for his blessings. A little to one side Saiah did the same, and Father Morat instinctively fell on his knees and looked up at the starry, black sky, and prayed.

The end of this prayer was never reached, as without warning, Isa detached the long dagger strapped to his forearm and plunged it into the back of Father Morat, transfixing him.

At the sound of the death cry, Father Richard rushed to his aid, but what could he do, as this White Father, like the other members of his Order, never carried arms. Before he could take any action, Father Richard was attacked by Isa and El Khadjem in whom he had such trust. Being a tall man, he warded off their sword thrusts with his hands and actually knocked down both of his attackers with his fists.

Noting that Father Morat was beyond human help and that Isa and El Khadjem were stunned, he decided that the only thing to do was to mount his horse and save Father Pouplard, of whom he had lost sight. However, just as he placed his foot in the stirrup, the third traitor, Bettina, came after him with a bell-mouthed blunderbuss and fired it point-blank into the body of the unfortunate priest.

There still remained Father Pouplard, who must follow the fate of his colleagues if the orders of Mohammed Bou Etteni were to be carried out. Abdallah, one of the Shamba of the caravan who had escaped from the Twareg group, found the young priest and tried to lead him to safety in the shelter of the rocks above the gully, where it might be possible to escape under cover of darkness.

As they were stumbling through the boulders, they were suddenly confronted by three veiled figures. Ida was one of them, and he raised his great sword, and split Father Pouplard's skull in half. The other two Twareg did their share by plunging their daggers into the priest's dead body. Thus, the Sahara had taken another share of victims and had added three more martyrs to the lists of heroes devoted to the cause of spreading the gospel in Africa.

As soon as the news of the massacre reached Father Kermabon, the superior of the White Fathers' Mission in Tripoli, he tried to have the bodies of the three priests brought back for burial in the Christian graveyard at Ghadames, but owing to their rapid decomposition in the desert heat it was impossible to carry them back the twenty miles to Ghadames, so they were interred where they had fallen.

Cardinal Lavigerie was grieved and shocked by the news of this new massacre and wrote as follows to the White Fathers in Algiers and in the other African missions:

My dear children—I have already had you notified by telegraph of our latest and most cruel ordeal. Fathers Richard, Pouplard, and Morat have shed their blood for these poor people whose apostles they intended to make themselves, and to whom they had already shown such goodness. It was the Twareg, the same Twareg who shed the blood of our first martyrs, who spilt that of these brothers. They brutally massacred them three days only after their departure from Ghadames.

Three of the assassins have been arrested by the order of the Turkish Pasha of Tripoli, but I have asked him, my dear children, in your name and mine, to spare these wretches, not wishing to take any revenge on the culprits than by persevering to save these people from their barbarous customs. I am sure that you will approve of this sentiment, which was that of our Master, forgiving His executioners from the cross and who now has with Him in heaven those three kindly victims of their duty. Praise God, that he added our brothers to that glorious choir of martyrs. Praise Him, because on account of their devotion, they have brought honour to the Church, our mother. Let us ask him that the blood spilt be ransom for these wretched infidel people. Do not let us be troubled by their difficulties and perils. It is in the name of God that we have taken on this task. May your hearts rise to Him to pray for the strengthening of your hopes. I join with you once more, my dear children, in this act of grace and this prayer in which I seem to feel our martyrs in heaven are now joining too. It is there that we will be reunited with them one day and all that we have suffered, according to the word of St. Paul, will be but a dream which fades in the presence of happy eternity.

Now, while this makes a page of noble prose and is filled with thoroughly Christian sentiments, it had the worst possible effect on the Senussi and Twareg of Tripolitania.

In this forgiving attitude they saw only the same weakness as had originally been shown after the Flatters Massacre. Thus the plight of the White Fathers in Tripoli and Ghadames became extremely precarious. In fact, it was evident that these missions must be evacuated, first of all, to Tripoli and then to Algiers, and it was not until 1894 that the mission house which Fathers Paulnier and Richard had hoped to establish in Timbuktu by way of the Sahara was finally organized from the west coast of Africa, after the French army under the future Marshal Joffre had occupied this ancient city on the Niger. Today, it is a flourishing concern, with White Fathers as well as White Sisters forming a base for the missions in Central Africa.

Cardinal Lavigerie died on 24th November 1892 in his cell-like room in the Archepiscopal palace in Algiers. He was appropriately surrounded by White Fathers and White Sisters now firmly established in Algeria with no fear of interference by the government of France who, though anti-clerical in their policies, recognized how much these men and women of the Order had done for their country. The Cardinal was buried beneath the sanctuary of the Cathedral of Carthage, which stands close to the Roman arena where Christian martyrs in Roman days met their ends among the wild beasts of Africa. But, although the arenas are no more and the White Missions are respected all over Africa, some of their members continue to become martyrs to the Christian faith.

7

VISCOUNT CHARLES DE FOUCAULD

ALTHOUGH the White Fathers claimed Father de Foucauld as a member of their Order and are today promoting his beatification, in point of fact he never belonged to this denomination, and this for an unexpected reason.

Foucauld did not consider the rules imposed by Cardinal Lavigerie on the brotherhood of the White Fathers harsh enough for the mortification of body and soul. He became a kind of freelance monk with rules of his own making. Paradoxically he was a man who exuded glamour and excitement wherever he went, whether as a gay cavalry officer or as a priest or a martyr missionary.

Born in 1858, of well-to-do parents, young Charles de Foucauld was given every advantage which money and social prestige could produce. Of this, he took full advantage and showed himself, at an early age, to be lazy, greedy, selfish and undisciplined. As he grew older these traits developed until, by the time he had entered the Military Academy at St. Cyr, all he thought about were the best means to give himself physical pleasure. Nor did army life, when he joined the Fourth Hussars, have any restraining influence, it only added to his joyous irresponsibilities. Good food, good wine and now beautiful women were the chief ingredients which made up the daily routine of the young officer. Finally, his behaviour became so scandalous that he was forced to leave the army in disgrace.

The next period of Foucauld's existence was one of readjustment, of explorations into the Sahara and unknown Morocco, where he went disguised as a Russian rabbi, travelling in daily danger of being killed or tortured.

He was also studying the customs and languages of the native inhabitants with a sense of the necessity for something spiritual to counterbalance the sensualities of the restaurants and race courses and boudoirs. The spiritual urge slowly took ascendancy until it completely overwhelmed the ex-cavalry officer. From now on, he wanted not only to *have* religion, but also *to be in it* himself. With the same enthusiasm as he had put into his sensual existence, he now flung his whole personality into the attaining of the ascetic.

Disdaining those orders which he deemed "soft", he became a Trappist, the most austere of all religious groups, then a hermit in Palestine and, finally, a missionary in the Sahara. From being the well-fed, exquisite, pleasure-loving sybarite, he developed such abnegation that his health began to suffer and his religious colleagues begged him to take greater care of himself and to eat and sleep a little more. He took scant notice and continued his ascetic life among the veiled Twareg in the middle of the Sahara, hundreds of miles from the nearest Occidental and with no one to talk to except these wild Twareg warriors with whom he had little in common. He made a point of learning their language and script with such success that he was able to publish a dictionary in Tamashek, the Targui dialect, and a treatise on Tifinagh, the Targui hieroglyphic writing.

He was always busy, trying to make conversions, for which purpose he translated the Gospels into the Targui language and reconnoitred the country. As a result, he was not only contributing to the glory of God in the Sahara but also to the glory of France's African Empire.

After years of this mortifying, yet constructive life, he was murdered by fanatics who saw in the stubborn, courageous little priest a menace to Islam as well as one to the political aspirations of the local chiefs.

In August, 1914, news had reached the Hoggar that Germany had invaded Belgium and then France. Foucauld had immediately volunteered to go to the front as a chaplain or stretcher bearer. The application had been turned down and he was ordered to remain at his post at Tamanrasset. Two anxious years followed with a steady rise of Moslem fanaticism and anti-French feeling.

Once more, the trouble was coming from the east where Italy's entry into the war on the side of the Allies had made her relax her hold on Tripoli. Simultaneously, the Turks, who were fighting for the Central Powers, began shipping arms and ammunition into the country, which enabled the Senussi to restart their raids into the French Sahara.

By 1916, with more and more French and Allied reverses on the Eastern and Western fronts, the situation in North Africa became grave. The tribes were on the warpath; the chiefs unco-operative, if not insubordinate. Fort Djanet, to the east of Tamanrasset, was besieged and captured. The garrisons of Fort Polignac, Fort Charlet and, finally, Fort Motylinski, had to be evacuated. The Senussi warriors were now very close to the Hoggar and it looked as if the French would soon have to abandon the whole of their southern territories.

The effect of the war on his doorstep had a galvanizing effect on Foucauld. His priestly role was forgotten, and he reverted to being an officer on active service. He became the centre of "intelligence" for the now scattered garrison commanders, and even issued orders as if he were directing the Sahara campaign. He made up his mind to transform his hermitage at Tamanrasset into a fort. He had a few soldiers from the Motylinski post, which had been regarrisoned, to help him. He chose as his site a knoll about nine hundred feet above the rest of the country and built there a stronghold with walls six feet thick, with no windows on the outside and only one narrow door. He filled it with stores and a few rifles and ammunition which the army had been able to send him. As long as he had only to deal with tribesmen without artillery, his stronghold would be impregnable.

"I have transformed my hermitage into a fort," he wrote to his friend, General Laperrine, who was commanding a division on the Western Front. "When I look up at my battlements, I cannot help thinking of the fortified convents and churches of the Middle Ages. How the ancient things return and how that which one thought gone forever reappears!"

The situation was precarious and Foucauld's life in constant danger. Moussa, the paramount chief of the Twareg in Foucauld's area, seems to have been the only one who remained sincerely loyal to the Christian "marabout". But he himself was having difficulties with his own people and had to be constantly on the move. Had he been on the spot, though, he might have saved the situation. The climax came on 1st December, 1916.

A little earlier in the year Si Mohammed Labed, paramount chief of the Senussi, had captured and occupied Ghat, towards which Father Richard had been making his way when he was murdered thirty years before; it was the capital of Fezzan about two hundred and fifty miles north-east from Tamanrasset. The defeated Franco-Italian garrison had abandoned quantities of modern small arms, and this all-powerful religious leader intended now to launch attacks against the French and their supporters, who included Moussa and his few loyal Twareg of the Hoggar.

Ouksem ag Chikkat, a Targui to whom Foucauld had shown much kindness and hospitality, had already gone over to the enemy, but the Moussa group of the veiled warriors still ignored all persuasive arguments and threats from Senussi headquarters. Si Mohammed Labed was baffled by this illogical devotion to the French cause, especially when it seemed to be lost in Europe, and there were rumours confirmed by Ouksem, that this was due to a white marabout who lived alone at Tamanrasset, and had some mysterious hold over Moussa and his Twareg tribesmen.

Si Mohammed decided that the removal of this infidel hermit was essential to the success of his projects. The capture of this man might also become a source of prestige and profit if he could hold him as a hostage. He gave instructions that the holy man be captured and brought to Ghat. He entrusted execution of this mission to a Targui chief, El Keraan, a personal enemy of Moussa, with authorization to use whatever methods he considered best and to employ as many men as he believed necessary to ensure success.

The sun was setting over the black pinnacles of the ill-famed Djebel Debnat, the enchanted Mountains of the Hoggar, when El Keraan and his thirty men rode into Tamanrasset. They had come a long way from their base, and were eager to accomplish their mission and get back to Ghat with their captive, before any French Meharist patrols had been alerted. But when they saw Father de Foucauld's fort on the high ground above the *oued*, they recognized that, even with their modern Italian rifles, any attempt to capture their victim by force would be a waste of time. A ruse of some kind must be devised if they were to succeed.

Some Twareg dissidents who had joined the Senussi suggested

that a freed Negro slave of Tamanrasset, called El Madani, might be used. El Madani was summoned from his hut, and after a good deal of argument and threats of torture, accepted the treacherous mission. El Madani led the raiders, now numbering forty or so, to the priest's fortress, where they concealed themselves in the trench which surrounded it. El Madani then knocked on the door in a way well known to Father de Foucauld. After a few minutes, the unbarring of the inner door was heard, followed by footsteps coming to the outer door. The priest's voice then asked: "Who is there?"

"Your slave, El Madani. I have the mail for you."

Now, not only was it quite normal for the carriers to leave the mail in the village if they were in a hurry and El Madani a likely person to be entrusted with it, but it also happened to be mail day. Nevertheless, Foucauld showed some caution. Drawing back the bolt of the outer door, he did no more than thrust forth his hand to receive the letters. But this was enough for his enemies. Fingers like steel claws gripped his wrist and jerked him out like a fish on a hook. Other men seized him, and, binding his arms behind his back, flung him into the trench.

After the first instinctive gesture of self-defence, Foucauld ceased to make any resistance. He neither struggled nor spoke. All he did was to scrutinize El Madani with a certain amount of curiosity mingled with compassion. The Negro, who had received much kindness from the priest, tried to avoid the burning, black eyes, which seemed to bore into him, but they followed him relentlessly. El Madani then slunk away and, according to his own account, took no further part in the rapidly unfolding drama.

While Foucauld lay crumpled in the ditch, most of the bandits poured into the fort, breaking down the doors, shouting with delight as they discovered what to them was a fabulous treasure— three dozen magazine rifles, boxes of cartridges, sacks of barley and flour, tinned foods, tea and sugar in quantities which they had never seen before, together with rolls of cloth, calico and linen. Such commodities were not to be bought anywhere in the Sahara. Fortunately, Foucauld's papers and diaries and translations from Tifinagh script meant nothing to these ruffians. They were tossed about but not damaged in the search for gold, which the raiders felt sure must be concealed in this Aladdin treasure house.

By this time, night had fallen and the Senussi, slightly calmed down after the excitement of ransacking the fort, began to wonder what to do next. Some of them tried ineffectively to force Foucauld to pronounce the *Chachada*, which amounts to recanting any faith in favour of Islam. Others, more practical-minded, tried to cross-examine their prisoner about French troops in the neighbourhood. Foucauld took no notice of the questions. He seemed to have detached himself from worldly matters and with eyes closed continued to pray. When El Keraan told him that his life depended on his speaking, he replied in Tamachek: *Baghi n'mout* ("This is the hour of my death").

The other raiders from Ghat, knowing that they would forfeit their reward if they killed the White Marabout, suggested that he might give information about the troops as well as about the gold, under torture. Before any decision about this proposal could be reached, the sentries who had been placed on the edge of the *oued* came running back to the fort. They had seen two Meharists on their camels, moving up along the dried water course. These, Foucauld appreciated, were the real mail carriers whom he felt he must warn. As he tried to raise himself so that his voice would carry, a young Targui called Sermi Ag Thora, who had been ordered to guard the priest, apparently lost his head and, placing the muzzle of his carbine to Foucauld's temple, pulled the trigger. The priest's body shuddered and stiffened, and then went limp. With what might have been a sigh of relief, it gradually collapsed and slid gently to the bottom of the trench. The eyes were open and staring sightlessly at the stars which flashed down from the tropical sky. At the same time other raiders took aim and shot the unsuspecting mail carriers and their camels.

The Sahara had claimed another lover, claimed him in the way this one would have wished. For among the papers later found in the fort was the following note in Foucauld's handwriting:

. . . consider that you must die a martyr, shorn of everything, stretched on the ground, naked and unrecognizable, covered with blood and wounds, violently and painfully killed, and furthermore, hope that this may take place today. In order that this favour may be granted, be faithful at all times to watch and bear your cross. Reckon always that your life must lead to this end, and recollect, accordingly, how unimportant are most things of this world. Reflect, often on this death so that you will be ready for it, and be able to judge everything at its true value.

For the raiders there were no pious thoughts. Their hostage was dead and recriminations would do no good. With Moslem resignation to the inevitable, they had to think of a way out of their quandary. Might it not be a good idea to take the White Marabout's body back to Ghat and trust to getting some of the reward? Or would Si Mohammed Labed be better pleased if the corpse of the infidel were left to be eaten by jackals and hyenas?

While these arguments were going on, the Targui contingent of the raiding party, which had no interest in rewards and little in Moslem fanaticism, had cut up the Meharists' dead camels, lit a brush fire and were roasting the flesh on the ends of their lances. With the oil and the tea and sugar and other supplies from the fort, there was the making of a feast usually associated with the wedding of some wealthy chieftain. The Senussi assassins sniffed the savoury odour of the grilling meat and, leaving their problems in the hands of Allah, joined the banquet.

It was a wild spectacle, with the red flames fed with desert scrub, flaring fiercely and lighting up these desert men, armed and exultant as they devoured the sizzling steaks and drank the mint-flavoured, sugary tea. Like the extravagant parties of Foucauld's youth, too, it was kept going until dawn. Then only did these men leave the smouldering fires, and, piling all they could on their camels, make ready to move.

By now they were in too good spirits to be concerned with the disposal of the body of their victim. Unfortunately, just before they got on their way, the mail carrier, coming from Fort Motylinski to collect Foucauld's outgoing letters, rode up to the fort. Before he could appreciate what was going on, he was shot dead, and his body left on the desert with the other murdered Meharists. Someone suggested killing those Twareg of Taman-rasset who had taken no part in the bloody doings of the night, to prevent them from identifying the members of the raiding party, but no one was sufficiently interested to dismount.

The expedition had been successful; there was enough food to keep everyone on full rations for some time to come; and enough rifles and ammunition to arm a powerful striking force which could bother the French and Italians for quite a while. This ought to satisfy Si Mohammed Labed, and make up for not having produced the White Marabout alive.

As the sun rose, the column of tall dromedaries sped away in a cloud of rosy dust, and disappeared into the Enchanted Mountains of the Hoggar.

It was only then that the Twareg of Tamanrasset dared to leave their huts and tents to investigate what had been going on during that night of shooting and fires and feasting, and find out what had happened to their friend, whom they had not dared to defend.

Consternation and grief followed the discovering of the body. No one quite knew what to do next. Finally it was decided to cover the priest's body with sand and heavy stones until some French officer came to Tamanrasset. This they did without even untying the bonds which held his arms.

Then they covered the three Meharists in the same way as they had Foucauld—where they had fallen. Such was their respect for the priest, and so great his prestige, that no one went inside the fort to loot or even find out what the raiders had done there. Instead, these poor people who needed food much more than the assassins from Ghat, bricked up the entrance of the fort and went despondently back to their miserable homes, knowing that they had lost someone who had become part of their lives and could never be adequately replaced.

Charles de Foucauld, Viscount, Cavalry Lieutenant and Reverend Father, never brought any Twareg to Christianity, but he established the kind of friendship among those warrior people which no officer nor White Father nor doctor, with all their authority and experience, ever approached. Whether he fell while in the service of God or of France, or of both, is of no real importance. What matters is that he died practising what he believed in—kindness and tolerance to all men regardless of their faith. His greatness comes from these Christian traits; his memory is kept alive in the wilderness of the Sahara because of them. When the governors and generals and bishops of Algeria, in their splendid graves, have outlived their grandiloquent epitaphs, Foucauld's name will remain in tradition and folklore among the wandering peoples of the Sahara, for whom he did so much with so little.

Today, the Catholic Church is working for the beatification of Charles de Foucauld and constant prayers with this intention are being said in all the churches of the world. Whether he is beatified or not, the ex-libertine, viscount and hussar must go down in history as a martyr and saint, as a man who, after giving way enthusiastically to every weakness of the flesh, destroyed his physical self in the emulation of Jesus Christ and in the service of God.

While most pictures show Father de Foucauld in his threadbare cassock outside his hermitage epitomizing the "soul", I like to think of him, too, as symbolizing the body. I like to imagine him in his sky-blue braided tunic and scarlet breeches, his plumed shako and shiny black boots, carefree and gay, riding at the head of his troop of hussars jingling through some sunny French village in the days when laughter came as a matter of course and world wars had not been thought of. I like to think of him thus, knowing that in a few years his motto will be: "Christ I proclaim, not by my voice, but by my way of living!"

René Caillé

Colonel Flatters

Charles de Foucauld

General Laperrine

One of Laperrine's Meharist scouts

8

GENERAL LAPERRINE

THE lives of Charles de Foucauld and General Henri Laperrine run parallel and are both so involved one with the other that the story of the Reverend Father should be completed with that of the General.

Both men came from aristocratic stock and were born two years apart, the Reverend Father in September of 1858, the General in September of 1860. Their respective forebears had been soldiers and both of them, after passing through St. Cyr and the Cavalry School at Saumur, joined cavalry regiments. Both men died violent deaths in the Sahara.

There, however, the resemblances cease. Whereas Laperrine was devoted to his career and determined to reach the top of his profession and did so, Foucauld saw the army as a means of having a good time and had no military ambitions whatsoever. Both young officers found themselves posted to the same regiment in North Africa, the Fourth "Chasseurs d'Afrique". Laperrine was the only officer who befriended Charles de Foucauld at a time when the rest of the commissioned young men were cold-shouldering the irresponsible subaltern who seemed bent on disgracing himself and his regiment.

When the Fourth "Chasseurs d'Afrique" were sent on active service to round up the rebel chief, Bou Amama, of whom we have already heard in connection with Aurélie Picard, a great change came over the woman-chasing libertine. Henri Laperrine noticed this and encouraged his friend to join him in studying the customs and beliefs of the Bedouins.

It was during this campaign that Foucauld confessed to the general-to-be how much he had been impressed by the fervour with which the nomads observed their religious duties, while he, a Christian, did not consider religion as in any way part of his life. Before Laperrine could witness this new way of living being put into practice, Foucauld had resigned from the army and gone off to explore Morocco. Nevertheless, destiny was shaping the courses of the two men so that they would soon merge.

Laperrine had appreciated during the Bou Amama campaign that the only way to pacify the people of the vast areas of the Sahara was to train troops who would be adaptable to this special kind of desert campaigning. Up to that time the oases garrisons were made up of French and native regiments, trained and equipped to the manuals of the Ministry of War; that is to say, for service to France. They were immobile for desert purposes, and equipped chiefly for duty in peaceful French garrisons, where their upkeep depended on the quartermaster's department which had merely to order and buy according to the daily needs of the units under their charge. Laperrine brought into being what were to be termed the Sahara Companies, or more commonly, the Meharists, a *mehara* being a tall riding camel, on which this new kind of soldier was mounted.

Furthermore, these Meharists were mostly recruited from the Shamba tribes of the nomadic Arabs of the northern Sahara, who brought with them their own dromedaries, for which they were responsible. There were also specially selected French officers and non-commissioned officers, who knew the Sahara and had sufficient stamina for the extremely harsh life on which Laperrine insisted for all members of his camel corps. Laperrine never expected a subordinate to do anything which he could not do himself; in fact, he went to extremes to give an example of hardiness, and by his way of living led his men and disciplined them. To set his men a good example, he was always perfectly turned out, almost as if he were going on parade in a French garrison town; but in spite of this trait of dandiness, he lived and messed with his men, insisting that everyone share the same fare as himself.

As more and more of these camel-mounted units were organized and trained, the Sahara became a country where trading caravans could move without fear of being pillaged by raiders; or, if they were attacked, knowing that in a very short while a

Meharist column would have caught up with the miscreants, and rescued the camels which had been stolen. This mysterious and unknown desert was gradually surveyed and mapped so that men with less knowledge of the Sahara than Laperrine could follow tracks on charts which led to oases or wells. Even the hostile Twareg were gradually tamed by the simple process of showing the other desert dwellers that they were not invincible and had developed their prestige chiefly through bluff. It was now that they were made to recognize that France meant business and intended to bring peace among the warring tribes which had been enemies from time immemorial.

Finally, defying orders from the Ministry of War in Paris who were continually urging him to go slow and cautiously with his punitive expeditions, Laperrine decided to risk a reprimand and teach these men, who had never been punished for the Flatters massacre, a lesson which would hurt. He sent out from In Salah what he termed a reconnaissance group, consisting of a few hundred recently recruited Meharists with forty Shamba N.C.O.s, and all under the command of one of his picked officers, Lieutenant Cottenest. This small group met and defeated a vastly superior force of Twareg warriors at a place called Tit.

This providential victory had a tremendous moral effect on the tribes of this part of the desert. Until that time the Twareg had led everyone to believe that they were invincible. After this battle at Tit no one could deny that they had suffered a crushing defeat. In fact, they retired into their inaccessible mountains, refusing to come out even to talk "peace" with Laperrine.

The Colonel, after consulting Foucauld at his hermitage at Tamanrasset where he had made his headquarters, countered this by banning all the oasis markets of the region to any men who wore the blue veil. This led the Twareg to form an army to take the oasis markets by force. This time Laperrine made no pretence of what he was doing, and sent a strong, well-armed column to destroy the army from the Hoggar. Such exaggerated accounts had been spread about the deadly machine guns at Tit that the Twareg army never gave the Meharists the chance to fight and fled back into their mountains, where they were received with such jeers from their women that internal strife set in, and Attici, the Amenokal, and his colleagues, who had been responsible for the Flatters massacre, lost much of their prestige.

This enabled that young Targui warrior, called Moussa ag Amastan, later to be Foucauld's supporter and friend, who had for some time been advocating peaceful relations with the French, to displace Attici. In fact, in 1903, he met Laperrine for a peace conference, bringing with him a number of influential Twareg who thought as he did. Laperrine, accompanied by Charles de Foucauld as interpreter, named the French general "Amenokal"—paramount chief of the Targui confederation of Twareg Tribes. He then made a triumphal tour of the Hoggar, so far closed to Frenchmen and to those who fought for the French.

During this tour, and the later pacification of the Twareg, Laperrine was greatly aided by Father de Foucauld, who had now finally established himself at Tamanrasset, where Moussa had his headquarters. In one of the official reports of his activities in the Sahara, he wrote about Father de Foucauld, "most charitable, always giving excellent advice, gay and charming—he had been the principal agent in the pacification of the Twareg in the Hoggar".

Still the chief credit must go to Laperrine, who had the imagination and the courage to bring peace to this desert country through the use of natives armed by the French and mounted on their own camels. If one considers that this French Sahara had an area of 1,200,000 square miles, or half the size of the United States, this feat, performed by one man, seems incredible.

I have followed many of these desert trails blazed by Laperrine, and have tried to imagine myself or anyone else, all alone, confronted with the task of opening up even a quarter of the United States without any reliable indication of available drinking water, and with no vegetation or trees bearing fruits—in fact, no vegetation at all—in a frightening climate liable to sandstorms and peopled by men whose instinct it was to kill anyone who encroached on their territory, especially if they were Occidentals!

With the outbreak of war in 1914, Laperrine found himself a divisional commander, and with the same courage and powers of organization which he had shown in Africa, made his division the most efficient in the French army. But, he was not happy away from his Meharists, as he knew that the peaceful conditions which he had established in the Sahara would not last. In fact, with the death of Father de Foucauld, Moussa Ag Amastan, who had rebuffed the blandishments of the Senussi chieftains, was finding it more and more difficult to keep many of his own Twareg tribesmen under control as they still wanted to avenge the humiliation of Tit.

Fortunately, General Lyautey was then Minister of War. He knew North Africa almost as well as did Laperrine, and appreciated that if the situation were allowed to get further out of hand, there might be another full-scale war on the hands of the already hard-pressed French army on the Western Front. He also realized that only one man could save the situation, and in December of 1916 appointed Laperrine as commander-in-chief of all the Sahara territories.

Within a week of landing in Algeria, the general was back among his beloved Meharists, and within a few more weeks not only had the fallen forts been recaptured, but the camel corps was pushing the Senussi raiders out of the territories which they had occupied. The general then rounded up the Arab chiefs who had gone over to the enemy, and made them realize their errors without taking any of their lives. The only people he did have executed were all those whom he could find who had in any way contributed to the murder of his friend Foucauld. He felt his comrade's death so much that he kept a list of all those involved in this assassination in a small notebook and continued to prosecute them until his own death six years after Foucauld.

I was told at the time when I lived in the Sahara that with the exception of Al Madani, who had led the murderers to Foucauld's hermitage, but whose guilt had never really been established, every member of the raiding party had been executed or imprisoned for life, and their names erased from the general's notebook.

Laperrine's death was in keeping with the way he lived, and took place in the Sahara Desert. In September, 1919, he had been promoted to command the Algerian Army Corps in the city of Algiers, whence he would have jurisdiction over the Sahara. Taking over this post with his usual enthusiasm, he began to make of the Corps the best-trained unit in North Africa.

General Laperrine soon found out that life in a garrison town, surrounded by staff officers whose army principles came from the École de Guerre in Paris, was very different from running his irregulars in the Sahara Desert, where he could make the laws both for his own men and the dissident tribes. He missed the vast expanses of the desert, where he could live and travel with his troops in a kind of intimacy which had no counterpart in a place where officers and men, separated by rank, never met, except on the barracks' square.

When the Ministry of War in Paris decided that with all the advances made in aviation during the war, the time had come to link up Algiers and Timbuktu by plane, Laperrine saw the opportunity to find his way back to the Sahara as an adviser on this project, and encouraged those in authority in Paris to put the project into effect.

These Ministry of War and Aviation people, realizing that the General probably knew more about the Sahara than anyone else, allowed him to counsel them regarding landing grounds in various parts of the desert, between the Mediterranean and the Niger, as without these landing grounds and refuelling stations it would be madness to try to fly across the Sahara, with its broken terrain which looked level and inviting from the air. It must be remembered that the flying machines of those days could not remain airborne for more than a very limited number of hours without refuelling. All these arrangements took time and it was not until the spring of 1920 that everything was ready for the first flight from Algiers to Timbuktu. The project had grown and there were now to be six Breguet bi-planes, which were the last thing in military aviation of that day, although their ranges of flight were comparatively limited.

General Nivelle, who commanded all of the garrisons in North Africa, including Morocco, was to be a passenger on one of these planes on this ambitious journey which had now been lengthened and would go from Paris to Dakar via Algiers, Biskra, Tamanrasset and Timbuktu. But General Nivelle's plane never went much beyond Algiers as he had to return to the base there due to engine trouble. At the same time, and for reasons which have never been made clear, the General was recalled to Paris by the Ministry of War. Before he left, he recommended that General Laperrine take his place. This recommendation was accepted and Laperrine immediately set off by automobile for Biskra where the squadron leader of the group of planes was awaiting further orders. He reached there on 6th February, 1920, and from then on was in continuous trouble, with badly functioning engines, and sandstorms which obliterated the landing grounds. There were several crashes and only three planes out of the original six which had set out from Paris reached Tamanrasset. In one of these was General Laperrine.

At that point arguments began as to which machine should carry Laperrine on the next stage of the journey. With his Sahara experience, it seemed obvious that he should be in the leading plane. Unfortunately the senior pilot of this group, Major Vuillemin, objected, saying that he must be accompanied by his observer who was familiar with the various instruments with which the plane was equipped.

This was a senseless argument, as it must have been obvious that a man who had a special knowledge of this part of the Sahara was more valuable than any instruments. Laperrine, for the first and last time in his life, allowed the arguments of a junior and inexperienced officer in matters Saharan to prevail. (It should be noted here that these Breguets had room for two people only, the pilot and the observer.)

It was decided that Laperrine should travel as a third passenger in a plane which was piloted by Warrant Officer Bernard, who also insisted on taking his mechanic with him, a private soldier called Vaslin. The primary reason for this was that Laperrine had declared that he had no knowledge of machinery or engines, and would not even take the responsibility of starting the engine by hand, as it was then necessary to do. As this machine did not carry enough fuel to go from Tamanrasset to the Niger in one jump, a dump of oil and petrol had been established at a half-way point.

Before setting out on this ill-fated flight the General had a session with the pilots and explained what landmarks they were to follow and the absolute necessity of never losing touch with one another in the event of a crash, which must be reported by the plane which reached its destination first so that a rescue party could be sent out immediately.

Major Vuillemin stated that he preferred to rely on his instruments and his compass rather than on landmarks which were all right for camel caravans but of little value to a modernly equipped airplane.

At 7.30 a.m. on 18th February, the two Breguets took off, and to the astonishment and consternation of the officers who had come to see Laperrine off, they saw Vuillemin's plane flying on an easterly course, whereas the General had insisted that a westerly course should first be followed. There was nothing which could be done now but to wait for the wireless message from Menaka on the Niger, which would tell of the safe arrival of the planes. On 24th February the message, signed by the major, came through: "Have landed at Menaka Stop. Lost contact with the General's plane in the Tin Zaouatin area."

Without a moment's delay every Meharist company in the area was mobilized to search this district. The group was under the orders of Lieutenant Pruvost, and for a fortnight every fold in the desert within fifty kilometres, in the area referred to in the radiogram, was scoured by the Meharists, who were determined to find their leader.

At the beginning of the third week, without any sign of the wrecked plane, Pruvost, whose men were running short of food and whose camels had been unable to find pasture or water, decided to return to Tamanrasset. Here he found Colonel Delestre, commander of the Timbuktu military area, who had seen Major Vuillemin, and from what he had reported was sure that General Laperrine's plane had landed in a desert region known as Anesbaraka and not in the Tin Zaouatin area, as reported. This Anesbaraka desert was frequented by nomads who would be sure to go to the assistance of Laperrine, whom they had known in the days when he had commanded the Meharist corps.

Accordingly, on 10th March, Lieutenant Pruvost, having replenished his rations and pastured his camels, set out again. For some reason, he chose the route which had no wells and little pasture, and by so doing, was partially successful in his mission.

As already pointed out, the Breguet planes carried only two people. When Major Vuillemin declared that he would not fly without his own observer, Laperrine had agreed to travel in the plane piloted by Warrant Officer Bernard. But this man had his own mechanic, Vaslin, with him, so that, incredible as it may seem for such a hazardous trip, the General had to travel on the lap of the mechanic.

To begin with everything went according to plan, and contact with Major Vuillemin was kept. Then 2½ hours later, that is, about 10.30 a.m., a local sandstorm hid the trail and the landmarks on the ground which, up to that time, the General had been able to recognize. Half an hour later, Bernard reported to the General that he had only enough fuel left in the tank to keep the plane in the air for one more hour.

It was then that Laperrine made the admission that he, who had crossed this same region eleven times on camelback, had no idea where he was. Bernard flew as close to Vuillemin as possible so that he would be able to note exactly where he was landing. He also sent out a radio message stating what he was about to do, accompanied by an SOS, but he was not able definitely to designate the actual region because neither he nor anyone else knew what it was.

The ground below looked flat enough for a safe landing, but when the plane was within a few feet of touching down, one of those small desert whirlwinds caught the machine and turned it over on its side, on to what was a patch of soft sand. Bernard climbed out of the plane, without even a bruise, and found Vaslin in equally sound condition. The General, however, seemed to be in great pain and he appeared to have dislocated his shoulder, and probably broken a few ribs. He did not complain, but said he would rest until afternoon before deciding what to do next. Soon after midday on 18th February, and in spite of the pain which was now acute, General Laperrine decided that he and his two companions must start to walk next morning in the direction of what was the regular caravan route to Timbuktu. At 7 a.m. the three men set out, carrying as much food and water as possible.

The night, which had been icy cold, now gave way to the fierce heat of the Sahara day and the walking became exhausting even for the two young and sound men. Yet it was the wounded General who encouraged them onward. When no caravan tracks were found, Laperrine decided that it was safer to return to the plane, the whereabouts of which Major Vuillemin must have noted. So the three men retraced their steps, the ordeal now being aggravated by lack of water. Luckily, there had been no wind and so they were able to follow their own footmarks until they reached the scene of the accident. Here they made a kind of shelter from the sun with blankets which they had carried with them. They divided the rations, and drew water from the plane's radiator to quench their thirst.

For five days and nights, the men remained thus, with the General suffering more and more and unable to eat due now to obvious, internal injuries. Once again, the courageous men decided that they should try to find the caravan trail in another direction, but as they struggled over the soft sand, it was evident that they must return to the plane.

It was now 3rd March. Bernard realized, too, that the General was getting weaker, but he did not seem down-hearted in any way and continued to encourage his companions with anecdotes of miraculous rescues in the desert.

On the morning of 5th March, Laperrine managed to sip his ration of water and munch a little chocolate. But, at 2.30 p.m. when Bernard issued the second water ration of the day, he found Laperrine dead. In spite of what must have been excruciating suffering, he had died without a murmur.

The two men covered the body with a piece of plane silk, and the next day they buried the General in the sand and built a small cairn with loose stones on which they placed their aeroplane's spare wheel, surmounted by the General's "kepi". Then they despairingly made an inventory of their rations, and found that there remained one box of sardines, two biscuits, one slab of chocolate and about six litres of water in the radiator. By the night of 13th March, this water had been consumed.

For the next twenty-four hours, their food consisted of toothpaste, which, combined with the intense heat of the day, made them very thirsty. In order to quench their thirst, they drank every drop of liquid available, including the glycerine in which floated their compass, and some eau-de-Cologne which was in the General's haversack.

On 14th March they decided that if no help came before the day was over, they would shoot themselves. It was then that the miracle which Laperrine had predicted occurred—Lieutenant Pruvost's search party appeared out of the dunes. The two soldiers fired the cartridges which they had intended for themselves, into the air, and they were soon being fed and watered by their French colleagues. The next thing they did was to disinter the body of the General. When they had done this and wrapped it in airplane silk, they roped it to the back of a camel. They then rebuilt the cairn, which stands today, beside the remains of the plane, to mark the scene of this tragedy.

The question which now arose was—how to get the two aviators back to Tamanrasset. Neither of them was strong enough to ride a camel, and it was therefore decided to tie them on the saddle like bundles of merchandise. With this done, the funeral caravan, which was itself running short of food and water, set out on its way back. Owing to the necessity of moving through an area where the camels would be able to find a little pasture, Tamanrasset was not reached until 26th April, where, in spite of the decomposed state of the General's body, the medical officer made an autopsy and found that Laperrine had lived through those two weeks under the plane, in that alternately torrid and icy temperature, with his left ankle broken, two fractured ribs which had caused haemorrhage of the lungs, and a dislocated shoulder. Such endurance seemed incredible, except for a man with the courage of Laperrine, whose optimism alone kept his two companions from committing suicide.

The commandant of the French garrison at Tamanrasset, remembering Laperrine's often repeated wish that if he died in North Africa he would lie in the Sahara, arranged for his burial alongside the tomb of his friend Father de Foucauld. The body was placed in a rough coffin of odd planks from Foucauld's fort and hermitage, and lowered into a sandy grave. Every member of the French garrison was present at the funeral, as well as hundreds of Twareg tribesmen, led by Foucauld's and Laperrine's old friend, the Amenokal Moussa ag Amastane, the paramount chieftain.

On the same day a requiem mass was sung at the Cathedral in Algiers by Monseigneur Leynaud, the Archbishop, assisted by Monseigneurs Piquemal and Bollon, auxiliary bishops of the diocese. After the mass the Archbishop spoke of the General's remarkable career, and concluded his sermon with the last articulate words spoken by Laperrine to his companions as he awaited death in the desert to end his sufferings: "It is I, my children, who am the cause of your misfortune. I have crossed the Sahara eleven times, and I was reputed to know it intimately; but the reputation was false. Neither I, nor anyone else, knows the Sahara."

On a wooden cross like that of Father de Foucauld, erected above his grave, was the following epitaph, roughly painted by local soldiers:

General Henri Laperrine
Commanding the Algiers Army Corps.
Grand Officer de la Légion d'Honneur.
Died gloriously for France on March 5, 1920, in the neighbourhood of Anesbaraka, Sahara, at the age of 59 years.
Miserecordius Jesus. Give him eternal rest.

The funeral was followed by a court of inquiry which led to no satisfactory explanation as to why so many stupid errors in judgment had been made by everyone concerned with the flight from Tamanrasset to the Niger. No one seemed able to explain their actions, but the chief blame seems to rest on Major Vuillemin, who not only refused to take the General as his guide, but having observed Warrant Officer Bernard's plane make a forced landing, did not land beside him, or at least make absolutely sure of the exact location of the landing place. This is one of those unexplainable instances of brave men losing their heads in moments of crisis.

9

ISABELLE EBERHARDT

~~~~~~

WITH the possible exception perhaps of a wealthy Dutch girl called Alexandine Tinne, who tried to cross the Sahara from east to west, that is, from the Nile to the Moroccan Atlas, women never explored the Sahara. Alexandine Tinne was more of a tourist than an explorer and was murdered by Twareg bandits, chiefly because it was known that she carried gold in her saddlebags with which to pay her guides. But there were no Gertrude Bells exploring the deserts of Arabia and Rosita Forbes those of Libya. Two ladies, however, were for many years intimately connected with those wildernesses immediately south of Algeria. One of them was Russian, the other French, Isabelle Eberhardt and Aurélie Picard.

These ladies knew more about the peoples of the Sahara than many of the explorers, and while one died destitute and despised by many, and the other respected and comparatively prosperous, both had dedicated themselves to the desert. Their physical love affairs, also, belong to those romances which prove that colour or creed, or similar backgrounds, are not necessarily essential to successful mating.

Isabelle Eberhardt was the daughter of Nathalie Eberhardt, who was the illegitimate child of a middle-class Lutheran-German and a Russian-Jew named Nicolas Korff. Without revealing her origins, Nathalie had married General Paul de Moerderer, an officer in the army of Tsar Alexander II. He had thus not only been led into marrying beneath him, but also to a partly Jewish woman in a country where anti-Semitism was almost as violent as in

Hitler's Germany seventy years later. Nevertheless, the General seems to have so loved his wife that he never reproached her for this duplicity. In fact, he did everything he could to make his family and his brother officers accept Madame de Moerderer as one of their own social standing. For this loyalty and devotion he was most ungratefully repaid.

In order to ensure that his children by this marriage should have the best possible education, the General engaged a tutor to teach them. His name was Alexander Trophimovsky, a pope of the Orthodox Church and a man of remarkable ability and intelligence. He was also good-looking and had great charm. What the General did not know was that this pope no longer practised his religion and was, in fact, a nihilist.

With the General frequently absent on military duties, his wife, although courteously treated according to her married rank, had no friends in this narrow aristocratic Russian society, and found herself dependent on Trophimovsky's attractive companionship. Soon she fell under his influence and charm and then allowed him to become her lover. The General suspected nothing until the day that Madame Moerderer disappeared with the tutor, who had, incidentally, likewise deserted his own wife and family.

For a while the lovers wandered about Europe with the Moerderer children, who were apparently still supported by the General. At one of their temporary stopping places a son who was named Augustus was born to this strange couple, and in 1877, a daughter who was named Isabelle.

By this time Trophimovsky and his mistress had settled in a villa near Geneva. Here the ex-pope undertook the education of the young Moerderers and later on, of his own son and daughter. Their education was extremely thorough and extremely revolutionary, so much so that the General's children, who did not like work, anyway, rebelled and returned to Russia. Trophimovsky does not appear to have been upset by this desertion and concentrated his teaching on his daughter, who was showing herself to be an eager and apt pupil.

As soon as she had passed through the elementary stages of her education, Trophimovsky began to teach her French, German, Italian and Arabic; she already spoke Russian fluently. He guided her in her reading and led her away from anything which might make her take Christianity seriously. It was probably for this reason that, when she became interested in Islam, she developed into an enthusiastic and then almost fanatic believer in the teachings of Mohammed.

In any case Isabelle was not a normal child and one of her early peculiarities showed itself in the wearing of boy's clothes. From the time that she had any say in the choosing of her wardrobe, she dressed as a sailor and later as an Arab. She had her hair cut short and, with her slight figure, she had no difficulty in passing as a man. She was, furthermore, physically strong and could out-tire her father in his gardening, for which he had an obsession, and out-ride him in the foothills of the Jura. Her future did not look promising. There was little money and no social life for anyone with such a shady background. Nor was there any obvious occupation in Switzerland for a girl with her kind of education.

Then, one day, she read an advertisement in a French newspaper which had been inserted by an officer stationed in the Sahara who was bored with the monotony of his life there and wanted someone to write to him. Isabelle immediately replied and a correspondence began which was to lead her to her Fate in the deserts of North Africa.

The officer's name was Eugène Letord who soon found out that this girl with whom he had intended to carry on a flirtatious exchange of letters was a scholar avid to know about the life among the Arabs.

While finding his garrison duties tiresome, Letord took a great interest in the nomads of the desert and the sedentary citizens of the oases. He appreciated that their grievances against their French masters were well founded and refused to be condescending to them as were his brother officers. No one, therefore, could have been more acceptable to Isabelle who, through the communist teachings of Trophimovsky was in favour of emancipating "oppressed peoples".

Soon Letord was urging Isabelle to give up her futile existence in Geneva and come to Algeria where she would find the way of living for which she obviously craved. With her knowledge of Arabic and her leanings towards Islam, too, everything would be made easy for her.

There was nothing which Isabelle wanted to do more, and as if to add to the incentive to cross the Mediterranean, she was seeing a great deal of one of the Turkish vice-consuls in Geneva. This Rehid Bey was a practising Moslem and found in Isabelle an intelligent student of Islamic beliefs. Soon, she could justifiably declare herself a Moslem. All that was now required were the means to reach North Africa.

Then Fate struck a third time! Isabelle had been doing some writing, for which she was showing definite talent. Her articles had to do with Arabs and were attracting a certain amount of attention because of their rather revolutionary approach to her subject. One of those who had become interested in Isabelle's strange instinctive flair for places and peoples she had never seen was an Algerian-Frenchman called Louis David who was touring Switzerland with his wife.

They met Isabelle in Geneva and suggested that she visit them at Bone. Isabelle was delighted, but felt that she could not leave without her mother. Persuading her was not very difficult. Madame de Moerderer was, by now, completely disillusioned by Trophimovsky, who had not only shown himself to be a quite impractical man with ideals which he could not work out, but was also going through the fortune which the General had generously left to his former wife when he died. Accordingly, in the spring of 1897, Isabelle and her mother crossed the Mediterranean.

Isabelle immediately realized that she must have nothing to do with the French inhabitants, who lived disdainfully aloof from the people of the country. She saw little of the Davids and rented an essentially Arab house as far as possible from the European quarter. She appreciated, too, that a Moslem woman could not go out alone or unveiled so she abandoned her frocks and, henceforth, dressed in burnous, *gandourah* and turban. By this means she could sit in the cafés and talk to Berber Moslems and pray in the mosques. It was here that she made her final and irrevocable declaration of faith, and caused her mother to do likewise.

Everything that Isabelle saw delighted and inspired her. The food, the smells of the street, the talk for the sake of talking, the sleeping on a mat instead of on a bed, the using of the fingers at meals instead of knives and forks. Without any effort, she slipped into the native way of living. The only Occidental trait which she kept up was compiling notes of all she saw. She also had stories published in the local French papers, which augured well for her future as an author.

Then, when everything was moving favourably along for the first time in her life and in an atmosphere of serenity which she had never known, her mother died. Isabelle was broken-hearted. Without realizing it, she had relied a great deal on the love of her mother to guide and protect her. Now she was alone and barely twenty years old. Trophimovsky appeared from Switzerland and tried to assume the indifference to human emotion as taught by nihilists, but he was just as grief-stricken as his daughter. In fact, he cried unashamedly as they buried Nathalie de Moerderer, under the name of Fatma, in the Moslem cemetery at Bone.

While Isabelle never forgot her mother, she was now at liberty to carve for herself a short and almost unbelievable career. For a while she remained in Bone, alternating ecstasies of religious fervour with learned Moslems and ecstasies of love-making with any young man who took her fancy. She also began to smoke *kief*, unofficially forbidden flower of the hemp, known today as marijuana, which many Moslems took as a substitute for the Koranically forbidden wine of the grape. Not that Isabelle shunned alcohol—she drank absinthe whenever she could get it. In fact, she seemed openly to have transgressed this tenet of Islam while being almost a fanatic Moslem where everything else was concerned. She was, also, spending the little money which her mother had left her as if it would go on indefinitely.

Isabelle's last link with her old life came in May of 1899 when her father died. She returned to Geneva and felt unaccountably sad at the disappearance of someone for whom she had never really cared. However, she was now even freer to live as she pleased. There would also be more money as the villa had been left to her. Before she could sell it, Trophimovsky's legitimate wife appeared from Russia and opposed the execution of the will. The best that Isabelle could do was to mortgage the estate. This she did and then took the first ship available to Africa. She was, at last, on her way to the Sahara where she hoped to find her pen-mate Letord.

The train at that time went only as far as Batna north of the Aures foothills whence she must travel south on horseback. Before setting out on this first stage of her emancipation from the past, she decided that the break must be absolute. She, accordingly, relinquished the names of her mother and became Si Mahmoud Essadi. This not only entailed the constant wearing of male attire, which she had been doing off and on for some time, but also the assuming of a male personality and writing and speaking of herself as if she were a man.

Riding past the still unexcavated Roman city of Timgad, she traversed the famous gorges of El Kantara where the torrent is still spanned by the bridge erected by the Third Legion in the year A.D. 45. As she came out on the other side of the defile, she suddenly saw the desert for the first time.

She reined in her horse and stared, staggered by the spectacle of this great golden wilderness stretching out before her. While she had hoped that it would be something like this, she had really never believed that her hopes would be fulfilled. As she allowed her horse to move on towards Biskra, she knew that she had taken another irrevocable step. This glittering wilderness must be her home forever.

In what was later to become the many-hotelled oasis made fashionable by Robert Hichens' best-seller, *The Garden of Allah*, Isabelle had expected to meet the man with whom she had corresponded for so long, Eugène Letord. But, when she arrived, she found that he had been transferred to a garrison further south in the Sahara. She also found that she could not go further and join him without the authorization of the Bureaux des Affaires Indigenes. This, she discovered, was hard to obtain. No French officer could understand why a Russian woman should disguise herself as a native of Algeria, especially in the garb of a man, and go into the torrid heat of the Sahara in midsummer. It all sounded most suspicious. However, with her usual obstinacy, Isabelle had her way, obtained her permit, and arranged to join a caravan, leaving next day for Touggourt, under the command of Captain de Susbielle, who was to be later a colleague and friend of Father de Foucauld.

Having achieved this much, Isabelle then proceeded to mess everything up. Gossiping in a café on the eve of her departure, she met two nomads who told her that the captain was one of those Frenchmen who specially despised the natives, and being his friend would be bad for any relationship she might wish to establish with the people of the south. Isabelle, who was always on the defensive where Moslems were concerned, deliberately missed Susbielle's caravan, thereby creating for herself an enemy who could have helped her much and would now do her harm.

Her journey to Touggourt was as haphazard as the rest of her behaviour. Riding her horse, she joined up with nomads' caravans, with soldiers of the Foreign Legion, with holy marabouts travelling south. The fact that she seemed to be a young Arab, with not only a first-rate education, but also a thorough knowledge of the Koran, made her an acceptable and often respected companion of these Moslems. In fact, by the time she reached Touggourt with its hundred-thousand palm oasis, she felt thoroughly pleased with her first venture into the Sahara. This elation was dampened when she met the very angry Roger de Susbielle.

However, with her usual effrontery, she pleaded the urgency to join Eugène Letord at El Oued, and so earnestly that the captain relented and grudgingly gave her guides for the last trackless fifty miles to El Oued. He also warned the commanding officer of that oasis garrison, as well as the Bureaux des Affaires Indigènes, about the peculiar creature who was on her way there.

Once again Isabelle was disappointed. Eugène Letord had been moved on again. Nor were the officers to whom her friend had recommended her, without ever having seen her, favourably impressed. Apart from what Captain de Susbielle had reported, none of them could countenance an Occidental, and especially one of the female sex, masquerading, as they imagined, in the costume of a Moslem native of the male sex. But Isabelle did not care. This sandy desert glittering all around her filled her with an ecstasy which she had never known before. In fact, she once more vowed that this region, and this oasis in particular, would be her home for ever.

Before she could put this pledge into effect, she had to go north. A bout of malaria made it essential to move to a temperate climate. Accordingly, Isabelle rode back into the land of trees and grass and towns, and finally reached Bone where she wanted to see her mother's grave. There she also accidentally encountered Eugène Letord.

The strange thing about the meeting, too, is that neither was disillusioned by the other. They both fulfilled what they had, so far, only imagined. They spent the whole autumn together, riding and talking and smoking *kief* and drinking absinthe. There is no record of their having become lovers, which is perhaps the reason they continued always to be such firm friends. The only reason which caused them to part was that Isabelle was running low in funds and had to get back to Geneva and see what had been done about liquidating her property.

When she reached Switzerland, she found that her own lawyer was obviously in connivance with Madame Trophimovsky and that there would be little money available for her. Nevertheless she waited, hoping that some kindness if not honesty would be shown her. The wait was in vain, but not entirely so, from a quite different reason.

In the pension where she was living Isabelle met a Russian girl called Vera Popova, a medical student and a political revolutionary. She had a dynamic character and convinced Isabelle that she had a future as a writer. This, in fact, was true, although Isabelle had no idea how to make anything out of her talent. Then, through another Russian, Lydia Peschkoff, the explorer and author, it was suggested that, in order to get into worthwhile print, Isabelle should go to Paris. The suggestion was followed up by letters of introduction. Isabelle accordingly went to Paris with her letters. From a constructive literary point of view, the visit was a failure.

It was the year of the Paris Exhibition of 1900 and the city was playing host to every kind of celebrity, so that Isabelle in her threadbare coat and skirt made no impression on the men and women to whom she had been introduced. She was too shy in the midst of these elegant and distinguished people to push herself forward or wear her turban and burnous which would have, at least, made her a curiosity. But, that Fate in which she so implicitly believed had something else in store for her which would assist her to fulfil her ambition to live in the Sahara.

In one of the salons to which she had been invited as a courtesy to Madame Peschkoff, she met the American widow of Antoine Duc de Vallombrosa, the Marquis de Mores. He had been Charles de Foucauld's closest friend at the Cavalry School at Saumur and, while never posted in a military capacity to North Africa, had gone there to do some private exploring of the Sahara. Here, in 1896, he had vanished and it had been reported by nomadic Berbers that he had been assassinated by marauding Twareg.

An inquiry had been set in motion but no clues had been found and no murderers arrested. The only evidence that Mores had ever been in this area was his revolver which a man called Ben Messis had picked up near Kebili south of Ghadames and had later given to Father de Foucauld. The Marquise was, nevertheless, convinced that the Bureaux des Affaires Indigènes had done little to force an issue and had, in fact, hushed up the incident for political reasons.

When, therefore, she met Isabelle and learnt that she knew the country about El Oued, where her husband had been last seen alive, she asked if she would go out and make a private investigation. All expenses would be paid and a bonus if anything new were brought to light. Isabelle, who was longing to get back to the desert and was almost penniless, accepted the offer enthusiastically.

On 21st July, 1900 she crossed to Algiers where she again met Eugène Letord. Then she went on by train and horseback towards Biskra and the south. On the day that she reached the edge of the desert, she wrote: "O Sahara, menacing Sahara, hiding your beautiful dark heart behind your inhospitable and dreary solitude!"

She reached El Oued this time without difficulty, and she rented a small house in this sand-surrounded oasis. She had, apparently, forgotten her mission. In fact, by the time she had established herself in her new home, she had spent everything which the Marquise de Mores had advanced her. Nor did she ever make any real attempts to investigate the Marquis' death. This was not deliberate dishonesty, but partly a kind of fatalistic irresponsibility which characterized the whole of her life, as well as the fact that the French appeared to be deliberately reticent when the name of Mores was brought up.

Once settled, Isabelle set about making friends with the local inhabitants and keeping well away from the officers of the Bureaux des Affaires Indigènes and the French garrison. She also bought a three-year-old white stallion which she called "Souf" after the name of that part of the Sahara. She was a splendid horsewoman or, outwardly, horseman in her male dress which did more to bring her close to the desert nomads than her Islamic piety and knowledge of the Koran.

One evening, in an oasis garden, she met a cavalry sergeant of the Spahis called Sliman Ehnni. He was making his career in the French native army and spoke French fluently. Sliman was good-looking, and had a kind of feminine charm which appealed to the masculine-minded Isabelle. In all other ways, he seems to have been a Berber of quite limited education who had never thought in terms beyond his military duties in France's North African army. However, he fell in love with the scholarly eccentric who was attracted by the sincerity of this man who already spoke to her of a permanent future together. He was also an admirable lover, which was always an important factor in Isabelle's relations with persons who, although dressing as she did, belonged to the opposite sex.

The liaison, therefore, prospered and eventually the Arab N.C.O. and the Russian voluptuary were living openly together. This gesture completed her ostracization by the French garrison who, already outraged by this European's life in the native quarter, decided that she must be left to her own ruin.

Needless to say Isabelle did not care what the French thought about her. She had no money and, outside of her diaries and notes which would one day form bases for her books, made no attempt to do any regular writing. Yet, she was completely happy with this fatalistic Sahara life and especially with Sliman Ehnni, who was giving her the kind of love which she had, so far, lacked. In her diary, she wrote: "As for Sliman, nothing is changed except that I am becoming more and more attached to him and he is becoming truly a member of my family, or rather *my family* in himself. May it last like this forever, even here, among these unchanging grey sands."

These feelings, however, did not prevent Isabelle from appreciating her lover's ignorance of anything approaching the literary, and of his purely materialistic and unambitious ideals.

While Sliman made plans to buy a café as soon as he left the army, and later on a grocery store, Isabelle tried to imbue him with Suffi mysticism. Finding that this was completely beyond his understanding, she set about interesting him in her favourite authors. This was not a success as, while he enjoyed reading Lotti's *Roman d'un Spahi*, he found other writers beyond the comprehension of his essentially desert Moslem Oriental mind.

But this did not worry Isabelle too much, she could forget her education and background in the physical ecstasies which her lover gave her. There was now very little money to spend and some of this was borrowed, but that did not bother her either. The oasis people were accustomed to a hand-to-mouth existence and a belief that God would always provide. That Isabelle Eberhardt, or Mahmoud Essadi as she was known throughout this Arab community, did not continue this existence of fatalistic bliss was due to her Islamic fervour which had also taught her the doctrine of *In sha Allah*.

While the native inhabitants in general had resigned themselves to the French occupation of North Africa as a lesser evil to that of the previous rule of the Turks, the religious fanatics were still recalcitrant. They preferred the indolent corruptness of the Moslem governors to the roads and railways and sanitation of the Christian conquerors.

These North African fanatics, like those of others of the Moslem world, had formed themselves into religious fraternities whose objectives were to keep Islam in the puritan form which Moham-med had preached. They were, evidently, Xenophobic and, whenever revolts occurred among France's restless Sahara subjects, it could usually be traced to some member or marabout of one of these fraternities. Furthermore, the French had found that it was almost impossible to put pressure on these religious groups headed by politically able men who were regarded by their followers as saints.

Isabelle had been brought into contact with a powerful fraternity of the El Oued region known as the Quadrya. It was not, like some of these groups, essentially militant and appealed to her because of its mystic attributes. At the head of these Quadrya was a certain holy man called Hussein ben Brahim. He had become acquainted with Isabelle in the camp of a nomad chief, and, impressed by her remarkable knowledge of his faith, had invited her to visit him at his *zaouia*, which is something between a monastery and a seminary where selected members of the Order were trained.

After talking to Isabelle for a while, he was even more impressed by her Islamic fervour and erudition which she assured him was in part due to her being the daughter of a Russian-Moslem father (which in fact was untrue). He also appreciated that she had sincere leanings towards mysticism and the makings of a fanatic. He probably also had an idea that, being a European with fluent French, she might be useful in giving him information about the doings of the local French governors.

At any rate, Isabelle was initiated into Hussein ben Brahim's *zaouia* without the usual formal examinations, which had the opposite effect on the French from that which the holy man had expected. Now convinced that Isabelle was a spy or an agitator or both, the Bureaux des Affaires Indigènes and the French military authorities put her on a widely circulated blacklist.

The Moslem members of rival fraternities were equally suspicious. It was unheard of for a European to join one of these groups and unbelievable that Sidi Hussein should have encouraged one of the female sex. Neither the Berber nomads nor the French military people would believe that Isabelle was a true seeker after serenity who wanted only to be left in peace with her mysticism, her horse and her lover. To try and prove this she retired more and more from public view.

Unfortunately for Isabelle's peace of mind, she had not taken into consideration the petty-mindedness of French military bureaucracy. If they could do nothing legal to harm her they could hurt her personally by separating her from a native of Algeria in the service of France. Sergeant Sliman Ehnni was suddenly transferred to the Spahi regiment at Batna, miles away and north of the Aures Mountains. Not only was this a tragedy from the sentimental point of view, but also from the practical. With Sliman gone, the small means of livelihood from his army pay vanished, and without money Isabelle could not even consider following her lover to a new garrison. Then Fate intervened again, bringing with it disastrous consequences.

Si Hussein ben Brahim had a brother named Si Lachmi. He was a man of splendid appearance who wore rich clothes, lived well, while at the same time continuing to maintain his prestige as a desert man who could manage a horse better than any of his tribesmen. He was also a rogue. However, in spite of the doubts which many of the more worldly members of the Quadrya Fraternity felt about his piety, he had had himself appointed Grand Master of the Order. From this he derived much profit which allowed him to go frequently to France where his religious attributes were not generally known.

Isabelle had met Si Lachmi some time before at Touggourt and had been taken in by his claims to mysticism. He, likewise, had been led to believe that Isabelle might be a useful link between him and the French authorities with whom he was apt to have "misunderstandings". When, therefore, he appeared in El Oued at about the same time as Sliman had been transferred to Batna, Isabelle went to him with her financial predicament and was given a present of 170 francs. This money enabled her to pay off her debts in the oasis but did not leave sufficient to let her reach Batna.

There was, however, another marabout of the same family as Si Hussein and Si Lachmi who might help. His name was Sidi Eliman and he was, at that moment, at a neighbouring oasis called Behima. Hearing that Si Lachmi was going there, Isabelle asked if she might accompany him. To this Si Lachmi agreed and the journey across the desert was carried out in the state becoming to a great marabout. Four days later Isabelle was stricken in a way that would mar her life in North Africa for some time to come.

While attending a combined meeting of members of the Quadrya and Rahmanya fraternities, Isabelle was attacked by a fanatic called Abdallah ben si Mohammed, who tried to kill her with a rusty old sword. That she did not die under the repeated blows was due to a clothes-line which happened to be strung across the room and broke the first slash at her head. From then on, Isabelle managed to dodge the wild onslaught until the man was overpowered and disarmed. This was not easy, as her attacker was in a state of fanatical frenzy. When, finally, he had been bound with ropes, Isabelle was able to ask him why he had done this and if he had any grudge against her; but Abdallah screamed back that he did not know her and had never even seen her before. He had done what he had by the orders of God!

Isabelle felt baffled, but before she could ask any more questions, the loss of blood from the wounds in her shoulder and arm made her faint. The next day, she was transported to the military hospital at El Oued where the garrison doctor took charge. She was in atrocious pain from the muscles which had been slashed and was also in despair lest she should die without seeing Sliman again.

In the meanwhile a controversial situation was materializing. On the one hand, the members of the Quadrya Fraternity had been convinced that Divine intervention had saved Isabelle's life— she was already respected for her unusual knowledge of the Koran and matters Islamic—and now, with what had occurred at Behima, she was being regarded as a maraboute. Even Si Hussein was inclined to attribute Isabelle's survival to a miracle. However, on the other hand, the French were far from pleased by this latest Eberhardt incident and were making plans to counteract

this holy aura which was glowing around Isabelle. As soon as she
had been discharged from the hospital, Isabelle left El Oued on her
horse, Souf, to join Sliman, the people of the Quadrya having
furnished her with the necessary funds for the journey.

The reunion was not as happy as she had hoped. Her lover was
quartered in barracks outside this ugly Occidental town where
he had none of the liberties of an oasis garrison. She had very little
money left and had to live miserably in a room in a mud house.
It was cold, too, among the Aures Mountains and both she and
her horse suffered from this sudden change of climate. No one
appreciated her destitution. The fact was that, when she had had
the money, from her mother's legacy and then from the Marquise
de Mores, she had spent it so lavishly that her behaviour had given
her the reputation of being a Russian of great wealth. That she
now lived in hovels and dressed like a beggar was attributed to
eccentricity.

This fantasy Isabelle did not deny, hoping that as long as she was
believed rich she would be left in peace. Her hopes were vain as,
without warning, she received orders to leave North Africa
immediately. The French authorities gave no reason for doing
this and she, being an alien, had no recourse but to obey. Sliman
tried to save her by asking permission from his commanding
officer to marry Isabelle. Being himself a French citizen, this
would have made Isabelle one too, but the request was refused.
In deeper despair than ever, she made her way to the coast and
took a fourth-class, deck passage to Marseilles.

She landed in France in May, but did not stay long as, in the
middle of June, she was summoned to Constantine to give
evidence in the trial of Abdallah ben si Mohammed who had tried
to kill her at Behima.

Owing to the singular personality of this chief witness, the trial
took on the proportions of a *cause célèbre*. Every Algerian newspaper sent reporters to Constantine, and there were a few specially
delegated from Paris.

Under cross-examination, Abdallah stated that God and his
angels had ordered him to destroy this foreigner who was
causing disturbances among the Moslem fraternities of the Sahara.
He assured the judge that he had never seen Mademoiselle
Eberhardt before the attack and knew nothing about her outside
what God had revealed to him. Nothing would shake his declara-

tion and members of his family confirmed that Abdallah had been divinely inspired and had been in a trance for days before going out to find his victim.

Isabelle, once more described as a rich and eccentric Russian, said that she knew nothing about the motives of the accused and had never done anything to stir up trouble among the fraternities. She added that she felt no grudge against Abdallah and confirmed that he was a stranger to her. She concluded her evidence by saying that she forgave her assailant and hoped that he would not be punished. The prosecution took the line that the whole business was a political conspiracy directed against the French; that it was treason and that Abdallah must pay for his crime with his life. The defending counsel blamed Isabelle for creating such a situation and called for the acquittal of his client.

The court, with the usual harshness of the Algerian French of that day, sentenced Abdallah to penal servitude for life. Simultaneously, and this time definitely, it gave orders for Isabelle's expulsion from North Africa. There was nothing for her to do, therefore, but take another fourth-class passage to Marseilles without even being able to see Sliman.

As her money was very low when Isabelle reached France she went to live with her brother Augustin, who had married a poor workman's daughter. All three led an existence of abject penury. In fact, Isabelle had so little that she could not even buy herself women's clothes which would have enabled her to find employment as a secretary or shop assistant.

She still wore her burnous and turban, so that the only way she could contribute to her board was to join her brother on the Marseilles quays as a dock labourer. Being, moreover, classified as an Algerian native, she received the lowest pay of any of the riffraff which eked out an existence when ships had to be loaded or unloaded.

In spite of this unbelievably hard work for a woman, and the squalor of her lodgings, she managed to do some writing. A novel of great merit and widely read after her death began to take shape. It was called *Le Trimadeur* and told of the hideous existence of the dock labourers who, without any unions to protect them, were at the mercy of unscrupulous, slave-driving foremen.

The only encouragement which Isabelle received during this more than degrading period of her existence was from Eugène

Brieux, the brilliant, controversial and successful French play-
wright of that day. He was living at Nice, and she sent him some
of her stories with a letter of introduction.

Brieux, who was opposed to the way in which France was
ruling North Africa, saw not only the literary value of Isabelle's
writing, but also a means of promoting the Arab cause. He sent
her several hundred francs as an advance royalty and tried to place
the stories. The French were, however, unwilling to read anything which came out in favour of Arab emancipation. Thus, the
editors approached, while noting that Mademoiselle Eberhardt
could write dramatically and convincingly, returned the manu-
scripts to Brieux, who told Isabelle not to be discouraged and to
continue working.

This gave Isabelle a great moral uplift. She began to feel that
she was not such an outcast as the French authorities had made her
feel. Her happiness was further enhanced by Sliman's transfer to a
regiment of Spahis quartered near Marseilles where he would have
to serve the remaining months before his discharge.

On 17th October, 1901 Sliman Ehnni was married to Isabelle
Eberhardt, first of all at the *mairie* in Marseilles, and then before the
Moslem Kadi, the first marriage being necessary owing to
Sliman's French nationality which gave Isabelle the same status.

With the little money which was left over from Brieux's
"advances" on her stories Isabelle had bought a scanty woman's
wardrobe, sufficient for the wedding. While waiting for Sliman's
liberation papers from the army, the lovers lived in a miserable
lodging near the harbour. But they were legally united now and
no one could part them, so what did it matter where they slept?
Furthermore, there would soon be no obstacle to Isabelle returning to Africa, where her order of expulsion had been based mainly
on the fact that she was an alien.

There was one more disappointment in store for Isabelle. A
week or so after her marriage she learnt that the villa in Geneva
had at last been sold, but that the whole of the price paid had been
swallowed up by legal fees. Isabelle shrugged her shoulders
fatalistically. The end of the Trophimovsky home at least severed
her last ties with Europe.

In February of 1902 Sliman obtained his discharge and, with
just enough money to pay their fare, the bride and bridegroom
sailed for Bone where Sliman's family lived. Here for a while

they would be welcome, as well as boarded and lodged free of charge.

The delight, too, of finding herself on African soil again gave Isabelle renewed energy, so that she made up her mind seriously to go about promoting her husband and to make him something more worthwhile than a devoted lover. The main obstacle to this ambition was Sliman's elementary education and the fact that he had learned nothing useful for civil employment while serving in the army. There was also his lack of desire to be anything but what he was.

Nevertheless, Isabelle persevered and, while appreciating that she could never make of Sliman the future Arab administrator who would right the wrongs of his oppressed compatriots, she was equally resolved that he should not follow his inclination to earn a living as a grocer or a waiter. She, accordingly, began to give him concentrated lessons in mathematics and geography, while making him take pains to improve his reading and writing of French.

With this education of her husband progressing slowly, Isabelle decided that it would be better for both of them if they left the obscure and almost degrading life in the native slums of Bone. She had been having articles and stories printed in the Algerian newspapers and periodicals and, while the remuneration had not been high, it had been sufficient to give her encouragement to continue working. She accordingly had Sliman say goodbye to his family and moved with him to Algiers.

Here she met what she once more regarded as another instrument of her fate, Victor Barrucaud, who certainly did much to alter the pattern of her life.

Victor Barrucaud was the editor of *Les Nouvelles*, a liberally inclined North African newspaper, favouring the cause of the Algerian natives. He had never seen Isabelle, but he had defended her in his newspaper after the Constantine trial and protested against her expulsion from Algeria. He was still under the impression that she was the wealthy, eccentric Russian as reported by the French police.

When, therefore, she called on him for the first time wearing the shoddy female costume which Sliman had insisted that she must put on when she went into the streets, he was much taken aback. But after talking to her, he realized the originality of her thoughts, her good education and general culture. He also appreciated how her store of knowledge about all kinds of Berber and Islamic matters could be made use of, especially in a paper like *Les Nouvelles*. Apart from the vivid memories which she had retained of her life in the desert and with the Quadrya brethren, she had filled many notebooks with ideas which would be good for articles.

Isabelle was, likewise, attracted by Barrucaud and found in the lovely Moorish villa which the publisher owned above Algiers an ideal house in which to work. She hated the squalor of Algiers where the Europeanized natives drank and gambled and fought, and were rightly treated by the French as the scum of humanity.

Barrucaud, hoping for a sensational story, was also instrumental in making it possible for Isabelle to visit that remarkable woman, Lalla Zeyneb, the maraboute and head of the Rahmanya confraternity which had its *zaouia* at El-Hamel near Bou Saada on the edge of the Sahara.

In this news-gathering he was disappointed, for, in spite of his pleadings, Isabelle never revealed what had passed between her and the saintly Lalla Zeyneb; in fact, she never recorded any details of the interview. However, she returned to Algiers rejuvenated and with an energy which she had lost during these past months of misfortune. It seems also as if the benign influence of the maraboute had helped her materially.

Sliman met his wife on the threshold of their dingy quarters in the Bab el Oued quarter with the news that through Barrucaud's influence he had been appointed to the post of *khodja*, native secretary and interpreter, to the French *commune mixte*[1] at Tenes on the Mediterranean coast, one hundred miles west of Algiers. It was not a position of much importance, but from the financial point of view there would be little further to worry about and Isabelle would have leisure for her writing.

Although Tenes was a lovely place with a temperate climate, it was peopled by a crowd of disillusioned French men and women

[1] *Communes mixtes* used to be towns in the essentially French part of Algeria and away from the Sahara, where the Arab population was in a majority. In such places the mayor, as in Algiers or Oran, was replaced by an *administrateur*, whose authority covered the adjoining native villages. He was assisted in his duties by an *administrateur adjoint* and a *commission municipale*, composed partly of Frenchmen and partly of Berbers who were elected by their respective peoples.

with too little to do, who quarrelled among themselves, but held aloof from the native population. Thus the arrival of a European woman with a shady background, married to an ex-N.C.O. of the Spahis, loosened a flood of exaggerated gossip. At the same time Sliman once more assured Isabelle that what he would really like to do would be to run a cheap coffee shop—Café Maure.

While Isabelle would not countenance such a project, she was resigned to her husband's intellectual shortcomings. She loved him sincerely as well as passionately and found that his strangely tolerant attitude towards her, especially for a Moslem, suited her diversified, vagabond life. One week she would be living in the luxury of Barrucaud's villa in Algiers or in the domesticated atmosphere of her Tenes home, while the next she would be off on horseback into the desolate mountains of the Ouarsenis, ecstatic in her solitude.

"Vagabondage means escape," she wrote. "For anyone who understands the value of solitary freedom, for one is only really free when one is alone, the act of leaving everything is the bravest and most beautiful of all. It may be a selfish happiness, but it is happiness for him who understands what it means."

Those words I have memorized ever since I first read them. They sum up Isabelle's philosophy, a philosophy which was the basis of hers and any honest person's design for living—*"For one is only really free when one is alone."* And she went on to state: "To possess a home, a family, property or some sort of public function, to have some definite means of existence; in fact, to be a cog in the social machine—these are the things that seem necessary and indispensable to the great majority of men. All property has its bounds and all power is subject to some law, but the tramp possesses the whole vast earth, whose only limits are the unreal horizon and his empire is intangible since he governs it and enjoys it in spirit. . . ."

And what a truth that is which few of us dare to admit or try to understand or practice. With material belongings, it is so difficult to be happy. I have never possessed a house or piece of land or even any furniture, and the most ecstatic times of my life were spent away from human beings in the Sahara. The vaga-bondage of Isabelle Eberhardt is the spirit, too, of the Sahara, the only spirit which makes any serenity possible. In fact, with the soundlessness of the Sahara, it is the solitude from all human interference which produces that charm which I have already tried to explain in connection with the lure of the Desert. In other words, the Bedouins mind their own business, they never ask one where one is going, or why; they never intrude on one's thoughts, they never "make conversation", or expect one to talk if one has nothing to say. By this method they give one the blessed sensation of being alone, together with a feeling that one is surrounded by friends who are eager to be of assistance if needed.

In addition to finding herself, and with peace of mind, Isabelle was learning more and more about the Moslems and their beliefs. While the Ouarsenis mountains behind Tenes were not the desert, they had the same kind of wild solitude and their inhabitants were nomadic. These Berber mountaineers loved and revered the white burnoused Si Mahmoud and while a few knew that she was a woman, these respected her male identity. The tribesmen considered her to be a holy creature and consulted her as much on interpretations of the Koran as on legal and medical questions.

However, in spite of this complete detachment from anything actively political, Isabelle's association with the now notoriously pro-native *Akhbar* newspaper was causing more and more concern to the French inhabitants of Tenes. The *administrateur*, eventually, trumped up a charge of subversion against her which implicated his rival, the assistant *administrateur adjoint*, Robert Randau, who had always so befriended Isabelle.

Randau, riled by this petty behaviour, brought a counter-charge against his superior, who then accused Sliman of corruption. A war of insinuations and denunciations was taken up by the press. As an immediate result, both the *administrateur* and his assistant had to resign and Sliman, the only person to have been proved guiltless, was transferred to the "khodjaship" at Guegour in the Djebal Amour highlands which run down to the Sahara south of the Atlas range. It seemed as if Isabelle's longing for the Sahara was destined to remain a longing. Then, in the summer of 1903, everything was changed.

There had been a great deal of Arab unrest in the northwest Sahara under the leadership of Bou Amama, whose insurrection had been responsible for Charles de Foucauld's rehabilitation in the army. Captain de Susbielle, with whom Isabelle had fallen out in Biskra during her first trip to El Oued, had just managed to save his oasis garrison at Taghit from overwhelming desert warriors.

But in other areas, the French garrisons had not been so successful. A French convoy, moving south to reinforce threatened oases, had been massacred by tribesmen. In fact the Bedouins who had declared themselves for France were beginning to wonder if they had not made an error in judgment.

Over the border, the Sultan of Morocco, on whom the French government had been depending to round up rebels who slipped into his territory, which was still a sovereign state, was showing complete indifference to the situation. In the far south, the Twareg were coming out into the open again, ready to waylay any caravans moving through the Hoggar. In Paris, questions were being asked in the Chamber of Deputies and in the press, while the Flatters disaster was being once more discussed.

It was, accordingly, decided that France must act boldly and independently to counter this growing revolt and a brilliant young colonel, Charles Lyautey, who had lately distinguished himself in Indo-China, was appointed to deal with the dissidents. Without further ado, he established his headquarters at Ain Sefra, a semi-desert town at the foot of the hills which run down from the Atlas and merge with the desert. Simultaneously Barrucaud despatched Isabelle to headquarters to cover the military operations for his *Akhbar* and with a further commission to contribute articles for other Algerian newspapers. Before leaving Algiers she was furnished with an introduction to Colonel Lyautey.

No two persons could have offered greater contrasts. Lyautey was rather a dandy, always faultlessly dressed, cultured, good-looking and wealthy—surrounded by a staff of elegantly turned out staff officers drawn from the best families of France. Everyone about him had to know his business, show implicit obedience to orders and instil that disciplined *esprit de corps* which makes a good fighting force.

There was Isabelle, on the other hand, whose whole existence had been that of an outcast, persecuted by the French government, dressed in well-worn Arab clothes, penniless and at times ill, with no one to respect her except a few intellectuals, her Spahi husband and a number of holy Moslems.

Lyautey, in spite of this adverse outward appearance and the odd reputation, immediately recognized Isabelle for what she was really worth. In a few weeks she had become not only his friend but his confidante. He, furthermore, appreciated how her knowledge of Arabic and Islam could help him in his task.

Thus, from being the suspect of all the Bureaux des Affaires Indigènes in North Africa, she suddenly found herself as the special agent of the French Military Intelligence. In fact, it was the collaboration of the brilliant young colonel and the derelict Russian vagabond which made the pacification of the western Sahara, and then the whole desert, possible.

For the first time in her life Isabelle was completely happy. Not only did she enjoy the confidences and companionship of Lyautey, but she was surrounded by other men with whom she could discuss matters of mutual interest.

Many of these men were members of the Foreign Legion, some of whom had had the same kind of education as Isabelle. Furthermore, when she found Occidental association tiresome, she could be off into the desert on the horse which Lyautey had given her. Dressed as an Arab nomad, speaking the desert dialects fluently, she could live the life which pleased her most and, at the same time, gather valuable information for the French general staff.

Little by little, Lyautey's tactics of force, where needed, and propaganda by Isabelle when possible, led to the gradual penetration into the Sahara, south of Ain Sefra. By the late spring of 1904 even Bou-Amama had decided that his cause was lost. The people of Morocco, too, were finding out that under Lyautey's firmly benign rule they could go to and from their markets without fear of being plundered on the way.

Lyautey was not completely satisfied with the general situation. On his western flank, there still remained groups of fierce Berber tribesmen—fanatic Moslems who detested all infidel races on principle. These men were, he learned, more or less under the control of the head of the Zianya fraternity, a marabout of legendary fame called Sidi Brahim ould Mohammed.

Lyautey decided that this man must be made a friend of the French before he could report that his campaign was successfully over. The great difficulty was how to reach safely the remote *zaouia* in the Atlas Mountains. Then he remembered that Isabelle was a member of the Quadrya fraternity and could probably easily make her way to Kensada, the capital of this theocratic state.

Isabelle accepted the assignment enthusiastically and, after several days of riding, accompanied only by a negro slave called Embarek, she reached the forbidden city of Kensada. Here she presented a letter of introduction from the head of the fraternity in Ain Sefra. In it she was described as a Tunisian student seeking mystic knowledge and, as such, was admitted to the *zaouia*.

She found it to be a kind of fortress in which she realized she was mentally as well as physically isolated from the world of French soldiers and dissident Arabs. In fact, it had an atmosphere of silent, peaceful mystery which she had not encountered since her visit to Lalla Zeyneb at El Hamel. This atmosphere was enhanced when she met Sidi Brahim, whose life was given up to showing his pupils and followers the path to truth.

To begin with Isabelle was delighted to find herself at such close quarters to the Suffism in which she had tried so long to perfect herself. She almost forgot the object of her mission and sincerely played the role of the eager Tunisian disciple.

After a while, though, she realized that, to all intents and purposes, she was a prisoner in the *zaouia*. She discovered that Sidi Brahim was aware of her identity and suspected the reasons for visiting him. This knowledge cleared the air and, becoming practical, Isabelle asked the marabout if she could leave the *zaouia* and see the rest of the town. This permission was granted and soon she was on intimate terms with her host, discussing matters political as well as spiritual. She then found that the holy man was favourably disposed towards Lyautey, provided he did not try to interfere with him or the fraternities of North Africa. This Isabelle could unreservedly and sincerely guarantee.

Eventually, after several more discussions with the marabout and some severe attacks of malaria for which this district was notorious, she asked permission to leave Kensada. This was granted and she was even furnished with an escort which made her journey back easier and quicker than the journey out. However, the malaria which she had contracted at El Oued pursued her and by the time she reached Ain Sefra she was so ill that she had to be put to bed in the military hospital.

There was no doubt either that this fever was only one of the minor ills attacking a body which had not only over-indulged itself with *kief* and absinthe, but had also frequently been deprived of nourishing foods. Isabelle, who certainly felt as ill as she was, asked Lyautey, who came daily to talk to her, whether he could have Sliman brought to Ain Sefra. Without further ado Lyautey fulfilled the sick woman's request and quite soon the lovers were reunited.

In view of Isabelle's state of health Sliman was told that he need not, for the moment, go back to Guegour. He accordingly rented a small mud house in the lower town of Ain Sefra, which lay astride a narrow river bed in which there was rarely any water except after heavy rain had fallen in the foothills behind Ain Sefra.

Isabelle, in spite of the doctor's pleadings and warnings, decided that she could get well much quicker in her own house with her beloved Sliman. Accordingly, she left the hospital and joined her husband. This was on 20th October, 1904.

During that day and the night which succeeded it there had been thunder and rainstorms in the hills. By dawn, muddy water was running down the *oued* which divided the town in two. Neither Isabelle nor Sliman, nor, for that matter, any of the inhabitants of this quarter seemed to have worried over the possibility of the river rising to a dangerous level. Yet that is exactly what it did.

As the dawn gave way to an unusually bright sunrise, the stream assumed the proportions of a torrent carrying all kinds of debris before it. Then, without warning and before anyone had had time to appreciate what was happening, the water had rushed up to the level of the mud houses which crumbled like pastry as the wild flood undermined their walls.

On the high ground above the native quarters the French officers and their men watched helplessly as the village disintegrated. It was impossible for any of them to venture down the hillside and, if they had been able to do so, they could not have done anything to rescue the animals and human beings which were being whirled along with uprooted date palms in the muddy flood. Lyautey had to forbid volunteers who wanted to go and save the people who clung desperately to the roofs of houses until the foundations gave way and they went to join the struggling bodies which were being swept towards the Sahara. This was especially hard on him as he had just heard that Isabelle had defied the doctors and joined Sliman in this disaster area.

When towards evening the water receded as quickly as it had

risen, first aid parties were despatched to help survivors. Among
those who lived in the lower part of the town, there were few.
Only Sliman remained near where his house had once been.
Somehow or other, the torrent had swept him upwards and had
left him clinging to a less vulnerable building which had with-
stood the watery attack. He was incoherent with terror and grief
and could remember nothing except that Isabelle had been
standing beside him when the river leaped out of its bed and
engulfed everything in its path.

It took twenty-four hours to find her body, crushed under a
beam. In keeping with her singular way of living, Isabelle could
now claim the distinction of being the first Occidental to have
been destroyed by too much water in the Sahara rather than by
too little.

Colonel Lyautey had the woman for whom he had cared so
sincerely buried in the Moslem cemetery in Ain Sefra and placed
a marble stone over her grave. On it, her adopted name, "Si
Mahmoud", was carved in Arabic and below it, her European
origin carved in French. Isabelle's age at her death was twenty-
seven, but into those twenty-seven years had been crammed more
adventure and misery than is usually the lot of someone who has
lived out his normal life span.

This misery, too, had been of her own doing, or let us say by
her own errors of judgment and disregard of public opinion.
She was a fatalist also, who believed that there was no free will.
She was convinced that everything which befell her had been
destined and made no effort to break away from what she could
easily have avoided.

The story of Isabelle Eberhardt Trophimovsky Ehnni is apt to
generate impatience and often lack of sympathy because she was
worth so much more than what she achieved while she lived. This
was proved, moreover, after her death. Victor Barrucaud had
collected all her writings, including some water-logged notes from
Ain Sefra and, after editing them, began to publish them. People
now read with astonishment what this derelict drifter—this *kief*
smoker and absinthe drinker—had written.

When *Dans l'Ombre Chaude de l'Islam* appeared it was acclaimed
as a classic. A street was named after its author in Colomb Bechar
and another in Algiers. Yet, in spite of this astonishing talent, these
romantic and poetic gifts, the French who had been acquainted

with her denounced her as a European who had betrayed her own kind. Only one person who had known her, the Countess de Brazza, the widow of the Congo Explorer Savorgrande Brazza— and she was a woman of ancient lineage who might well have condemned one such as Isabelle—told me what kind of creature she really was, emphasizing her inspiring love story which, in spite of her vagabondage, undoubtedly dominated her life. Sliman Ehnni must also have been a splendid person, in spite of his educational shortcomings, to inspire such emotions.

I prefer to think of Isabelle as one of those rare human beings who was sincere in all she did and unaware of the meaning of the word "convention". She had beauty as well as poetry in her mind, too, for no one with ugly thoughts could have written:

> There are three different tints in the sky of our lives; the past is rosy, the present is grey, the future is blue. Beyond this blue which shimmers before our eyes, there gapes an abyss without bourne and without name—the abyss of metamorphosis into the eternal life.—*The great charm of life comes, perhaps, from the certainty of death.*

Isabelle was a believer and there is no doubt that she looked forward to a happy release from the miseries and worries of life when the end came. It is a cult which belongs to all religions, to all beliefs and disbeliefs. It is the only conviction which can breed serenity and what we Christians call "the peace which passes all understanding".

10

THE MURDER OF THE MARQUIS DE MORES

IT WILL be remembered how ineffectively Isabelle Eberhardt carried out the commission given to her by the Marquise de Mores to elucidate the disappearance of her husband in the Sahara.

As a matter of fact, even if Isabelle had made any real effort to bring this story to light, she would have met with failure, as the murder of this brave officer was carried out to all intents and purposes by the orders of the French government. It is an example of to what extremes politicians will go to achieve their ambitions.

To my mind it is also one of the most hideous and unnecessary of those too-numerous Sahara tragedies, and had as its victim this friend and contemporary of Father de Foucauld and, at one time, an officer in one of the dragoon regiments which Colonel Laperrine had commanded. In fact, this death in the desert of one of France's most courageous officers was contrived in a cold-blooded way which surpassed any of those plans so deliberately prepared for the killing of Father de Foucauld and Colonel Flatters. This time, the doomed man was the Marquis de Mores, Duc de Vallombrosa, who had shared Foucauld's quarters at the Cavalry School at Saumur. While more serious-minded than his room-mate, he had been rather amused by de Foucauld's pranks and escapades and had joined in some of them, but never to the extent of allowing them to interfere with his work.

The Marquis de Mores had been posted to a "crack regiment" of curassiers near Paris when his friend was joining the Third Hussars at Pont a Mousson on the Franco-German border, where his riotous behaviour led him to be expelled from the regiment.

When the time came for the Marquis de Mores' promotion he had been appointed to a regiment of dragoons also stationed near Paris and had met there, and then married, a rich American widow from the Middle West, who had persuaded him to resign from the service and accompany her to South Dakota, where she owned extensive properties. De Mores had agreed, and in 1882 went to the United States, where he took up cattle breeding. He wore the traditional costume of the cowboy but, except for his magnificent horsemanship, could not compete with the business problems which were as much a part of the lives of these Dakotan farmers as their riding.

Having lost his wife a great deal of money through innovations which did not work out on an American ranch, the Marquise decided that it would be wiser and more prudent to take her handsome, aristocratic husband back to the setting to which he belonged. But the "call of the wild" had got into de Mores' blood and the social, fashionable life of Paris into which he had been born and could take his wife who loved it, bored him. He had himself appointed to supervise a project in Tonkin, which was to establish a railway to link up places inland which, until then, had depended on coolies to carry provisions to the French inhabitants. In fact, in order to reach those who lived in the furthest outposts it sometimes took three years, and cost the Minister of the Colonies over a million-and-a-half francs per annum.

The governor of Tonkin, Monsieur Richaud, on whose staff de Mores found himself, was greatly in favour of the plan to link up interior outposts with Tonkin, and appreciated that his new assistant was the kind of enterprising young man who could supervise this railway scheme and bring it safely to a constructive conclusion. The Minister of the Interior of France, from whom depended the credits for such an enterprise, was a certain Monsieur Constans, who had preceded Monsieur Richaud as Governor of Tonkin, and in that capacity had gone in for somewhat questionable financial deals, the facts of which were, unfortunately for the Ministry, still in the files of Richaud's office.

As in most French colonies of those days as well as in some of Great Britain's, most officials sent to administer the country under their government's sovereignty had as one of their objectives the making of money deviously and quickly without being found out. There were those fabulously wealthy nabobs of India who were so rich that they had the ice to cool their drinks sent all the way from the ice houses of New England to Calcutta, in the new fast-sailing clipper ships.

Warren Hastings, who was impeached in 1778 for his peculations in Oudh, while acquitted, was nevertheless following an old established custom. In the French colonies of Indo-China, Tonkin and Cambodia, it was even easier for an administrator to line his pockets, as the native inhabitants had much less intelligence than that of the Indian and none of their education, while there was nothing even resembling that East India Company to keep an eye on the business of its employees.

Monsieur Constans was one of those officials who felt that it was perfectly normal to pad payrolls or even send in contractors' estimates countersigned by himself which were considerably higher than the money which the contractors would receive.

Constans, not wishing to involve himself in something which might bring disaster to his career as well as publicize his peculations in Tonkin, refused Richaud's request for funds for the railway, so that Richaud, who had become a close friend of de Mores, showed him Constans' incriminating file. De Mores, who was a man of great integrity, persuaded the governor to give the gist of Constans' machinations to the Minister of the Colonies in Paris.

As an immediate result of this, Governor Richaud was recalled, and set out for France, taking with him the incriminating file. But neither he nor the condemning papers ever reached France.

One morning, while crossing the Indian Ocean, Richaud, who had been in perfect health the day before, was found dead in his cabin, while by orders of the Minister of the Interior, his papers were put under lock and key by the ship's captain and delivered to Constans. At the same time Constans had an article published in the press, making aspersions on Monsieur Richaud's integrity and suggesting that it was to face a court of inquiry that he had been recalled from his post in Tonkin.

De Mores, on hearing of the mysterious circumstances of the governor's death, had taken passage to France, reaching there just in time to have published in the same newspaper which had attacked Richaud, a rebuttal of all the aspersions made about his friend and questioning his mysterious death at sea. At the same time, he made public papers from the incriminating file which he had taken the precaution to have copied.

It was election time, too, and every time that Constans attempted to make a speech to his constituency, he found de Mores opposing him and proclaiming that, not only was the Minister of the Interior's governorship of Tonkin dishonest, but also that he was the author of other questionable matters which he, Mores, had managed to dig up in France—to say nothing of Monsieur Richaud's sudden death while crossing the Indian Ocean on a French ship.

This inevitably involved other members of the French government and raised enthusiasm among voters for the handsome, ex-cavalry officer, who was also a brilliant and merciless orator.

It thus came about that every official from Monsieur Maline, the Prime Minister, down, felt that it would be safer to have the Marquis de Mores out of the way. In fact, with his personality and obvious honesty, it looked as if Mores might become a leader of a reactionary government—all the more so, as he had the wealth of his Marquise from Dakota to back him.

Félix Faure, the President of the Republic, was particularly embarrassed. He not only had at the time a personal scandal with which to deal, but also was in a delicate international predicament over the Dreyfus affair and the Fashoda situation on the Nile. There Captain Marchand was refusing to take orders from General Kitchener, who was insisting that he evacuate this part of the Sudan.

The opportunity to be rid of de Mores came when the Marquis, who was not really interested in politics, decided that he could help France better by making his way into the Twareg country, where Colonel Flatters and his men had met their ends so dramatically fifteen years before. So, instead of fighting corrupt and disreputable politicians, he crossed to North Africa to organize his caravan.

The first indication that something peculiar was afoot was the arrival of a telegram signed by the French Intelligence Officer and Military Attaché in Tunis, to Lieutenant Lebeuf, the officer commanding the oasis post of Kebili, which is in southern Tunisia, just north of the Great Eastern Sand Desert. The telegram, after announcing the arrival in Kebili of a caravan led by the Marquis de Mores, stated: "You must not forget that de Mores' expedition is a private enterprise and in no way officially authorized, so that you are not to assist him in any way whatsoever. You must see, too, that he proceeds south by way of the Berresof oasis. Please keep me informed of everything connected with the Mores' caravan."

The second indication that this was no ordinary explorer was the receipt of a contradiction to this official order from Tunis in the form of a message from Colonel Cauchemetz, commanding the Gabes district in which Kebili lay, also addressed to Lieutenant Leboeuf, as follows: "You will give me much pleasure by receiving the Marquis de Mores as my friend and in helping him in every way possible."

The next phase in this premeditated drama came to light from a native source after de Mores' death.

In May of 1896 Si Hamma el Aroussi, marabout of the Tidjani *zaouia* at Guemar, despatched a messenger on a trotting camel to Messine, southeast of Ghadames, where were encamped a group of dissident Shamba tribesmen with their chiefs, El Kheir ben Abd el Kader, and his nephew Brahim, and Abdallah El Kheir. The message carried by the camel courier read as follows: "Come to Berresof at once where you will kill a Frenchman who has a great deal of money and is travelling without any official escort. Whoever kills him will not be arrested. I give you my guarantee that all those involved in this business will receive the *amam* [official pardon];" (signed, Si Hamma el Aroussi).

What this message, therefore, amounted to, was the murdering of a Roumi who had been disowned by his own people which would, at the same time, pay good dividends. El Kheir did not consider the pros and cons of the project, but set off at once with seven of his most trusted retainers. On the way through Ghadames he paused to tell other Tidjanis what was afoot, repeating Marabout Si Hamma's message regarding the *amam* for all those concerned in this raid.

Some of the Twareg, who heard the news, decided that this was a splendid opportunity to complete what had been begun at the wells of Bir el Gharama with Colonel Flatters, and the scene was thus laid for the destruction of one of the bravest and noblest characters in France at that time, for no other reason than that he could not tolerate corruption in the government of France, and had the courage to say so.

The next phase in the unfolding of this frightening story was the setting out of de Mores and his caravan from Tunis. As had been the case so often before in these Sahara disasters, de Mores was one of those men who would not listen to the advice of men more experienced in Sahara ways than he. The handsome Marquis declared that as a cavalry officer he not only knew horses, but men also. He, accordingly, picked his Arab escort by the standards used in the selecting of French soldiers and their mounts, and trusted them to supply him with the necessary provisions of food and water as well as good camels.

The first glimpse we have of de Mores on his trek south is at Kebili, where Lieutenant Leboeuf, who knew de Mores' history and had just received that strange telegram message from the Intelligence Officer in Tunis, as well as the contrary message from Colonel Cauchemetz, was sitting on the veranda of the officers' mess with the medical officer, Doctor Larouse. Suddenly, as he sipped his vermouth, he caught sight of a large caravan entering the open square in the centre of the oasis.

At its head stalked a superb white dromedary, on which was mounted a man most unusually dressed for a traveller in the Sahara—perfectly cut khaki riding breeches with white gaiters, a bright yellow jacket and a broad-brimmed, beige felt hat, usually associated with the western ranches of the United States. Inside the costume was a creature superbly proportioned with broad shoulders and narrow hips and the features of an ancient Greek statue, while a small, curly, black moustache covered his upper lip.

"That can only be the Marquis de Mores!" exclaimed Leboeuf.

"Whoever he is," added the doctor, "he is the best-looking man I have ever seen, and those clothes must have been tailored in Paris. Look at his hands, too, they seem to have been lately manicured."

"I wish that I could speak as well of those wretched pack camels in the caravan," went on Leboeuf. "They're all right for travelling in the hard desert, but they'll never make those long treks in the soft, sandy areas. I wonder who the scoundrel was who landed him with those animals. Probably those cameleers who look like a lot of cut-throat ruffians."

At that moment, de Mores, who had dismounted from the white dromedary, approached the two officers and handed them a leather bag containing the mail from Gabes. At the same time, he introduced himself while the doctor and the lieutenant did likewise. However, when Leboeuf made some derogatory comments on the Mores' caravan, the young man assured him that his chief guide was Si el Hadj Ali, the nephew of the Turkish Governor of Ghat, who had made all the plans and purchases.

Leboeuf, who had served all of his soldiering life in the Sahara, refused to be impressed, declaring that being the nephew of the Turkish Governor of Ghat did not guarantee his integrity or make him a man who would go out of his way to help or protect a Frenchman. He then asked de Mores who the others in the caravan were. The Marquis reeled off the names of his personal servants—a negro guide for the next stage of the journey, an interpreter and twenty cameleers, twenty-nine men in all. Leboeuf, whose business it was to know the identities of men who usually escorted caravans of this kind, had heard of none of them.

De Mores shrugged his shoulders, stating that, while the personnel of his column had not been guaranteed by the Turkish authorities in Tunis, they seemed to be honest nomads. "Men who went exploring in the desert," he added, "had to run some risks."

This time it was Leboeuf who shrugged his shoulders and, changing the subject, invited de Mores to dine in the officers' mess of the fort that night. De Mores accepted on the condition that his hosts would treat him as one of them, a lieutenant of about the same ranking seniority as Leboeuf, and his fellow officers.

Leboeuf was uneasy and during the afternoon paid a call on de Mores and asked permission to have a look at his camels. What he saw, both as it concerned the camels and the cameleers, did not reassure him.

Suddenly de Mores turned to Leboeuf and asked, "If you received the order to arrest me, what would you do?"

"Being a soldier, Monsieur de Mores," he replied, "I would carry out my instructions." And then he added, "But why do you ask me such a question?"

"Because I was given so much trouble by our own people in Tunis that I came to the conclusion that something unusual was going on as far as my trip was concerned." He paused before continuing. "If I am murdered during my journey south, it will be by orders of responsible men in France who want to see the last of me, and not on the initiative of plunder-minded desert bandits."

Leboeuf could only show his surprise, and assure de Mores that he had received no orders to arrest him. On the contrary, he had heard from Colonel Cauchemetz, commanding the district of Gabes, to do all he could to help de Mores.

De Mores smiled. "Yes, Cauchemetz was once in the same squadron of dragoons as I, and while somewhat my senior, was always most friendly."

That evening, with the setting sun turning the desert into a sea of gold, de Mores sat relaxed with the officers of the Kebili fort. They had dined as well as it was possible to dine in a remote post of the Sahara and had washed their meal down with passable Algerian wine.

Now, before each of them, was their favourite liqueur, and de Mores, feeling himself back among his own kind of people, was talkative. He confided to his comrades that he had with him fifteen thousand francs, at that time worth about three thousand dollars, which he would use as presents and bribes. He added that his main objective was to try and lessen the danger which France ran from penetration into the Sahara "by her old enemy" England. He wanted to establish relationships with the dervishes of the Mahdi of Omdurman who had been giving quite a dusting to the British army in Egypt and the Sudan.

The young officers listened with enthusiasm to this good-looking dragoon, who had the ability to speak well and charm an audience. Only the older Leboeuf remained glum.

"Did you tell anyone else about these projects?" he asked.

"As a matter of fact, I did," replied the Marquis. "In fact, I made a speech about it to an audience of French farmers and business men in Tunis who acclaimed my words with such enthusiasm that I did something which perhaps was rash and foolish. I sent a despatch to Lord Salisbury, Queen Victoria's Prime Minister in England, telling him of my intention of trying to join hands with the Mahdi. It is a wonderful opportunity. We know that Captain Marchand is on his way to Fashoda and if he is held up there by the British, he will have me and the Mahdi's followers to back him up and force an issue with Great Britain! It's about time, too!"

At that, the young officers rose to their feet and, with cheers, drank to de Mores' project and to its success.

Only Leboeuf did not raise his glass. When the cheering had

died, he said: "God help you, de Mores! England is not a country likely to be amused by that kind of venture. If you are afraid of being murdered on this trip, it is of the British you must beware. Moreover, I am convinced that the French government does not want a war with England, and they will certainly back her up if there is any kind of unofficial war declared, brought about by your rashness."

"Of that I have no doubt," laughed de Mores. "As the French politicians would, anyway, like to see me out of sight for ever!"

Leboeuf glanced at the doctor, but did not say any more. The doctor, too, seemed to have been infected by the delightful enthusiasm of this godlike creature who, all alone in this unknown desert, seemed ready and prepared to take on the British, who were at the time the most powerful nation in the world.

He called the mess waiter and ordered champagne. Leboeuf could not help smiling at this, and when the sparkling wine had been poured, raised his glass and said: "To your success, Monsieur de Mores; although you are undertaking a very difficult and dangerous task!"

"I know it," replied the Marquis. "I have enemies and I may be killed, but bear in mind that my worst enemies are not in front of me over there in the desert."

"There is still time to give up your plan," said Leboeuf.

"No, no," interposed de Mores, quickly, "give up now? No, a hundred times, no! This is no longer my personal affair. It is a national matter and I believe in God's protection."

His words, which were becoming tinged with jingoism, were interrupted by an orderly who handed a written message to Leboeuf, who quickly opened it and read it aloud. The telegram came from General de la Roque, commanding the division at Constantine, and was addressed to the Marquis de Mores, and to the effect that Twareg guides would await him outside the oasis of Berresof.

"That's odd," said de Mores. "I never asked General de la Roque to find me guides, and I certainly made no suggestion that they should wait for me at Berresof. This has something to do with the troubles which I have already had with our people in Tunis and their politics. By what authority does the French government try to interfere with the travelling plans of a private individual, even when he has ulterior motives? In any case,

gentlemen, good night. And thank you for your hospitality. I'll
see you all tomorrow, I hope."

As he disappeared into the Sahara night, Leboeuf said, addressing his subalterns: "Listen to me, my friends. As commanding
officer of this post, I am the only one really responsible for the
safety of the Marquis de Mores, but the situation is so grave that
I feel I need your counsel. De Mores is obviously afraid of an
ambush at Berresof. On the other hand, our immediate chief,
Colonel Cauchemetz, has instructed me to do all I can to help de
Mores and no one has ordered me to arrest him. Under these
circumstances, should I insist that he take the route which he
evidently deems dangerous?"

"Certainly not!" declared the other officers unanimously.

"Then, if he does not wish to go by way of Berresof, I consider
myself free to allow him to go in whatever direction he pleases."

"Most assuredly, and long live de Mores!" cried the officers,
once more raising their champagne glasses.

But in spite of this enthusiasm and friendly precaution, the net
was being drawn closer and closer around the unfortunate, too
courageous and rather reckless, Marquis de Mores.

The Caid of Kebili was a certain Ahmed ben Hammadi. He
was a strange man, said to have been guilty of several shady
business transactions, and not averse to extorting money from
the oasis people, who thought they might be in trouble with the
French government for non-payment of taxes. There were times,
too, when there had been rumours that this conniving chief,
reputed to be fabulously rich, and certainly the owner of the finest
house and most beautiful gardens in Kebili, would be relieved of
his scarlet and golden burnous of chieftainship. This rumour was
especially prevalent in March of 1896 at the time when the
Marquis de Mores was approaching Kebili.

When it looked as if this degradation might take place, Si
Ahmed was summoned to Tunis by the government authorities.
He returned almost immediately, with his official appointment
not only confirmed but renewed. Everyone in the oases was
astonished at this sudden turn in the fortunes of the Caid who had
seemed destined for demotion. Si Ahmed also appeared to know
all about de Mores and his projects and called on him in his official
capacity to arrange for a suitably provisioned caravan to take the
Marquis on his way.

The café in Bone where Isabelle Eberhardt first began to drink absinthe and smoke *kief*

The flooded desert where Isabelle Eberhardt was drowned

Sliman, Isabelle Eberhardt's husband

Isabelle Eberhardt when a young girl

While Si Ahmed and de Mores were discussing ways and means, Lieutenant Leboeuf joined them and invited de Mores to lunch. While Leboeuf did not like Si Ahmed's crooked business ways, he knew that he was the only contractor in Kebili who could make adequate arrangements for the journey south.

When Leboeuf left de Mores' camp, Si Ahmed followed him, inquiring about de Mores' status in France. Leboeuf replied that he was a *grand seigneur* and added that he expected Si Ahmed to supply him with the best guide available, and to this request Si Ahmed made the following disquieting reply: "And he will need someone trustworthy, as I have heard that certain men are lying in wait for him at Berresof."

Leboeuf took note of this declaration, but did nothing further, though he urged Si Ahmed to look after de Mores as if he were his son. With that, they parted after Si Ahmed had invited Leboeuf to bring de Mores and the officers of the fort to a banquet that evening in his garden in the oasis. Leboeuf accepted the invitation, and went on his way. Si Ahmed did likewise, but stopped at the house of one of his best Sahara guides, a man of uncertain age, called Brahim El Hacheyn, to whom he entrusted de Mores, giving him the following surprising recommendation: "This man, de Mores, is an enemy of the French government, and it is essential that he does not come back alive from this expedition. Take this letter to the Targui, Bechaouiben Chaffaou, whom you will find at Machiguig. In it, he has been told that whoever kills the Roumi will not get into any trouble and will also receive a reward. You will lead de Mores to Machiguig. Be attentive and inspire him with trust, but try as far as possible to keep him isolated from his own servants so that at the right moment, he will be alone."

The dinner in the lush, blossom-scented garden was a great success; all the traditional courses for the gala repast were served. Gazelle roasted whole, game stew, sweetmeats and piles of golden couscous, followed by coffee and mint tea. When Si Ahmed was asked whom he had appointed as de Mores' guide, all the officers laughed. "But Brahim is the biggest scoundrel in the region!" they all exclaimed.

"All the better," said de Mores. "I prefer a scoundrel who knows that I'm aware of his reputation to a lot of men who pretend friendship and then knife you in the back."

12

Then turning to Leboeuf, he inquired what kind of crimes this man had committed.

"Only a few murders," replied Leboeuf with a laugh. "He has no scruples about killing when he is to be paid for the job!"

De Mores chuckled. "Splendid! At least I know that he isn't afraid to kill when an emergency arises."

Leboeuf then went on in more serious tones: "I'm not too worried about Brahim who is quite an old man, but I *am* worried about your camels. They are not the kind, or in condition, to make the trek which you have in mind."

"I am taking care of that," interrupted Si Ahmed. "I am sending a letter by Brahim to a friend of mine at Mechiguig who will supply suitable animals."

With that, the party broke up and everyone, even Leboeuf, went to bed that night feeling that the Marquis de Mores would now travel with a certain degree of security. Yet, as it turned out, everything, as in a Greek tragedy, was leading relentlessly to one of the worst catastrophes in the history of the Sahara.

On the morning of 20th May, 1896, de Mores, faultlessly dressed and riding on the back of the huge white dromedary, led his caravan out of the oasis square. Accompanying him for a short distance were Leboeuf and two of his staff on horseback, while the Caid had come to pay his respects in a light carriage drawn by two grey barbs. It was a most unusual conveyance for a Saharan Arab, but then Si Ahmed was an unusual man with a mentality which suggested something more of a Levantine than of a desert nomad.

At the edge of the oasis the party halted while Leboeuf inspected and interrogated the men of the escort and examined the animals. He still did not entirely approve of their desert worthiness, and had the Caid send out to nomads, who were pasturing their sheep in the neighbourhood, for animals which were in first-rate condition. About the men, he was better pleased, for while he did not know most of them, except for their bad reputations, he was delighted to find included in the escort five Meharists who had served their time under the French flag. On these men he knew that de Mores could rely under any circumstances.

While the Caid drove back to Kebili after the midday meal,

Leboeuf and the other two officers lingered on. For no reason which he could define, Leboeuf still felt uneasy; in fact, he delayed the departure of de Mores until the following morning and it was not until 21st May that the final goodbyes were said, and the caravan, led by the man in the cowboy hat, disappeared into the haze of the desert.

Until 3rd June nothing untoward happened, and on that day the caravan camped in a fold in the ground surrounded by hillocks covered with scrub, which would afford an admirable cover for anyone who wished to approach the camp without being seen. The heat was insufferable, and no breeze stirred to relieve the furnace-like atmosphere.

De Mores did not feel apprehensive, although through his own fault he was now in the hands of the most ruthless of enemies, the men who had been waiting in ambush for him at Berresof and had now arrived at the camp.

Soon after leaving Kebili, and at the suggestion of the treacherous guide, Brahim, he had dismissed the cameleers and guides and Meharists who had been engaged by Leboeuf, on the grounds that he had not sufficient provisions to feed all these men, and that they would be unwelcome in Targui country.

On 26th May an old Shambi with a strain of Targui blood appeared in de Mores' tent. He was called Ali Ben Messis, and was two years later to help Father de Foucauld learn the Targui language. It was he, too, who was able to reveal to the Marquise de Mores some of the details of what had happened to her husband and had actually retrieved de Mores' revolver which the Marquise had, in turn, given to Ben Messis. The butt was engraved with the name of de Foucauld's friend and had led to the employment of the old Shambi as teacher of Temascheck.

Ben Messis spoke fluent French and had been one of the non-commissioned officers whose bravery and knowledge of the country had contributed greatly to the victory of Lieutenant Cottenest at Tit. Without introduction or ceremony, he warned de Mores that he had been betrayed and urged him to return to Kebili without delay.

De Mores laughed off this warning, but Ali Ben Messis insisted that he had heard about the whole plot and had joined the caravan in order to frustrate it. However, like so many others who had met their deaths through not heeding the counsel of their well-wishers, de Mores dismissed this old man, who was clearly a true friend of France. Now he was alone.

On 3rd June some of the cameleers who had been out to look for a well, returned to the camp, bringing with them a tall, veiled Targui. Immediately El Hadj Ali, the nephew of the Turkish governor of Ghat, concerning whom de Mores had talked so confidently to Leboeuf when he first arrived at Kebili, went to greet him. Rather taken aback by the familiar way in which the two men were addressing each other, de Mores asked El Hadj Ali if he knew the Targui.

"Well. And for a long time," replied El Hadj Ali. "He is Bechaoui ben Chaffaou, about whom the Caid of Kebili spoke the other night. He is one of the chiefs of the Targui tribes near Ghadames."

"What is he doing here?" inquired de Mores.

"He is camped near here with his flocks," came the ready reply, "and has a request from the Caid at Kebili to assist you."

"I would like to talk to him," went on de Mores, and called his interpreter, Abd el Hack, who had been educated at the French College of Tunis, and had been in charge of the Tunisian section at the Exhibition at Lyon in 1894. The three men went into de Mores' tent, where the first sentence of the Targui, translated by Abd el Hack, caught de Mores off balance.

"Give us arms and ammunition, and I will have my tribesmen join you to go and fight the British."

De Mores' reply was quick and to the point.

"Tell this man that we want to hire camels which will take us to Ghat where I wish to see the head of the tribal federation there."

Abd el Hack translated this to the Targui, but Abd el Hack heard El Hadj Ali, who spoke Tamacheck, say in an undertone: "This is the man, de Mores. But I warn you that he is a brave man and a crack shot, who never missed his mark."

"How about his escort?" asked the Targui.

"They are all on your side, except this Tunisian here, and the old Ali Ben Messis. We must get rid of them; so promise him the camels and I will have him send back those which come from Gabes, with our cameleers."

The Targui promised the camels and after a lot of bargaining, the price of their hiring was settled and the pact reached by de Mores shaking hands with the Targui.

When he had gone, Abd el Hack told de Mores that he had heard El Hadj Ali whispering to the veiled man. Ali Ben Messis then joined in the discussion and warned de Mores that this Bechaoui was a notorious outlaw, who was not even trusted by his fellow Twareg. Even then de Mores maintained his attitude of minimizing the dangers which these loyal retainers told him were on his doorstep. He was not even suspicious when, on 7th June, the Targui would not remain with him or help him with camels unless he dismissed Ali Ben Messis, who was a friend of his fellow Shamba tribesmen, and consequently an enemy of the Twareg. He added that if Ali Ben Messis did not leave the camp, the Twareg would kill him.

De Mores conveyed this information to Ali Ben Messis, who replied that he would only leave if de Mores wished it, and would give him a letter of recommendation. This de Mores did, and that evening the only man who could have saved his life rode off in the direction of Kebili.

The end came quickly and relentlessly, as with the concluding scene in the Greek tragedy. With Ali Ben Messis out of the way, the treacherous El Hadj Ali and the villainous Bechaoui ben Chaffaou thought that the rest of the execution of their plan would merely be a matter of the right timing. But while de Mores was still completely trusting, and took no precautions to have himself guarded, except at night by the young and faithful Abd el Hack, there was something magical about this tall soldier with his winning smile, which made both Twareg and Shamba tribesmen hold back and not cut his throat while he slept. In fact, among themselves, these desert warriors referred to de Mores as El Seid, the title of the Spaniard known as El Cid, who had helped to drive the Moslems out of Spain in the middle of the eleventh century A.D.

Some of the bolder Shamba did penetrate into de Mores' tent and removed one of the boxes of his baggage, believing that it contained gold which everyone had talked about so much. When nothing was found but maps and papers, the thieves scattered them furiously about the desert. They had, nevertheless, managed to steal the carbines belonging to the Marquis' servants.

When de Mores came out of his tent in the morning and saw what had happened, he seemed to have had the first inkling that some of the warnings he had received were based on foundations worthy of his consideration. No longer smiling, and speaking as an officer to one of his men, he sharply told the leaders of the Targui and Shamba groups that he did not feel that there were enough provisions to feed everybody for a journey as far as Ghat.

"The caravan will first of all go to the oasis of Sinauen," he announced, "only a few hours' march from the camp and buy stores at once for the long desert trek to Ghat."

Neither the Shamba nor the Twareg showed any emotion at this pre-emptory order, although they appreciated that if their victim reached Sinauen he would be in contact with the French army, which would mean the end of their sinister projects.

Bechaoui immediately gave the necessary orders and the loading of the pack animals began. When all was ready de Mores found that instead of his white dromedary there was a baggage camel for his convenience. Sharply he inquired of Bechaoui what had happened to his *mehara*. Bechaoui replied that it had strayed, but a search party had been sent out and it would rejoin the caravan before long.

"It had better," snapped de Mores, patting his revolver which hung in its holster from his belt.

At 7 a.m. the caravan set out in a cloud of dust in the direction of Sinauen. As they started de Mores' servant, Mohammed, together with El Hack, asked that their carbines be returned to them.

"Where are they?" demanded de Mores.

"El Hadj Ali has given them to the Twareg."

De Mores looked about for El Hadj Ali, but he was out of earshot leading the caravan.

"All right," replied de Mores to El Hack. "If the need arises, I will give you mine."

At the same time, he glanced at the grouping of the caravan. While the pack animals straggled over the desert, he noticed that close to him on his right were three fully armed Twareg, and on his left, three Shamba equipped in the same way. It looked to him almost as if he was a prisoner closely surrounded by armed guards. He realized simultaneously that not one of his own retainers had any arms. He had his own carbine laid across his knees, and his revolver at his side. But the wretched animal on which he rode would be useless if he tried to escape any attack from the now obviously hostile men.

This superb horseman, who at Saumur used to astonish his instructors by jumping his horse over and out of the double gates at the railway level crossings when the whistle of the Paris express could be heard approaching, was practically immobilized by the kind of camel which could not even trot like his white dromedary. But still de Mores' treacherous companions did not seem to dare to attack and the caravan moved on slowly through the sagebrush country.

At 9 a.m. it reached a crossroad in the desert track, and de Mores guided his camel towards the north, towards Simauen—towards safety. Unfortunately, at that particular place camelthorn bushes took the place of the sagebrush and encroached on the track, which obliged the bandits to ride closer to their victim.

This forced the issue and these men, who had not dared to attack de Mores when several yards separated him from them, now closed in until they almost touched his camel. The nearest Twareg on one side leaped on to de Mores' camel and tried to seize his carbine, but he held tightly. At the same time, one of the Shamba endeavoured to get hold of his revolver, but all he managed to seize was the holster, while the revolver remained attached to de Mores' belt by a strap.

It was all a wild scramble in which the attackers got in each other's way. Down went de Mores' camel, breaking the carbine under its weight. Its rider got himself clear, but not before one of the Twareg had wounded him in the forehead with a lance which sent the famous cowboy hat flying. Then, all of a sudden, de Mores was on his feet with eyes blazing, and his revolver in his right hand. He had been the crack revolver shot at St. Cyr and Saumur and his excellent marksmanship now showed its worth. Within a minute, one Targui and one Shamba were lying dead in the bushes and a third limping away with a broken leg. Nevertheless, the other assassins closed in. De Mores, quite cool, shot down three more veiled men, while the leader of the Shamba cried out in alarm: "That is not a man, but a *djennoun*!"

Even the reputedly fearless Bechaoui crept away into the cover of the bushes. This gave de Mores the opportunity to climb on to a small knoll whence he could at least see what his betrayers were doing.

But now an equally murderous element assailed him—the sun. He had lost his hat in the initial skirmish, and now he stood bareheaded with those merciless sun rays pouring down on him. The sun is the most treacherous enemy in the Sahara. Even when the temperature is near freezing point, no one ventures outdoors without some kind of headgear. There is no hazy atmosphere to obscure its powerful rays as in places further south like central Africa or Java—the sun beats down on the desert with nothing to arrest its force and, furthermore, reverberates from the ground and strikes up into the eyes of its victim.

It was now a little after 10 a.m. and de Mores knew that until 6 p.m., eight hours away, he must undergo the torture of the sun, which would undoubtedly lead to a paralysing sunstroke. For the moment, he had time to tie his handkerchief around his brow which gave him a little relief. He was also able to look about for his personal staff, Abd el Hack and his servant, Mohammed. Their whereabouts soon were clear, as he heard the young man begging for mercy, somewhere in the sagebrush, and then the scream followed by the gurgle of a creature having its throat cut. He also heard Mohammed being pursued through the undergrowth, but before he could dash to his rescue, he heard his cry of pain, as a Targui broadsword cut him down.

A few minutes later, shots fired from the rear warned him that he would have to be alert to attacks from all directions. Any thought he might have had of escaping to Kebili had to be put away. But no one dared to make a general attack as every time a head appeared out of cover, the deadly revolver cracked and another Moslem went to his reward in Paradise.

Even Bechaoui could not disguise his admiration for the cool bravery of the Frenchman. "If two of us had the Roumi's courage," he exclaimed, "he would have been dead an hour ago!"

In fact, Shamba and Twareg began chiding each other for not daring to rush the lone soldier on his knoll.

De Mores, too, was beginning to suffer as the nausea, prelude to sunstroke, swept through him. He, nevertheless, remained calm and never missed an opportunity to send a veiled man or an Arab rolling in the dust, while the women who had followed the caravan let out howling lamentations as they found another of their men dead.

Then, above one of the bushes, de Mores saw a piece of white linen attached to a Targui lance. It was the treacherous nephew of the Turkish governor, El Hadj Ali, who wanted to parley.

When de Mores had him approach and demanded what it was he wanted, El Hadj replied that if de Mores would surrender and demand the *amam*, he would come to no harm. On the other hand, if he continued to try and fight it out, his enemies would continue the siege of the knoll until their victim died of thirst or exhaustion or hunger, or all three.

"I will never surrender," replied de Mores without hesitation.

"The blood be on your own head, then," retorted Ali. He had come quite close to de Mores on his hands and knees, and with that got up to show that this parley was over. But, he had caught his burnous on one of the camelthorn bushes and could not get away. De Mores took the opportunity to pull El Hadj Ali down.

"You have betrayed me," he said, "and I shall now keep you here as a hostage. If you try to get away you won't get far, I promise you."

With that, he kicked El Hadj Ali in the stomach, he rolled to the ground and the attackers, seeing what had happened realized that de Mores had no intention of giving in and pressed as close to the knoll as they dared. But this only led to more casualties from the deadly revolver, so they then began a devilish manœuvre —running around the knoll, shooting as they went or making darts at their victim!

To counter this, de Mores whirled like a dancing dervish in the frightful heat, firing his revolver whenever he had a target which he was sure of hitting.

El Hadj Ali seized this opportunity to try and creep away, but de Mores seemed to have eyes on all sides of his head, for just as the Turkish traitor felt that he was far enough away to make a run for his life, de Mores' revolver cracked once more and El Hadj Ali, with a cry of pain, went rolling down the side of the knoll.

Nevertheless, the torment continued, turning in all directions and, together with the sun and parching thirst, the ordeal was getting the better of this brave cavalry officer. If only he could lie down for five minutes and rest—if only he could get a mouthful of water. But there were no such possibilities and with an aching head and burning eyes, he kept on, feeling as if he were dancing in a fiery furnace.

Suddenly the Shamba chief, El Kheir, darted up the slope when de Mores was firing in the opposite direction and let go his rifle point-blank into the Frenchman's back. At the same time another Shamba lodged a bullet in de Mores' head which came out on the other side, smashing his jaw. Even so, he did not fall. The bandit let out a scream of triumph which changed to a howl of consternation as the tall figure, obviously mortally wounded, raised his right arm and fired that deadly revolver full in the face of a charging Targui, who had felt it safe to attack the lone Roumi.

Then only did the bareheaded soldier, who had once so proudly worn the plumed steel helmet of a cuirassier, pitch forward and lie still on the baking sand.

Bechaoui ran up the slope, stumbling over the treacherous El Hadj Ali, who gasped out—"Water!" However, instead of water, he received a sharp blow from the Targui's sword which finished his misery and his life. At the same time, El Kheir drew his long dagger and drove it with such force into de Mores' back that it pierced him through, with the point of the blade coming out near his stomach.

So ended the life of the Marquis de Mores, Duc de Vallombrosa, the nobleman and ex-cowboy who, like his friend, Father de Foucauld, had much the same kind of rash bravery which led them to heroes' deaths at the hands of men who could never reconcile non-Moslems penetrating into their Sahara; and yet we may ask ourselves—were rashness and self-assurance the real causes of this soldier's death? No one seems to have the answer.

What must be admitted is that while the commander of the Kebili oasis fort heard indirectly of what had been going on near Sinauen, and took his men there to verify the story, reporting to Paris the facts of the case which he had collected from local shepherds, who with the loyal Ben Messis, had been distant eye-witnesses of the murder, only the Marquise de Mores seems to have been officially notified of her husband's death.

There were no eulogies on the end of this hero, known to so many members of French society as well as to political and military circles. His death, which followed fourteen years after the massacre of the Flatters column by the Twareg, promoted no serious inquiries nor any attempt to round up the murderers. Nor could the Marquise arouse any interest at the Ministries of War, or Colonies, or from the French military and civil officials at El Oued, who must have been well acquainted with the desert grapevine which has an uncanny way of finding out what has been going on anywhere in the Sahara. Every direct question asked about de Mores was met with evasion, and suggestions that Madame de Mores should not try and penetrate the mysteries of the Sahara. Yet there were many Frenchmen who knew what had happened, while others were aware of how the murder had been planned.

It is also interesting to note that Gabriel Hannotaux, in his detailed history of France's colonial expansion over Northwest Africa which covers the period from the seventeenth century until 1930, while telling of the Flatters disaster and the murders of the White Fathers, never mentions the name of the Marquis de Mores.

We can only surmise that the French government hoped to get rid of someone who knew too much about their shady colonial politics. What we certainly have are the official instructions from the Intelligence officers at the French Military Attaché headquarters in Tunis, not only to offer de Mores no assistance on the flimsy grounds that he was travelling in a private capacity, but also to make sure that he travelled via Berresof, where the Shamba-Targui ambush had been laid. Or was it that Lord Salisbury took seriously de Mores' letter about leading an expedition to help Captain Marchand's small column on the Nile? It would certainly have strained Anglo-French, already antagonistic, relations seriously if General Kitchener, facing Marchand at Fashoda, had suddenly found the French contingent reinforced by Twareg warriors, led by a fanatical French officer, determined that the tricolour should fly over the Sudan.

In other words, did Lord Salisbury tell the French government that if Marchand's already rash move were supported by another French-led column, it might lead to war? And did the Prime Minister in Paris then see in the death of de Mores a double escape from the embarrassment which the young officer's political speeches had caused to his cabinet while, at the same time, appeasing the British, who meant business on the Nile and were not going to allow anyone else to interfere?

I have never been able to find out from any French sources what the truth of the story was, or whether it was just another case of a man who took the Sahara for granted and discounted the fatality which caused so many brave men to go to their deaths there. In fact, I had never heard of the Marquis de Mores until I

began to do research for my biography of Father de Foucauld.
Here, first of all, I discovered de Mores as one of Foucauld's
closest friends at Saumur, and then read the story of that loyal
Shambi guide, Ben Messis, who after being so ungratefully dismissed after warning de Mores what there was in store for him,
apparently kept in touch with the caravan on its way to Sinauen
and had retrieved the Marquis' revolver and presented it to Father
de Foucauld as a kind of introduction to the monk when he met
him on his way from Beni Abbes to Tamanrasset, some time in
1907.

My next glimpse of de Mores was in a book about Isabelle
Eberhardt which immediately showed that some mystery surrounded the gallant officer's death.

The details of that heroic fight I read in the files of the Governor-
General of Algeria, Monsieur Steeg, who I suppose felt that I was
a very inquisitive man with no knowledge of or interest in French
political questions. What I read in the governor's files were also
confirmed by de Mores' grandson, the Duc de Vallombrosa,
whom I knew during the 1919 Peace Conference in Paris.

It is certain that de Mores had talked too much, especially about
his view on the British side of the question. He had also bragged
about the money he had with him, and there was nothing which
set those nomads of the nineteenth century more quickly on the
warpath than the prospect of plunder, especially when it was said
to be gold. One cannot make a plan or talk about anything in the
Sahara without it becoming known thousands of miles away.

There is no doubt that in de Mores the French lost a man who
could have helped the pacification of the Sahara as ably as
General Laperrine, as there is nothing which a Targui or Shambi
respects more than physical courage, as was seen by Bechaoui's
exclamation of admiration when Marquis de Mores was fighting
his last fight on that sun-baked knoll, south of Kebili.

11

THE FINDING OF PETROLEUM
IN THE SAHARA

〜〜〜〜〜〜〜〜〜〜〜〜〜〜〜〜〜〜〜〜〜

LOOKING at the Sahara today, the stories which appear in this book may sound incredible. Yet, thus was the great empty, unproductive desert during the period that I lived there, and throughout the centuries before my time. In fact, it was the actions of these adventurous pioneers who had dared to affront the Sahara that led to its modernization and to the destruction of that ineffable peace of mind by the finding of oil in the subsoil.

What one is apt to ask oneself is why oil and other valuable underground products were not discovered and exploited many years before. It was obvious that Iraq and Saudi Arabia, the greatest oil sources of today, are geographically and geologically part of the Sahara, as is also Arabia, and should therefore have the same basic conditions for bringing petroleum into being as their more westerly neighbours. Nevertheless no one, until quite recently, ever thought of France's desert empire as productive of anything worth while.

In fact Mr. Hallis D. Heldberg, the chief of the Gulf Oil Corporation of America, wrote in the magazine *Petroleum Development*, on three separate occasions, in 1949, 1951 and 1952, "In North Africa, one can discover no indication of petroleum. In no part of this country are there any signs which suggest worth while sites for exploration of the undersoil. This applies particularly to the northern Sahara."

The French now naturally declare that Mr. Heldberg wrote these reports because he did not want France to become a petroleum-rich rival of the American oil companies.

On the other hand we must also take into consideration that the nomads had never reported any patches of tar on the desert or found water impregnated with the odour of petroleum during their wanderings over land where some of the richest oil wells have been drilled.

There were no records of any Bedouin tribe reporting the presence of material akin to tar or of something unusual seeping out of the ground, as had Noah and his kin in the regions round about what is now known as Mosul on the banks of the Euphrates some five thousand years before the birth of Christ. In the sixth chapter of the Book of Genesis we have this passage: "Make thee an Ark of gopher wood and patch it within and without with pitch." We are also told, in the same book of the Bible that the people of Babylonia used this same pitch or asphalt to cement together the bricks of the Tower of Babel. Today, the sites of the Ark and the Tower of Babel building have become the fabulously rich oil fields of Mosul.

Gertrude Bell also made a note that bitumen and asphalt were bubbling out of the ground when she passed by Mosul in 1905. At that time the automobile era was in its infancy and the only use for petroleum was to keep lamps alight.

In the Sahara there were no Noahs to make their arks waterproof and no sons of Shem to build a tower and mortar it with asphalt and no Gertrude Bells to draw the attention of geologists to the riches of the Arabian subsoil. In fact, had a Bedouin noticed any tar during his wanderings over the Sahara, he would have undoubtedly regarded it as something completely foreign to his interests as a shepherd.

It must be admitted that neither the French nor the Americans wanted to go to the expense of prospecting for oil with no certainty that their search would be, in any way, rewarded.

The first man to suggest that oil lay under the Sahara Desert was a certain Conrad Kilian, a geologist who had the Sahara fever in his system and had given up a great deal of time to the exploration of the Tassili Highlands in the Hoggar Mountains. He had started this after one of the Shamba followers of the Flatters disastrous expedition, who had managed to escape the mass murder of Colonel Flatters and his men, reported that the Colonel had come upon a fabulous emerald mine but had been unable to bring back any sample emeralds because of the savagery of the

Twareg bandits. Kilian found no emeralds but he did discover prehistoric paintings, of hippopotami, crocodiles, elephants and giraffes as well as other creatures, such as those men in armour, the Garamanti, who rode in horse-drawn chariots, all of whom no longer belonged to Sahara life.

It was rumoured that the Garamantes, these hunting charioteers who lived at the eastern end of the Hoggar some two thousand years ago, had at one time worked the fabled emerald mines in the country now occupied by the veiled Twareg. This often repeated rumour once more led an Algerian businessman to equip an expedition to find the emeralds.

To help in such a venture he required an able geologist with a thorough knowledge of the country to be surveyed. For this purpose he was recommended Conrad Kilian, the son of the older geologist.

The expedition failed to find any signs of emerald mines or, for that matter, any emeralds at all. Nevertheless, during the surveying, Conrad Kilian became convinced of the oil-bearing properties of the land he covered. He reported this to the French government both in Algiers and in Paris. However, the authorities scoffed at his reports. Only his father, who had implicit faith in his son's judgment, sent a team of experts to check the reports. Every one of the experts confirmed what young Kilian had stated.

Nevertheless, for the moment, no one in Algiers or Paris showed the slightest interest in what was to change the whole aspect of North Africa and, for that matter, of France as a world power.

Everyone was too busy fighting the losing war against the rebels of Ben Bella and Ferhat Abbas to think of oil wells and all that went with them. In fact, it was not until the end of 1955 that oil drillers were sent out to Edjeleh on the borders of Tunisia where Kilian said that he was positive of evidence of a rich oil field.

On 6th January Kilian's prognoses were confirmed as the oil suddenly gushed from the well in such unexpected quantities that a great deal was lost in the desert sands. Following Kilian's advice, another drill was put down at Tiguentourine, fifty miles south of Edjeleh, which gushed on 6th June. In May another huge oil field had been discovered at El Adeb Larache, seventy-five miles southwest of Edjeleh, and so it went on. It was now obvious that the Sahara could supply France with more than her needs in petroleum.

However, like all those brave men who had defied the spell of Sahara the mysterious, Kilian was to pay with his life for his interference.

The French government did nothing to reward the courageous and far-seeing man who had given France untold riches. He was given no compensation, and drifted into a life of penury. Eventually he died, apparently by his own hand, in a state of great poverty. Nevertheless, the police authorities who found him hanging from a beam in his poor lodgings declared that they had never seen a man who had died by hanging with his eyes and mouth closed. While his end was recorded as suicide, rumour had it that he had been a victim of the international oil war which, it appears, is always raging behind the scenes when new oil fields are being exploited.

Kilian knew too much about the petroleum possibilities of the Sahara. He had also made friends with Twareg of the Fezzan who were his sworn allies in all his undertakings. It was, therefore, worth while for any who wanted to undermine the oil monopoly of the French in the Sahara to get rid of someone who knew the exact location of the potential oil fields and could also influence people on whose territory the black gold was to be found.

As far as I was personally concerned with this first oil strike which took place near Edjeleh in January of 1956 at an unmarked spot some sixty miles south of Ouargla, I knew nothing. I was no longer living in the Sahara. I took note that this initial well was within the pasturing area recognized as being under the domain of the tribal federation of Bedouins, to which I belonged.

The actual first strike was called Hassi Messaoued, which means Fortunate Well. By that time I had long ceased to live my shepherd's carefree life in the Sahara, but had I been still there I would have called this first evidence of oil the Unfortunate Well.

For thousands and thousands of years this vast wilderness had remained unchanged. From time immemorial the nomads had pastured their sheep and their camels at the same places and at the same time of year. Small cities had grown up around places where there was sufficient water to bring an oasis into being and there was nothing to suggest that life in the desert would not remain unchanged until the end of time.

Ben Messis, the friend of the Marquis de Mores who fruitlessly warned him of the ambush

The square in Kebili from which de Mores set out on the journey to his death

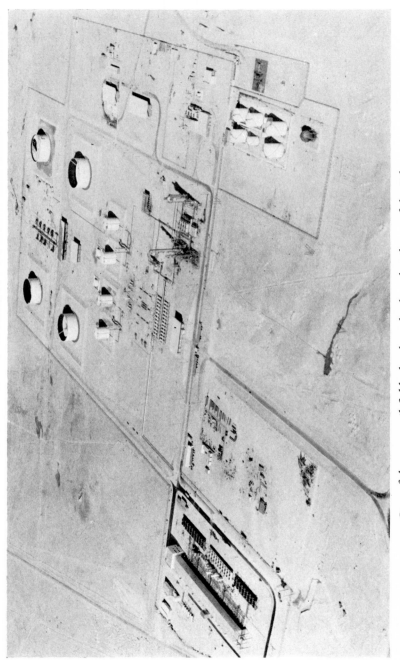

One of the many oil fields that have broken the silence of the Sahara

The only communication with the outer world was by un-reliable and ancient buses or by a small single-gauge railway which ran from Algiers to Djelfa, a dismal hamlet within eighty miles of the oasis of Laghouat. Not more than six chiefs of my federation of tribes in addition to myself owned an automobile, and in order to go to Algiers some three hundred miles to the north, I had to drive over an untarred rough road which took me the best part of ten hours.

The military governor of the area had access to a telephone, but only he or one of his staff could use it.

Owing to this lack of modern inventions, there was no fussing or worrying over material problems. On the few occasions when I protested about setting out two hours late on some expedition, my friends used to say: "Why do you Occidentals always become so excited over saving time? What do you do with the time you have saved? And, anyway, worrying about it won't do any good."

And gradually, I absorbed this peace-giving philosophy and found that by letting everything take its course without fussing and under the slogan of *In sha Allah*, we all had peace of mind and never lay awake turning over some problems which we knew we could not solve by thinking about them. We had blissful tran-quillity and accepted this blessing without comment.

Then, as already described, the oil wells came into being with-out warning in districts which until then had consisted only of stone and sand. Tarred roads started to spread out over the desert, telephones were installed linking the remotest oases and petroleum cities with Algiers and then with Paris. Horrible, hideous cor-rugated iron villages sprang up around the equally hideous derricks. These mushroom settlements had air-conditioned resi-dences and restaurants which were for the use of European technicians and engineers. While for the manual labourers air-conditioned cinemas and recreation rooms appeared out of the waterless plains. Airports were built to accommodate the jet planes which daily brought in spare parts for the oil drills, as well as fresh meat and fish, fresh eggs and vegetables for these men, a great majority of whom had never eaten anything but couscous.

Luckily, I repeat, I had ceased to live in the Sahara before all these innovations came into being, but I have kept in touch with my old friends, both native and European, who have continued in the old desert way of living. What these one-time peaceful

13

companions complain of most is the unbelievable change of mentality which these oil discoveries have brought to the cameleers and shepherds, as well as to the nomad inhabitants of the Sahara.

These men, in my time, felt contentment and happiness if they earned enough to give them one square meal a day and the possession of a black tent under which they could rest and a burnous in which to wrap themselves.

Today, as soon as they have earned a few hundred francs, these Bedouins, born to be simple shepherds, go to the nearest oasis to buy themselves showy, impractical, plastic sandals, then a wrist watch, the possession of which is a clear rise on the social ladder. When they reach the rung of imported American blue jeans and American cowboy shirts, they feel that a superior status has been reached. The day that they can buy bicycles they consider themselves equal to Caids or even Aghas. The next step in this upward social progress is the motor-cycle or scooter. From then on, they will despise their one-time companions who have wisely stayed with their flocks, and have, of course, lost all reverence for their tribal chiefs. They neglect their religion and spend their spare time drinking forbidden wines and spirits in local cafés, while they talk socialistic politics which they do not understand.

This is how it is now, and is deplored by the tribal chiefs and the French administrators who have stayed in Algeria to help the irresponsible native governors, and those also who have been unable to separate themselves from the desert and have retired to live in some oasis. What causes these men most concern is what will happen to these comparatively rich Bedouins when the sources of their incomes dry up. Because dry up they will, once the oil wells of the Sahara are working concerns, and can be taken care of by a few specialized foreign engineers. When this occurs, the day labourer's fabulous wages will vanish like a Sahara mirage. What then? What will he do? He knows no trade and is usually illiterate.

With his new bicycle and plastic shoes and his recollections of two square meals a day, followed, if he likes, by two hours at the cinema, it is unlikely that he will return to tending sheep and camels. His mind, too, will be filled with communist notions, meaningless to him as Islam already preaches the doctrine of equality among men, but which can be made much use of by

Algeria's new dictators; and their friends and colleagues who rule China.

The Chinese have already infiltrated into some of the towns and oases of North Africa and will have little difficulty in moulding these newly unemployed petroleum labourers into militant communists.

Then there is another very difficult question. Who is to reap the benefit of the newly found oil? When the first well gushed Algeria was still under French rule. Today, however, Colonel Boumédiene, a one-time regimental sergeant major in the French army, with no formal education, rules an independent nation, and declares that as he governs the country, so will he govern the oil industry. He does not seem to be anxious to give credit to the French for having found the oil and put it to practical use with their capital and equipment and under French technical supervision. It is the French, too, who have built the pipe-lines from the Sahara to the Mediterranean, and it is the French, too, who alone can refine the oil and market it.

Incidentally, the Sahara produces twenty-five million tons of oil each year, while the natural gas reserves amount to more than 2,000 billion cubic metres. This is good, but not as great as the oil production capacities of Saudi Arabia and Persia.

There does exist a commercial agreement between the Republic of France and the Algerian Republic. This agreement covers 102 closely printed pages, but, after reading the document through twice, I am no more enlightened as to what it purports to establish than after reading one of those long legal documents which lawyers delight in composing, wherein "the party of one part" promises to do something for "the party of the other part" and adds that, in future, "so and so" will be the "party of the one part" and someone else "the party of the other part".

All that I can do for the benefit of my readers is to translate from this agreement some of the more contradictory and nonsensical clauses, hoping that someone will be able to draw some sense out of the confusing sentences.

Article 31 reads: "In order to realize these industrial projects, the French government agrees to bring to Algeria a financial contribution in the form of a long term loan not reimbursable."

"A guarantee of credits for supplies. . . ."

"The necessary technical assistance for the construction and operation of the industries concerned, as well as the recruiting of a professional personnel. Also the free access of the sub soil products to the French markets under the most favourable conditions to the producer."

Article 32: "Prior to putting this agreement into effect, the French government will contribute 200 million francs a year to the Algerian government, consisting of a loan of 160 million francs and 'co-operation' of 40 million francs not reimbursable or considered a loan.

"The sums which are loans will carry interest at 3 per cent and be repayable in twenty years."

After this follow two completely contradictory articles in this French agreement.

"To clarify the present protocol. The headquarters of the petroleum association will be established in Paris and half the capital will remain in the hands of the French government."

A little further on in the agreement, we have "Le Siège Social (head office) of the Franco Algerian companies shall be, for all administrative purposes, located in Algiers."

The agreement then adds that, "the working of the hydro-carbonates is a matter of business;" furthermore, "that the oil deposits are *immeubles*" (*immeuble* is usually employed as a noun and means in French a several-storied building which brings in revenue. Used as an adjective, it can only signify that the oil is immovable, which is obviously contrary to fact). The buildings, machinery and all the materials used for working the oil deposits as well as the storing and transportation of the raw oil are likewise immovable (*immeubles*)—and so on and so on until one feels that one is reading a work by Lewis Carroll.

In fact I, who was born, brought up and educated in France and write better French than English, have found myself stumped by French words in this agreement. For example, what is the meaning of *tréfoncière*? This word appears in no Anglo-French dictionary and not even in the French Larousse. Nor does the context give me any clue to what *tréfoncière* might signify.

This agreement is in a paper-bound volume entitled *Accord entre la République Française et la République Algérienne Démocratique et Populaire concernant le règlement de questions touchant les hydro-carbures et le développement industriel de l'Algérie* and takes the form of letters exchanged between Monsieur Jean de Broglie, Secretary of State at the Ministry of Foreign Affairs and Monsieur Abdelaziz Boteflika, President of the Council of Ministers of the Republic of Algeria.

Each letter opens with the words "Monsieur le Ministre", and terminates with the respective writers' high consideration for the addressee.

Can one imagine anything more ridiculous than the vagueness of the language of the agreement which might baffle a seasoned company lawyer, whereas the document has been prepared for Algerian officials who not so very long ago were non-commissioned officers and provincial grocers in Algeria with less education than men of the same status in Europe. A French Minister speaking of his high consideration to men who have no background but the hovels or tents in which they used to live is absurd and without sense, when a few years ago the French were trying to kill off all Algerians. I knew one of the present cabinet ministers when he eked out a miserable existence peddling fake Oriental carpets on the sea front of the French Riviera and the Côte Basque. I remember giving this almost starving illiterate creature a few francs, for old times' sake when I had known him in Algeria, to buy himself a cup of coffee when I found him shivering outside the Hotel Carlton in Cannes; in this hotel he now stays with the *haute consideration* of the Prime Minister and the hotel management which, at the time of our meeting, would have physically kicked the pedlar out of the hotel garden if he had dared to appear there with his grimy carpets.

I do not suppose that any of these executives of the "République Algérienne Démocratique et Populaire" has any definite understanding of what the *Accord concernant le règlement touchant les hydrocarbures en Algérie* means than I have.

Tied up in all this contradictory legal verbiage, the Algerians could default on their contract without even knowing that they had done so.

This might lead to all manner of complications and possibly to war with the intervention of third parties or nations who are oil poor and could take over the Franco-Algerian business with little trouble.

The French hope soon to be pumping thirty million tons of oil every year out of the Sahara, which is more than what is required for their domestic consumption. This pumped oil runs through a pipe-line over 400 miles long which crosses the Atlas range at a height of over 3,000 feet.

The pipe-line begins at Haoud el Hamma not far from Hassi Messaoud. The next pumping station is M'Sila, which drives the oil up over the watershed of the Atlas Mountains via the Seltana Pass. This pass has been artificially created by cutting away part of the mountain range, thus allowing the oil to pour down the northern slopes of the Atlas. The oil is run then into great tanks on the Mediterranean coast at Bougie. Thence it flows to piers where French tankers of an average 65,000 tons take the precious liquid to France for refining.

Incidentally the Algerians today own no tankers, so they cannot sell their oil to outside nations unless they come to fetch it. To counter this problem, the French government is prepared to build tankers for the Algerians, who will, of course, have to pay for them.

To go back to the nonsensical *Accord* between the French and Algerian governments, I did happen to find two articles which made some sense. The first is that the Algerians will be held responsible for the recruiting of native personnel to work in the oil fields while all technicians and specialists in oil matters (French or foreign) will be selected and appointed by the French government.

I happen to know that this has not been a success, especially as it concerns Americans. These veteran oil drillers and executives from Texas were brought to the Sahara at the request of the French to teach the French and Algerians the ABC of the oil business. However, no one in North Africa seemed to want these instructors or would even listen to them. In fact, the French behaved as if the Americans had come to the Sahara to take over France's newly born oil empire.

The French technicians declared that the Americans acted as if they were supermen, asserting that no one could run an oil business as well as they.

The Americans complained that the French were jealous of their skill and experience, and were forgetting, apparently, that these men from the United States had been in the oil business for a hundred years, whereas they, the French, had had only five years' experience. As one Texan is reported to have remarked: "All I can say is that the French can have their oil. The way they run the business in the Sahara, there won't be anything left in five years but sand and abandoned derricks."

The second article in the agreement which seemed to me quite lucid was to the effect that after the oil had been pumped to the coast at Bougie, it would be divided equally between the French and the Algerian companies.

The great difficulty about all this Sahara oil business which has now arisen is—How to dispose of the oil profitably? The drilling and pipe-lines have already engulfed eight hundred million francs and it seems that a further five hundred million francs will be required to bring this Sahara venture on to a sound footing. The world bank has been tapped twice for loans and French investors do not seem to favour putting their money into the great Sahara oil bonanza.

The French government has also been deeply disappointed to find that it is easier to dig oil from the wastes of the desert and pump it 400 miles over plains and mountains to the coast than to sell it. Neither Middle Eastern Arabs, nor Russians nor Americans are eager to help the marketing of a commodity which they respectively regard as their monopolies.

The only advantages which I can see for France in these fabulous oil strikes is that it makes France independent of all other countries for the flying of their aeroplanes and the running of their tanks and other motor vehicles.

It makes me sad to think that all the peace and serenity of the Sahara Desert which I enjoyed for so many years has been wasted for no good purpose.

The whole state of affairs is confusing and I can see no solution. No native Algerian, be he of the desert or the oasis, has any mechanical sense, or can even see beyond the day. So, unless France is prepared to fight for it, some other Occidental power, with the same views as Boumédiene, will step into the scene and become master of what may well be the biggest oil reserve in the world. Because of this black gold, France is surrounded by enemies. It is even said among French politicians that the United States financed the Algerian "fellagah" rebellion in order to be able to cash in on the oil prospecting. All this mess and confusion breaks my heart.

The Sahara and its people were, in my day, the greatest peace-giving element which I had ever known. Now all this tranquillity is gone, and from Edjeleh on the eastern border of the Sahara to Tindouf on the west, the oil pumps unceasingly play their monotonous chant as they draw the black gold from the once silent desert. All I can say is, "Alas, alas for the Sahara as I knew it."

Then there is a further problem. How long can Boumèdiene really rule North Africa? He is a townsman and no desert nomad will admit being under the jurisdiction of a sedentary Berber. The desert people are the gentlemen of the tent and the sword who despise citizens, be they from modern towns on the coast or from Sahara oases. By the same token, the sedentary folk despise the desert people, whom they consider dull, ignorant people with no knowledge of the modern way of life, or of the politics of the Occident.

Furthermore, the Bedouins take no practical interest in oil riches of the subsoil of the Sahara, other than finding temporary well-paid employment. As far as this is concerned, all they need is enough petrol to make their cars run when they happen to want to travel by automobile. This oil will in no way help the sheep business except by the fact that it has led to intensive boring for water which will hold off the menace of drought and subsequent famines.

The people of the desert who descend from the great Berber tribes of Kabylia and the Arab invasions of the seventh and twelfth centuries are quite prepared to let the French have their oil, provided they leave the Bedouins to run their Sahara pastures and Atlas farms in peace.

I used to quote a verse from a sonnet called "Silence" by Thomas Hood as I lay waiting for sleep in my black tent:

> There is a silence where hath been no sound,
> There is a silence where no sound may be
> In the cold grave—under the deep, deep sea
> Or in wide desert where no life is found.

Today, alas and alas, I would be kept awake by jet planes and the monotonous song of the oil pumps; the desert would no longer be soundless.

Epilogue

~~~~~~

A SHORT while ago, that is to say at the beginning of May, 1967, I wrote to a bookseller in Algiers who used to supply me with all my reading material while I lived in North Africa, to ask him if he could furnish me with certain photographs to illustrate this book. I also asked him to tell me, if he could, what conditions were like in Algeria today with a native government at the head of this newly independent state. I added that I would be grateful if he could give me any information about my grandfather's former house, that Barbary corsair's palace already referred to. The reply which I received was singularly free of reticence and to my mind rather indiscreet from a Frenchman living under a suspicious and hostile rule. In fact, so indiscreet were my old friend's remarks that I will not mention his name.

The following is a free translation of what he wrote.

I would like to help you as much as possible as it concerns illustrating your new book. I fear, however, that there is little I can do. In fact, our printing press and archives have for some years now been acquired by the Algerian government. Furthermore, the official organizations which took over all the books and publications which we used to produce has neither any literary nor artistic interest in what used to be our main work. Thus all the documents and pictures with which we could have presented you have been lost if not deliberately destroyed.

Algeria, with the exception of its climate and beauty spots, is no longer the country that you used to know. In fact, the only resident Europeans are limited to the personnel of the embassies and consulates, as well as to some twenty thousand French people, most of whom are new-comers who have not settled permanently in the country as in olden days.

Economically, the situation deteriorates every day. The local currency, the Algerian dinar, has no international rate of exchange, and France alone recognizes it under certain circumstances. As to the exportable produce of Algeria, it is, as always was, almost exclusively agricultural but with their one-time superior qualities now gone, their demand abroad has disappeared.

All land belonging to foreigners and native landowners who have left Algeria have been expropriated and become "national property" and the running of these lands is more or less attended to by the State or the Committees of Management working on a Socialist basis.

The home of your grandfather still exists but it is in an abandoned state since the departure of the last European resident there. It is on the way to becoming a complete ruin and the garden uncared for is returning to a state of primitive jungle.

(My grandfather, with great pains, had planted one of the "show gardens" of Algeria.)

So this is what General de Gaulle has done to this country which used to be a rich paradise of vines and orange groves and olive yards and innumerable flowers and beautiful shrubs by handing it over to the ex-sergeant major Colonel Boumédiene. I suppose too that the other lovely residences occupied by the Anglo-American colony have suffered the same fate as my grandfather's place.

The Arabs have always been destroyers and rarely creative. Their homes are tents and, provided they can cultivate enough food for the day's needs, that is all that matters.

Some readers may challenge this by pointing out the Alhambra, the mosques at Seville and Cordoba as well as the Generalife gardens at Granada, as representing creative works of Arabs. However these palaces, mosques and gardens, still the most, beautiful in the world, were not created by Arabs but were brought into being by the Almoravides religious ascetics, a Berber tribe which came out of the Sahara in the eleventh century, occupied Morocco and then crossed to Spain, where they remained for two hundred years.

The true Arab, the descendant of Mohammed's followers, is a nomad tent dweller and a fighting warrior. Colonel Boumédiene and his bandit companions have inherited all the characteristics of their Bedouin predecessors and are running a country which

the French had made, perhaps, the richest and the most peaceful
country in the world in the same way as might an illiterate
nomad chief who had never lived in a house.

I am glad to have left Algeria when I did and more than glad
that my grandfather and mother died before they knew what had
happened to their home and the Algeria they loved.

These facts, supplementary to those given to me in the letter
from my Algiers bookseller friend during April of 1967, were
conveyed to me late in 1967 in London by a "Pieds Noir"[1] official.
I had known this man when he was a prosperous owner of vineyards near Blida to whom banks offered blank overdrafts of a
million francs or more because his business reputation was so
solid. Now I saw him walking along the Strand in a threadbare
suit, patched shoes and a beret. He looked hungry so I took him
into the nearest restaurant and gave him as much as he wanted to
eat and drink, reminding him of the lavish way in which he had
entertained me in Algeria. The unaccustomed food and drink
seemed to loosen his tongue and he answered all my questions
readily.

"All this mess in North Africa is solely the fault of our President
Dictator General de Gaulle," he began. "This so-called gentleman
deliberately betrayed us for his own advantage. We had the
richest vineyards in the world. We supplied I do not know how
many hectolitres of wine each year with which French-pressed
wine was 'cut' and strengthened. We supplied enough grain to
feed the majority of the French population. All the 'primeurs'
[early fruit and vegetables], for which French tables were famous
in winter came from Algeria. Our sheep industry gave France
meat and wool. We required no financial aid from the mother
country. And now what? The Algerian currency, the dinar, has
no rate of exchange outside Algeria. It is worth nothing. The
non-wine-drinking Moslems have ploughed our vineyards,
which had taken years and years to cultivate. The wheat and
barley crops are mismanaged or neglected and the grain given to
countrybred horses and mules. The nomad Arabs, the great sheep-

[1] Former European inhabitants of Algeria who have exiled themselves
somewhere in Spain in the hope that they may one day return to their lands
in Algeria.

breeders of the Sahara, will not sell their produce through the intermediary, Colonel Boumédiene, a sedentary native whom the men of the desert despise. Nor did most of the intelligent Arabs want the French to leave North Africa. They had been well-treated by the French Army, the French Civil Service, and knew that as long as these men, devoted to the country, remained Northwest Africa would prosper and be administered by lawful means, and be defended against enemy aggression. And all this prosperity both for Algeria and for France was destroyed by this General de Gaulle who betrayed native and French settlers because he wished to curry popularity with the French regular army, or at least the majority of it, which was tired of wars. He did not care what happened to the native population of Algeria, and less what happened to us who had made our homes in North Africa since 1848 and brought all our craftsmanship and industrious ways to the people, who had lived for centuries on the policy of *In sha Allah* ('If God wills it'). We built roads and farms, introduced railways and constructed large harbours for the distribution of our goods. And today, through de Gaulle's indifference to all that Frenchmen have done to promote Algeria, the paved roads have become dirt tracks. No one cares about running railways and people prefer to travel on foot or on donkeys. Our model farms and their equipment have been burned to the ground. The harbours will soon be unsafe and unusable."

"But there is still the petrol of the Sahara," I protested. "That is worth international money."

My companion shrugged his shoulders. "Hardly," he replied. "All the oil sold has to pass through the hands of Colonel Boumédiene and his dishonest associates, and you know how money was frittered away by Arabs between source and outlet when there were no Occidentals to control business. Besides there is no real outside demand for Sahara oil. Algeria has gone back to what it was before the French conquest of 1830, an impoverished, disorganized land with no future!"

"And is there nothing you can do to put things right?" I inquired.

My friend paused for a moment reflectively and added: "We must get rid of de Gaulle, either by the legal methods of the machinery of democratic voting or by assassination. Once he is out of the way the French, who are logical people, will see what that megalomaniac dictator has done to ruin France and Algeria. It is for that purpose that I am here."

I stared at my old friend and there flitted before my eyes a picture of the sunbathed square outside the Cathedral in Algiers, and then inside where my friend's beautiful daughter was being married to one of the richest and most eligible of French farmers in "the Sahel". My friend, who it was said had endowed his daughter with one of the largest dowries ever bestowed on a bride, stood resplendent in a morning coat.

The vision faded and I saw before me a sad, discouraged man in an obviously second-hand workman's suit and patched-up, unpolished shoes, who was thanking me for my generosity towards him. I protested that I had not given him the kind of meal that had been served at his daughter's wedding or offered him a glass, even, of champagne which had been so lavishly poured out at the nuptial ceremony in Algiers.

I wondered as I spoke to this man whether the goose-faced President de Gaulle had ever considered the cases of René Caillé, Colonel Flatters, the White Fathers and Cardinal Lavigerie or the Marquis de Mores, all of whom had given their all to make Algeria great. Probably not. The French officials I met in the northern Sahara and in Algiers, except those who had specialized in the subject or whose parents had been connected with the colonization of Algeria, were singularly uninterested in its history and could in no way help me to find books or maps that I needed for the purpose of telling my story. They likewise cared little about the fates of the "Pieds Noirs" who had tried to consolidate and improve on what the explorers and generals had attempted to establish in Northwest Africa.

In fact one colonel in Laghouat suggested that René Caillé and the Marquis de Mores and certainly Isabelle Eberhardt were a bit awry in the head to have attempted what they had. His attitude suggested that he considered their fates served them right since they risked their lives for such a futile cause.

So unless France produces a constructive and democratic government which will recognize Algeria at its true value, my one-time wealthy friend and his thousands of patriotic companions will probably die of starvation, if they are not first shot by one of General de Gaulle's private firing-squads, some of which have murdered his old friends of his soldiering days.

Appendix I

THE ISLAMIC FAITH

In view of the fact that a good deal has been said in this book about Islam and its effect on the people of the Sahara, it seems essential to give the reader a rough idea of what the Moslem Faith represents. This is a fairly easy task as I practised this Faith during the seven years that I lived with the Bedouins of the Sahara and can, therefore, give an accurate explanation of what Islam demands of its believers.

In the first place, it is incorrect to call a member of the Islamic Faith a Mohammedan. Mohammed never proclaimed himself as anything but a messenger sent by God to bring salvation to the idolators of Mecca. He always insisted that he was a mortal man like Moses or Abraham and had nothing to do, himself, with the doctrines of this new religion.

He declared himself to be a prophet like the patriarchs of the Old Testament sent by God to restore into the right path His people who had strayed.

He, furthermore, emphasized: "We believe in Allah and what He has sent down to Abraham and Ishmael and Isaac and Jacob and what has been given to Jesus and what has been given to all the Prophets of the Lord. We make no distinction between them."

A person who adheres to the teachings of Mohammed is a Muslim. Muslim signifies one who submits or surrenders himself (to God).

The more concise translation of "Islam" is Submission to God. Not an absolute submission to Him, but rather a striving after righteousness.

The whole of Islam hangs on the simplest of fabrics: "There is no God but Allah. He is God alone. He begetteth not and is not begotten, and there are none like unto him."

To this belief must be added that Mohammed is the "Messenger of Allah". Not "Prophet", but "Messenger". For while *nabi*, which means Prophet or Preacher in Arabic, is often used with reference to Mohammed, the word in the creed is *rasul*, which signifies "Messenger".

The words uttered by the muezzin when he calls to prayer from the minarets of mosques which many a tourist has heard when travelling in the Orient, are as follows: *La ilahah illa Allah! Mohammed Rasul Allah!* "There is no God but Allah. Mohammed is his Messenger."

This is important for, while Mohammed declared himself to be as mortal and sinful as any other Arab, he made the belief in himself as God's messenger imperative.

To begin with, Mohammed's conception of God was of Someone unimaginable and aloof. Then, little by little, God drew closer. God was present when men were gathered together. There was no reason to raise one's voice when praying, God could hear the lowest whisper.

One of the strongest impressions I got when living with my Bedouins was the same as that recorded by Charles de Foucauld during the Bou Amama campaign, that is, the "every-dayness' of God. He ruled our eating, our business, our loving, our travelling. He was our hourly thought, our closest friend in a manner impossible for people whose relationship with God is separated from them by rites of formal worship. It was this intimacy with God which caused me to practise the Moslem Faith. Had I remained aloof from Islam, I would have felt myself an outsider and a spectator, when my companions fasted or prayed or told their beads.

Nor was this practice too difficult for me as Mohammed believed in Jesus and in His claim to being the Messiah. For in the Koran Mohammed wrote: "Say unto the Christians their God and my God are one . . ." and further on: "God gave Moses the Book, and gave Jesus the Evangel, and gave Mohammed the Koran."

It would not have taken a great deal to make Mohammed into a Christian. Although disapproving of some Christian doctrines, he never openly declared himself against them. He undoubtedly hoped that, somehow, Islam and Christianity would come to an understanding and merge. That he was no more able to bring this about than to lead the Jews into his fold was due to what might be called a quibble. With the Jews, it was the Messiahship of Jesus which was denounced as a heresy. With the Christians, it was the unshakable belief in the Holy Trinity.

Mohammed was endeavouring to impose a monotheistic Faith on a people who, from time immemorial, had been worshipping a multitude of deities. In Mohammed's opinion, the Christians seemed to have complicated their fine, simple religion by inserting something unnecessary and incomprehensible.

To Mohammed the mystery of the Trinity and the Incarnation appeared to contradict the principles of divine unity. In their obvious sense they seemed to have introduced three equal deities and transformed Jesus into a mortal who was, nevertheless, the Son of God.

Then the Christian reverence for saints and images did not seem to be so far removed from the three hundred idols in the Kaaba at Mecca, which Mohammed had denounced and would one day break into pieces.

Mohammed detested images and there does not exist in the world today one statue or picture of the founder of Islam. Every Mosque bears witness to this. What we call arabesques, those geometric decorations made out of interlaced Arabic letters and interwoven inscriptions from the Koran, which are works of art in themselves, are the outcome of Mohammed's iconoclasticism. He would not have the likeness of anything alive reproduced by man in stone or paint.

Nor was the practising of the Moslem Faith too exacting. The creed demanded:

1. A belief in God. *La ilahah illa Allah.* There is no God but Allah.

2. A belief in God's angels. Of these, the four principal are: Gabriel the medium of revelation; Azrael who receives the souls of the dead departed; Azrafel, who is in charge of the trumpet; and Michael, who cares for all human beings.

3. A belief in God's Books, these books being the Pentateuch of Moses, the Psalms of David, the Gospels of Jesus and the Koran of Mohammed.

4. A belief in God's prophets. The most important of these are Adam, Noah, Abraham, Moses, Jesus and Mohammed. Prophets must be regarded as almost free of sin, the only sinless prophet being Jesus. Mohammed speaks of Him as the Word of God, Spirit of God, born of Miriam (Mary) and Worker of Miracles.

5. Belief in the resurrection of the body and in the Day of Judgment. The actions of all men will be judged on that day. The sign of its approaching advent will be the return to earth of Jesus Christ. The resurrection will be definitely physical. The pagan Arabs of Mecca contested this, asking Mohammed how it could be possible to re-assemble all the bones of the dead departed. To this, Mohammed replied that if God was able to create a human being from a drop of sperm, He could just as easily collect the bones of the dead and put them together again.

6. Belief in the predestination of good and evil. Allah's will accounts for everything that happens, all that has happened or ever will happen.

In addition to those beliefs, Moslems have five obligatory duties.

1. The daily recital of the creed. Condensed to its shortest, it amounts to: "I testify that there is no God but Allah and that Mohammed is His Messenger."

2. Prayer five times a day. At dawn, noon, mid-afternoon, sunset and two hours after sunset. Mohammed used to say: "The five daily

prayers are like a fresh river which runs by the entrance to one's home. He who washes himself five times a day will keep himself pure and clean."

This, however, did not prevent him from being particular about the bodily cleanliness of Moslems. They had to make their ablutions before praying and before and after eating. Furthermore, being aware that water was not usually available in the desert, Mohammed allowed sand to be used as a substitute. I found this to be a most cleansing element. My companions and I used to rub it all over ourselves and then brush it off. It was rather like polishing one's limbs with an emery board.

3. Fasting. This is observed throughout the month of Ramadan. During these twenty-eight days nothing can be eaten or drunk from before dawn until after sunset. That is, "from before and until after a white hair and a black hair held at arm's length are indistinguishable".

Owing to the Moslems observing a "lunar year", the fasting months do not recur at the same seasons. Hence, when Ramadan falls in June, the fasting and the ban on drinking during the long torrid day can become a trying ordeal.

What I found most inspiring was how my companions conscientiously obeyed their religious duties. It would have been quite easy for any of them to forget the noon or mid-afternoon prayer without anyone noticing the omission, yet without any watches to consult, my friends stopped whatever they were doing at noon and at four-thirty—hunting, travelling, or doing business—and went through the elaborate motions of praying as a matter of course. When we happened to be going somewhere in a bus, the driver automatically halted the bus and the passengers all tumbled out on to the desert and prayed.

Then, during the fasting period, any Moslem could have gone into his house or tent to take a sip of water without anyone being any the wiser. But he just did not cheat. He followed his conscience, however unpleasant it might be.

4. The fourth duty of a good Moslem is that once during his lifetime he should make the pilgrimage to Mecca. This had been a custom dating back to the oldest days of the Kaaba. Mohammed saw that this pilgrimage would draw together the Faithful from all parts of the world where Islam was practised, from Pakistan, from Indonesia, from Persia and North Africa. All these people of different races would be assembled together because of Islam. They would all have to wear the identical pilgrim dress and talk to each other in Arabic, which it was obligatory to learn in order to pray or read the Koran. However, with his usual practical attitude towards life, Mohammed added a rider to this obligation, which absolved any who could not afford the journey and the upkeep of the home while absent in Arabia.

5. Almsgiving. These are legal alms to the community chest and the destitute. While there was no penalty for disregarding charity, this obligation was usually practised by the rich towards the poor. This explains why beggars are encouraged in Moslem countries. It is very rare to see a well-to-do Moslem turning away a beggar.

Although it is not one of the tenets of the Moslem Creed, Mohammed declared that Jesus was not put to death on the cross. He explained that God substituted someone for Jesus at the last moment and that the Messiah was carried straight to Heaven.

In brief, therefore, those are the principles of this new religion for which Mohammed was prepared to risk his life among the pagan Arabs of Mecca. He was offering his people a God as sublime as the Christians, but more intense, more in keeping with their harsh lives. It was a religion for the shepherd and for the warrior of the burning, boundless wilderness of Arabia.

Christianity contains whole fields of morality and whole realms of thought which are outside the religion of Mohammed. The fundamental ideal of Moslem life, even as the founder of Islam, is more material than the life of the founder of Christianity. There is no ethereal life in Islam, in the true sense, for Mohammed's character was admitted by himself not to be ethereal.

Nevertheless, Islam is not an easy religion to practice. With its fasts, its numerous daily prayers, its contemplations, its pilgrimages, its almsgiving, it is not made to appeal to the lazy and the selfish. There is no outward show and there are no worldly recompenses as with some of the other recognized Faiths of the world.

I have often been asked whether the Koran is the Bible of the Moslems or a history of Mohammed, or a collection of sayings of the same kind as those attributed to Confucius or as a volume of Moslem laws. No one that I have so far read seems to be able to explain concisely this work on which Islam is founded.

Without any idea of adding fresh comments to what Oriental scholars have already contributed, I will endeavour to outline what the Koran actually represents.

"Koran" is an Anglicized form of the Arabic *Qur'an*, which is derived from *qara'a*, meaning to read or recite.

The Koran consists of 114 *suras* or chapters, the longest of which has 286 verses, the shortest three. Each *sura* has a title taken from some word or sentence occurring somewhere near the beginning of the text. The title does not necessarily have anything to do with the subject matter of the *sura*.

For example, the seventy-fourth *sura*, entitled "The Greeks", opens with: "The Greeks have been defeated in a land hardly . . ." which is a reference to their rout by the Persians in 615 B.C. However a few verses further on the Greeks are forgotten.

The Koran consists of a series of revelations made to Mohammed at various times by an angel of God. As the various messages were delivered, they were committed to writing on anything that was handy, a palm leaf, a piece of bone, oyster shells, on bits of wood and stone, on strips of leather. These scraps were thrown into a box without any indication as to the order in which they should be read.

It was not until after Mohammed's death that his father-in-law, Abu Bakr, had all these bits and pieces copied on to a scroll. This was done with unimaginative devotion, so that when it was finished every revelation of Mohammed was set down in no particular order so that it really made no sense. (Voltaire, who wrote a play entitled *Mohammed*, declared that the Koran was utter nonsense.)

It was not until a century or so later, under the Caliphate of Othman, that a group of scholars were ordered to make an orthodox version of the Koran, giving it some sort of order by deciding what Mohammed could only have thought before the Hijra (the flight from Mecca) and after his establishment at Medina. They took such pains that the first official edition of the Koran, put into circulation about A.D. 900, is a readable volume, in which the thoughts and chapters are consecutive.

Appendix II

GLOSSARY

Abba Night gown garment made of wool or silk and worn over jacket and trousers and under the burnous.

Agha Second ranking chief among Sahara dwellers.

Ain Spring; e.g. Ain Mahdi.

Al Hamdullah "Praise God". Said at the termination of a meal or task or journey.

Amenokal Elected chief of a Twareg tribal confederation.

Bash Agha Senior ranking chief in Sahara. Head of a federation of tribes.

Bassour A kind of palanquin placed on the backs of camels and hung with curtains for the transportation of women and children when moving camp.

Burnous A long cloak with a hood, made of camel hair or wool, also of cloth for ceremonial occasions. Chiefs wear scarlet burnouses embroidered with gold.

Bismillah "In the name of Allah". Said when starting to work or eat or set out on a journey.

Beselaama "Peace be with you". Usually used at the end of a meeting or at the moment of parting.

Ben or *ibn* The son of; e.g. Mohammed ben Isa, Mohammed the son of Isa. Mohammed ibn Saud. There are no surnames among Arabs. People are identified by so and so, the son of so and so.

Bint Daughter of, used in the same way as ben or ibn.

Caid The head of one of the tribes making up a federation. It is the third ranking chief in the Sahara.

Chesh Headcloth worn over turban, called Kufaya in Arabia.

Couscous Semolina cooked over steam; it is the staple dish of the Sahara inhabitants as rice is that of most Asiatics.

Debourca A kind of drum made out of pottery with a skin fitted over one end.

Djebel Low mountain; e.g. Djebel Amour.

Djinn (plural *Djennoun*) Evil spirit.

Erg Sand desert.

Fantasia A display of dancing and horsemanship performed at some festival such as the marriage of a paramount chief.

Fondouk A lock-up for merchants and their wares.

Gandourah The Sahara name for the Arabian abba.

Hammam Steam bath, the original of a modern Turkish bath.

Imam A mosque attendant. He is in charge of religious ceremonies and leads the prayers when said collectively.

In Sha Allah If God so wills.

Kadi Arab judge, attorney, official receiver. He is connected with anything having to do with Moslem law including marriage and divorce and crimes.

Kasbah Literally "Fort". Today the native quarter of a foreign dominated town.

Marabout (feminine *maraboute*) Moslem saint, often supposed to be descended from Mohammed; also the tomb where he or she is buried.

Mufti A Moslem official who is an authority on religion and law. The Mufti sometimes explains the Koran in the mosque and preaches.

Mehari (plural *mehara*) Tall riding dromedary; used to be employed for warlike purposes by the Twareg and mounted soldiers of General Laperrine's camel corps.

Meharist Mounted soldier of the Sahara camel corps.

Mohkadem Holy official of the North African religious fraternities.

Nails Sahara dwellers' sandals.

Oued Dry river bed, sometimes called wadi and overflowing with water after heavy rains in the northern hills.

Ouled Nail Sahara tribe which specializes in training dancing girls and those of easy virtue.

Rizzou Raiding nomads; used to be applied to the plundering Twareg.

Rezzia Raid.

Raita A trumpet with a reed mouthpiece, producing a sound like a great number of bagpipes played in a small room.

Roumi (plural *Ruama*) Literally, Romans. Used later to denote all Occidentals.

Ramadan Month of Moslem year when all believers must fast from dawn until dark.

Sahara When pronounced in the right way, i.e. with the first *a* short, means dun-coloured and refers to sandy or rocky desert between the Atlas Mountains and the Sudan. When pronounced with the tonic accent on second *a*, the word means box or chest.

Salaam Alek Greeting on meeting someone and means "Peace be with you".

Salaam Aleikum Used when greeting more than one person.

Shesh The same as chesh, see above. Spelt with a capital S is probably the correct method, as the letter C does not exist in the Arabic alphabet.

Si or *Sidi* Sir. An honorific title prefixed before the names of important people; e.g. Si Ahmed Tidjani.

Shamba or *Shaamba* Plural of Shambi, a nomad shepherd of the central Sahara.

Shott Shallow salt lake or marsh.

Taleb Teacher in Arab schools, also professional writer of letters in Arabic and sometimes in French. Occasionally employed as a legal adviser.

Tamtam A large tambourine.

Tamashagh Script of Twareg language.

Tamashek Language of Twareg.

Tassili Foothills of the Hoggar (Twareg country).

Toubib Doctor.

Twareg (singular *Targui*, feminine *Targuia*) Origins unknown, but probably of Berber stock who inhabit the Hoggar or Ahaggar Mountains in the centre of the Sahara.

Zaouia A monastic retreat for men and women. Those taking monastic vows give the marabout in charge of the zaouia all they possess and, in return, are looked after for the rest of their lives. The zaouia are usually the homes of the fraternities, such as the Tidjanis, of which Aurélie Picard's husband Si Ahmed was the head, or the Kadrya which Isabelle Eberhardt joined.

Bibliography

Ameer Ali. *The Spirit of Islam*

Ahmed Khan Bahadur. *Essays on the Life of Mohammed*

Archer, J. C. *Mystical Elements of Mohammed*

Bazin, René. *Charles de Foucauld*

Benoit, Pierre. *L'Atlantide*

Blanche, Lesley. *The Wilder Shores of Love*

Boucher, Monseigneur. *La Vie Héroïque de Charles de Foucauld*

Bovill, E. W. *The Golden Trade of the Moors*

Byng, E. J. *The World of the Arabs*

Caillé, René. *Journal d'un Voyage à Tomboctou et à Djenné dans l'Afrique Centrale*

Campbell, Dougald. *On the Trail of the Veiled Tourag*

Cardier, Edouard. *Voyages de René Caillé*

Crosnier, Elise. *Aurélie Picard, Première Française au Sahara*

Carl, Louis. *Tefedest*

Dinet, Etienne. *Mohamet*

Eberhardt, Isabelle. *A l'ombre chaude d'Islam*[1]

French Bureau of Intelligence. *Commercial Agreement between the Republic of France and the Algerian Republic regarding the distribution of oil and gas found in the Sahara*

Herison, Robert. *Avec le Père de Foucauld et le Général Laperrine*

Hitti, P. K. *History of the Arabs*

Kheirallah, Doctor G. I. *Islam and the Arabian Prophet*

Kitter, G. W. *The White Fathers*

---

[1] The Marquise de Boishébat, an old resident of Algiers who had known Isabelle Eberhardt, filled in many gaps in her story. What this lady told me was confirmed by the Comtesse de Brazza, widow of Savargnan de Brazza, the explorer who put the Congo on the map. Madame de Brazza had been a close friend of Isabelle Eberhardt.

Leclerc, René. *Sahara*

Muir, Sir William. *The Life of Mohammed*

Owen, Richard. *The Saga of the Tiger (The Search for Mungo Park along the Niger River)*

Prorok, Byron de. *The Mysterious Sahara*

Pottier, P. *Le Sahara*

Pottier, R. *La Vocation Saharienne du Père de Foucauld*

Rodwell, J. M. *Translation. The Koran*

Rodd, Francis Renell. *The People of the Veil*

Ward, Edward. *Sahara Story*

Index

A

Abdallahi (Caillé's assumed name), 28
Abdallahi Chebir (Caillé's host in Timbuktu), 31, 32, 34, 35
Abd el Kader, 50
Abraham, 113
Adour, river, 99
Africa, North, Northwest, Central, 28, 45, 50, 85
Ag Chikkat Attici, 90, 111
Agha Khan, 50
Ahaggar, 78
Ahitagel, 88, 89, 90, 92, 98
Ahmed, Si, marabout of Tidjani fraternity, 9, 50–65
Ain Mahdi, 15, 50, 52, 57, 58, 63, 67, 68, 69
Ali, son of Si Ahmed Tidjani, 66
Allah, garden of, 20, 67
Algeria, 15, 85
Algiers, 13, 55, 100
Almoravides, 71
Amenokal, Twareg chieftain, 88, 90
Amguid, gorge, 94
Andjelous, 75
Andrews, Roy Chapman, 17
Antinea, 83, 84
Antony, Mark, 83
Arabia, 50
Arabia, Lawrence of, 11–13
Arabian desert, 11
Areg, 74
Arouane, el, scene of Major Laing's murder which Caillé visited, 33
Atalla Bouameur, Laghouat merchant 69
Atlas, mountains, 36, 39, 57, 76
Aures, mountains, 76

B

Bachir, Si, brother of Si Ahmed Tidjani, 50, 62, 64
Barbour, Nevill, 75n.
Baghdad, 26
Bamakao, 27, 42
Basses Pyreneés, 90
Baubacar, Sidi, Moorish friend of Caillé from Mogador, 37, 38
Bayonne, 99
Bedouin shepherds, 14; their way of living, and simplicity, their ignorance and their loyalty, 25; chiefs, 13
Bel Kacem, mulatto cook of Flatters expedition, 97
Bell, John, author's grandfather, 12
Bell, Gertrude, author's cousin, 11, 12
Benoit, Pierre, author of Atlantide, 83
Beringer, Monsieur, Public Works official of Flatters' expedition, 88, 92
Betika, son of Targui guide hired by Father Richard for trek to Ghadames, 112
Berbers, 13, 22, 36, 56, 74
Bir el Gharama, wells where Colonel Flatters was murdered, 91, 92, 93, 98
Biskra, 88, 146
Blad el Khouf, land of fear, 78, 79
Bonaparte, 28, 38
Boumédiene, Colonel Houari, President of Algeria, 77n., 84, 195, 199, 200, 202, 204
Bou Amama, dissident marabout, 61, 162
Bou Djemma, Targui guide who tried to save Flatters, 92

Bourmont, General de, commanding French army during first invasion of North Africa in 1830, 47

Bovill, E. W., 14, 75n.

Bouteflika, Abdelaziz, Minister of Foreign Affairs in Republican Government of Algeria, 84

Bou Bekher, el Hadj, son of Agha of Metlili sent with White Fathers to protect them in their first expedition south, 106

Bouchard, Pierre, White Father member of first disastrous expedition towards Sudan, 106, 107

Bordeaux, 48, 51, 52

Brazza, Comtesse de, 15, 166

Brazza, Savorgnan de, Count, Congo Explorer, 15, 166

Brame, Corporal, Colonel Flatters' orderly, 96

Briggs, Cabot, 74

Brosselard, Lieutenant, member of Flatters' expedition, 88

Burton, Richard, 11

C

Cabaillot, Monsieur, railway engineer with Flatters' expedition, 88

Cannibalism, among Flatters' expedition survivors, 97

Chatelier, Lieutenant le, officer with Flatters' expedition, 88

Chad, Lake, 86

Charbonnier, Father, member of order of White Fathers, 105

Cleopatra, 83

Cleopatra, Selene, 83

Constantine, Emperor, 84

Christians, 103, 119

Congo, 103

D

Dacine, Targuia, poetess and friend of Foucauld, 80

Dancing girls, Ouled Nail tribe, 72

Dakota, Marquise de Mores, home state, 170

Dante, Alighieri, 79

David, Father Superior of White Fathers in Laghouat, 15

Debourca, Sahara drum, 71

Deberré, French Naval officer who helped Caillé reach Senegal, 27

Delaporte, Monsieur, French Consul in Tangier, 41

Dentistry, as practised in the Sahara, 21, 24

Deserts, Sahara, Nefuhd, Mojave, Gobi, 17

Dianoux, Lieutenant, in Flatters' expedition, 88, 94, 95, 96

Dilke, Sir Charles, 12

Djaddour, Targui El Khadjem's negro slave, 112

Djinns, an evil spirit, 19

Djennoun, evil spirits, 19

Djenné, town on Niger, 30

Djerma, Sahara town between Tripoli and Lake Chad, 86

Doré, Gustave, painter, 7?

Donatists, Christian heresy, 74

Doughty, Charles, Arabian explorer, 11

Dromedary, 78

Duponchel, Colonel Flatters' chief engineer, 88

Duveyrier, Henri, lived with Twareg and believed them to be honest and trustworthy nomads, 86

E

Eberhardt, Isabelle, 15, 141–66

Egypt, 50

El Oued, where Si Ahmed Tidjani died, 63, 67 and ff. Where Isabelle Eberhardt settled in Southern Sahara.

Enchanted Mountains, home of Twareg, 98, 127

F

Falcon, hunting and feasts celebrating Aurélie Picard's wedding to Si Ahmed, marabout of Tidjanis, 59

Fantasia, nomad celebration for Aurélie Picard's marriage to head of Tidjanis, 58

False teeth, marabout of Tidjani's, 54.
Si Ahmed's explanation for these new teeth, 59
Federation of Larba Tribes, 13
Fez, Morocco, 39
Financial crisis in Si Ahmed's affairs rectified by Aurélie Picard, 59, 62
Flatters, Colonel Paul, 64, 65, 73, 85–98
Flocks of sheep, 19
Fondouk, Arab lock-up for merchants and their merchandize, 40
Fontainebleau, 70
Foucauld, Father de, 38, 39, 61, 73, 76, 81, 82, 120–8, 131, 133, 139
Foureau, Commandant, leader of first punitive expedition against Twareg, 65
France, Bodley's history of, 12
Franco Prussian War, 50, 52, 87
Franco-Kissour vocabulary prepared by Caillé, 43
Frenchmen who could never leave Sahara, 18
French school founded at Ain Mahdi by Aurélie Picard, 55, 68
Freycinet, Monsieur de, Minister of Public Works in France who encouraged the Flatters' expedition, 86, 87
Fromentin, Eugène, French writer, one of the first to visit the Sahara, 17

G

Gandourah, nomad's garment, 21, 77
Gambia, Gray's expedition to, 27
Garamantes, 74, 191
Garden of Allah, 20, 146
Gautier, Professor, 75
Gendarme, father of Aurélie Picard, 47, 64, 68
Geographical Society, of France, 27, 30, 41, 42
Ghourland, Southern Morocco, 37
Ghat, oasis, 109, 110, 113
Ghadames, oasis, 105, 109, 111, 112
Ghardaia, Mzabite city, 105

Girard, 101
Gironde, river at Bordeaux, 48
Gironde, Prefect of, 51
Guiard, Captain of French Medical Corps with Flatters' expedition, 88
Guitar, played by Arab orchestra at Kourdane, 69
God of the Christians, 34, 209
Governor General of Algeria, 12, 56, 61, 64, 99
Gold Medal of Geographical Society presented officially to René Caillé, 41

H

Haggard, Rider, 83
Hassan ibn Muhammed, Leo Africanus, 26
Herodotus, 78
Hilal, Arab invaders of N.W. Africa, 74
Hoggar, mountains of Twareg country, 76, 77, 78, 86, 88, 122, 123
Horse, first introduced into N.W. Africa and the Sahara, 74
Himyaritic, migration west, 74
Hyksos, shepherd kings, 74

I

Ida Ag Gemmoum, Targui chief, 107, 113
Imouchar, Shamba name for Twareg, 73
Irak, 74

J

Japanese, script, 76.
Samurai, 107
Jesuits, 104
Juba II, king of Numidia, 83

K

Khadjem, Targui guide from Tripoli, 112, 117
Kaikondy (today called Boké), starting place of Caillé's expedition from West African coast, 28
Kouroussa, village on River Niger visited by Caillé, 28
Koran, 57, 101, 102

L

Laing, Major Gordon, 26, 33
Laghouat, Oasis, 57, 67, 68, 69
Lamy, Commandant, 65
Laressore, Pyrenean seminary, 99
La Rochelle, 26, 27
Lavigerie, Cardinal, 56, 57, 98, 99–119
Lyautey, General, 133, 161, 162, 165
Lyon, Lavigerie bishop at, 100

M

MacMahon, Marshal, President of
    France, 55. Governor General of
    Algeria, 99
Madani, El, Algerian corporal of
    Tirailleurs with Flatters' expedition,
    97, 98
Madani, El, treacherous slave of
    Tamanrasset, 124
Marabout of Temacine, 110
Marjolet, Corporal, Colonel Flatters'
    cook, 96
Masson, Captain, 88, 92
Medea, Atlas mountain village, 61
Mehara, riding dromedaries, 89
Metlili, Southern Sahara oasis, 105,
    106
Menoret, Philippe, Father, 106
Mogador, 37
Mohammed, Bou Etteni, Si, Senussi
    fanatic in Tripoli, 112, 113
Mohkaden, Marabout of Tidjanis,
    65, 89, 95
Morat, Father, White Father, 110, 117
Moslems, 74, 100, 207–12

N

Nancy, 100
Napoleon, 27
Niger, River, 27, 28, 30, 31, 92, 104,
    109

O

Ouargla, oasis, 86, 89, 98, 106, 111
Ouarsenis, mountains, 159
Osman, King of Sudan at beginning
    of nineteenth century, 27

P

Park, Mungo, explorer of the Niger,
    27
Paulnier, Father Alfred, 106, 107, 110
Partarrieu, Monsieur, who helped
    Caillé in Gambia, 27
Pius IX, Pope, 103
Pobeguin, Sergeant of Flatters' mission
    eaten by cannibal soldier, 94, 96, 97
Pouplard, Father, 108, 110, 114, 117

Q

Quadrya, religious fraternity which
    Isabelle Eberhardt joined, 151, 153

R

Ramaya, Moslem religious fraternity
    associated with the Quadrya which
    Isabelle Eberhardt joined, 153
Rabourdin, railway engineer with
    Flatters expedition, 88
Red Sea, 113
Reichshoffen, battle of Franco-Prus-
    sian War, 51
Richard, Father, White Father who
    led Second Lavigerie expedition,
    109, 110, 111, 112, 113, 114, 117,
    118
Roche, Monsieur, mining engineer
    with Flatters expedition, 88, 92

S

Saiah Ben Bou Said, Father Richard's
    Shamba guide from Ouargla, 112
Saint Louis, Senegal, 27
Saluki, Sahara greyhounds, eaten by
    survivors of Flatters' expedition, 94
Senussi, fanatical tribe living on the
    borders of the Sahara and Tripoli
    and murderers of Charles de
    Foucauld, 109, 110, 123, 126
Senegal, 27, 86
Shamba, guide who escaped Flatters'
    massacre, 111
Shamba, tribe, 13
Sirocco, 18, 90, 91
Society of Missionaries of Africa, 162
Sorbonne, 99
Sudan, 27, 34, 85, 103, 109, 112, 119

T

Tadjemout, 91

Tafilalt, 37

Tanganika, 102

Targui, origins, 75, language, 75, dress, 77

Targui, singular of Twareg, 73, Targuia, female Targui, 77

Temacine, 62, 110

Tidjani, Fraternity of Ain Mahdi, 47, 50, 52, 53, 55, 57, 58, 59, 61, 62, 63, 65, 67, 68, 71, 89, 95

Timbuktu, 26, 30, 31, 41, 103, 108, 119

Tin-Hinan (prehistoric Targuia queen) tomb discovered by Byron de Prorok, 83

Tirailleurs, Algeriens, 89, 93, 97, 98

Tétu, Caroline, Caillé's bride, 43; bears Caillé children, 45

Tuat, 89

Tripolitania, 98

Tripoli, 109, 110, 112

Tunisia, 61, 68

Turks, 109

Twareg, 73–84

U

Uganda, 102

V

Verde, Cape, 27

W

White Fathers, order of the, 101; their dress, 102, 105, 119

White Sisters, order of the, 102; their dress, 103, 104, 119

Wissenbourg, battle of Franco-Prussian War, 50

X

Xenophobia, 89, 91

Y

Yahia, Jelloul Ben, Bash Agha of Larba Federation of tribes, 13

Z

Zaouia, Moslem Monastery in Carvent at Tlemcen, 60, at Guemar, 65

Zeyneb, Lalla, marabout of El Hamel, 188

Ziban, Sahara tribe, 13

Zorah, Si Mohammed's Sudanese wife whom he repudiated, after marrying Aurélie Picard 60

Zouave, guard at Ain Mahdi, 62